The

Middle East

and

North Africa

Regional Studies Series

The Regional Studies Series

Africa
China
Europe
The Subcontinnet of India
Japan and Korea
Latin America
The Middle East and North Africa
Russia and the Commonwealth

The

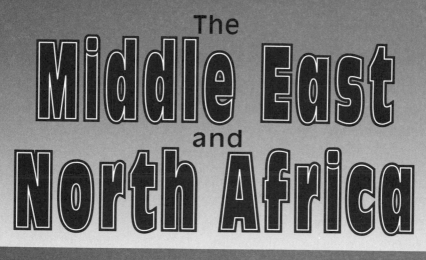

Middle East
and
North Africa

Regional Studies Series

Consultants

Reeva S. Simon

Phyllis Goldstein

Stephen Wasserstein

GLOBE FEARON

Pearson Learning Group

Reeva S. Simon

Reeva S. Simon has an M.A. degree from Harvard University's Center for Middle East Studies and a Ph.D. degree in history from Columbia University. She has written numerous articles on Islam, inter-Arab and Israeli politics, and the history and culture of the Middle East. She is the author of a book on Iraq between the two world wars.

Phyllis Goldstein

Phyllis Goldstein majored in political science at the University of Chicago and holds an M.A. degree in teaching from Harvard University. She has taught social studies at both the junior high school and high school levels and has edited many textbooks on world geography, history, and world cultures.

Stephen Wasserstein

Stephen Wasserstein has an M.A. in history from Brown University and has taught at the university level. He has written and edited many history textbooks.

Area Specialist: Gordon Darnell Newby, professor in the history department and in the department of philosophy and religion at North Carolina State University. He is chair of the Islamic Studies Section of the American Oriental Society.

Reviewer: Ira Zornberg, Assistant Principal, Thomas Jefferson High School, Brooklyn, New York.

Executive Editor: Stephen Lewin
Project Editor: Robert Rahtz
Art Director: Nancy Sharkey
Cover Designer: Armando Baez
Production Manager: Winston Sukhnanand
Marketing Manager: Elmer Ildefonso

Cover Image: The picture on the cover is a scene outside the College of Dentistry in Riyadh, Saudi Arabia.
Maps: Mapping Specialists, Ltd.
Graphs, Diagrams, and Charts: Keithley & Associates

Photographic acknowledgments appear on page ix.

ISBN 0-8359-0437-7

Printed in the United States of America

11 12 13 14 15   07 06 05 04

Globe Fearon
Pearson Learning Group

1-800-321-3106
www.pearsonlearning.com

CONTENTS

Chapter 1 *The Land* 1

What Is the Middle East? 1
What Elements Characterize the Region? 2
A Large Dry Region 7
Agriculture and Industry 13
  Case Study: From an Egyptian Village 16
Problems of Development 22

Chapter 1 Checkup 26

Chapter 2 *People and Culture* 31

The Cities 31
Problems and Patterns of City Life 33
  Case Study: Modern Cairo 35
Population Trends 43
The Villages 44
Israel 47

Chapter 2 Checkup 51

Chapter 3 *People of the Ancient Middle East
(c. 10,000 B.C.–A.D. 500)* 55

The Process of Change 55
The Ancient Middle East
  (4000 B.C.–500 B.C.) 60
The Egyptians of the Nile Valley 64
Anatolia and the Mediterranean Coast 66
  Case Study: The Book of Ruth 68
Persia, Greece, and Rome Rule the Middle East
  (500 B.C.–A.D. 500) 70
Judaism and Christianity 73

Chapter 3 Checkup 78

Chapter **4** *Muhammad and the Emergence of Islam (A.D. 500–1000)* 83

The Founding of Islam 84
Islam: the Religion 87
Case Study: The Example of the Prophet 92
Islam and the Individual 93
Islam As an Institution 96
The Expansion of Islam 100

Chapter 4 Checkup 103

Chapter **5** *The Development of an Islamic Civilization (750–1400)* 107

Bringing Together an Empire 107
Case Study: A Day in the Life of a Court Physician 116
Islamic Civilization (750–1000) 117
Invasion and Decline 126

Chapter 5 Checkup 130

Chapter **6** *The Rise and Decline of the Ottoman Empire (1280–1914)* 135

The Ottoman Empire, from Its Origins to the End of the Eighteenth Century 135
Case Study: The Ottoman Siege of Vienna 143
The Impact of the West 145
From the Era of Reform to World War I 150

Chapter 6 Checkup 157

Chapter **7** *Two World Wars and Their Impact (1914–1967)* 163

The Middle East After 1914 163
Turkey and Iran: Two Attempts at
  Modernization 166
Developments in the French Middle East 173
Palestine, a Troubled Land 176
  Case Study: The Pioneers 180
Egypt in the Twentieth Century 187

Chapter 7 Checkup 193

Chapter **8** *More Turbulent Years (1967–1989)* 197

Religious Revival 197
No War, No Peace 201
The Politics of Oil 210
The Iranian Revolution 214
  Case Study: The Fall of the Shah of Iran 217
Crisis in Lebanon 219

Chapter 8 Checkup 226

Chapter **9** *The Middle East and the World (1989–Present)* 229

War in the Persian Gulf 229
A Bitter Peace 235
  Case Study: The Problems of Oil Wealth 239
A Window of Opportunity 246
Winds of Change 251

Chapter 9 Checkup 255

Glossary 259
Bibliography 265
Index 268

Maps

The Middle East and North Africa: Political
Map 2–3

The Middle East and North Africa: Language
Map 6–7

The Middle East and North Africa: Physical
Map 10–11

The Middle East and North Africa: Rainfall
Map 14–15

The Middle East and North Africa: Oil and Natural
Gas Production 28–29

The Ancient Middle East 60

The Byzantine and Persian Empires, About A.D.
565 80–81

The Spread of Islam, to 751 100–101

Baghdad, About 775 110

The Crusader States, 1099–1204 127

The Ottoman Empire, 1481–1683 140–141

Arab-Israeli Conflict, 1948–1967 184

Israel and Its Neighbors 248

Graphs, Charts, and Diagrams

Countries of the Middle East and North Africa 24

Ten Largest Cities in the Middle East and
North Africa 33

Life in the Middle East and North Africa 42

Population Facts 54

Time Line: The Ancient Middle East: Egypt
and Mesopotamia 61

Time Line: The Rise of Islam 98

Time Line: Muslim Rule, A.D. 600–1400 108

Governments of the Middle East and
North Africa 206

Oil Prices, 1970–1990 210

Armed Forces of Countries in the Middle East and
North Africa 243

PHOTO ACKNOWLEDGMENTS: Cover Photo: © Barry Iverson 1991/Woodfin, Camp & Associates; Arabian American Oil Company: 22; Art Resource: 72(Fratelli Alinari), 172 and 186(SIPA), 204(Michas Tzovaras); Bettmann Archive: 38, 61, 62, 121, 123; British Museum: 129; The Corning Museum of Glass, Corning, New York: 111; Culver:149, 183; Gamma Liaison: 8(A. Borrel), 234(N. Quido), 235(Isikversen), 246(E. Baitel), 252(C. Vioulard); Historical Pictures Service: 153, 154, 155, 168; Frederic Lewis: 37(R. Gates); Library of Congress: 66; Magnum: 40(Abbas), 95(Steve McCurry),169 (Richard Kalvar), 175(Marc Riboud), 221(Raymond Depardon), 236 (Abbas), 240(Bruno Barbey); Monkmeyer: 33, 49, 188(Paul Conklin), 73, 113(Hilty), 125(Henle), 139(Bernard Silberstein), Oriental Institute: 71; Rapho/Photo Researchers: 56(George Gerster); Reuters/Bettmann Newsphotos: 222(Gebron Tabaja), 224; Shostal: 91, 96; Stock Boston: 36(Robert Caputo); Sygma: 9(Pascal Manoukian), 17(Owen Franken), 19(Jean-Louis Atlan), 45(Owen Franken), 85 (Elkoussy), 94(Alain Nogues), 215(Kalari), 216(Philippe Ledru), 238(Alain Nogues), 247(C. Spengler); Turkey Office of Culture and Information: 137; United Nations: 4(Ian Steele), 39, 69, 88(J. Issac); UPI/Bettmann: 203, 204, 208; Wide World: 192, 233.

Today, through my visit to you, I ask why don't we stretch out our hands with faith and sincerity so that together we might destroy this barrier [between Israel and Egypt]? Why shouldn't our and your will meet with faith and sincerity so that together we might remove all suspicion of fear, betrayal, and bad intentions?

Why don't we stand together with the courage of men and the boldness of heroes who dedicate themselves to a sublime aim? Why don't we stand together with the same courage and daring to erect a huge edifice [building] of peace. . . ?

–President Anwar el-Sadat of Egypt
speaking before the Israeli parliament,
November 20, 1977

1 *The Land*

The Middle East is the place where the continents of Asia, Africa, and Europe come together. Its river valleys were home to two of the world's first civilizations, along the Nile River and in the valley between the Tigris and Euphrates rivers. It includes some of the oldest inhabited cities in the world. Moreover, the Middle East is the place where Judaism, Christianity, and Islam—three of the world's great religions—began. For thousands of years, the region has also been a center of great economic activity. Long ago, that activity focused almost entirely on trade routes that crisscrossed the Middle East. Today much of the region's economic activity centers on the rich oil deposits of the lands that border on the Persian Gulf.

WHAT IS THE MIDDLE EAST?

In the past, the terms "Near East" and the "Levant" have been used to refer to the region of the Middle East. The term "Middle East" was first used by an American naval officer, Captain Alfred Thayer Mahan, in 1902 to contrast the region with the "Far East," as China and Japan were known then. The term was based on a Western point of view and was not used by the people who actually lived there. (What would they consider themselves in the middle of, or east of?) Residents of the area define themselves in terms of their religion, ethnic or cultural heritage, language, and country.

Think of the Middle East as a wheel. It is the "hub" for the continents of Asia, Africa, and Europe. The spokes of this wheel extend west across Africa to the Atlantic Ocean, east into Asia as far as Afghanistan, north to Europe through Turkey, and south to the Arabian Peninsula

1

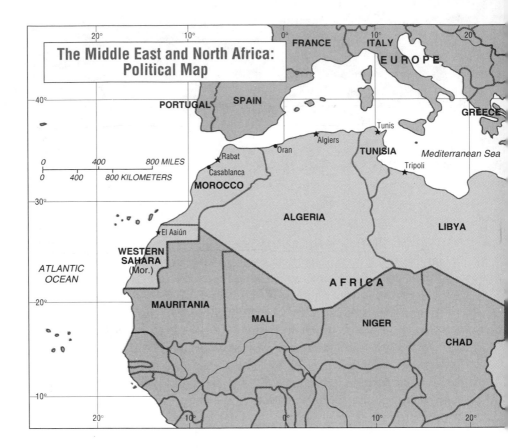

The Middle East and North Africa: Political Map

20° · 10° · 0° FRANCE · 10° ITALY · 20°
EUROPE
40°
PORTUGAL · SPAIN · GREECE
Tunis
Algiers
0 · 400 · 800 MILES
0 · 400 · 800 KILOMETERS · Oran · TUNISIA · Mediterranean Sea
Rabat · Tripoli
Casablanca
MOROCCO
30°
ALGERIA · LIBYA
El Aaiún
WESTERN
SAHARA
ATLANTIC · (Mor.) · AFRICA
OCEAN
20°
MAURITANIA
MALI · NIGER
CHAD
10°
20° · 10° · 0° · 10° · 20°

and the Indian Ocean (see the map above). Opinion varies as to which countries should be included in the term "Middle East." To most people the core generally includes Egypt, Israel, Jordan, Lebanon, Syria, Turkey, Cyprus, Iraq, Iran, Saudi Arabia, Yemen, Oman, the United Arab Emirates, Qatar, Bahrain, and Kuwait. Sudan in Africa and Afghanistan in south central Asia are also included in the Middle East in this book, even though these two cultures have strong non-Muslim features as well. Morocco, Algeria, Tunisia, and Libya are Muslim countries that are located on the continent of Africa. They are sometimes grouped together as "North Africa."

WHAT ELEMENTS CHARACTERIZE THE REGION?

Most people in the Middle East are **Muslims** (MUZ-luhmz), as followers of Islam are called. They share centuries of common history. They do

2

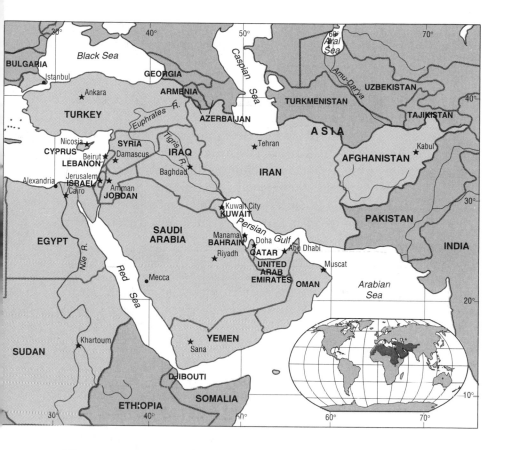

not, however, share the same **culture**. A culture is a way of life. It includes the way a group of people live and work. One part of culture is
religion.

Religion.   Although the majority of the people in the Middle East are
Muslims, Judaism is the main religion in Israel. Sizeable Christian communities exist in Egypt, Lebanon, and Syria. And within Islam itself
there are subdivisions. Most Muslims are **Sunnites** (SUN-eyets). But
Shiite (SHEE-eyet) Muslims form the majority in Iran and are a sizeable
group in Iraq, Yemen, Lebanon, and Oman. Groups that have broken
off from Islam (like the Druze in Lebanon, Syria, and Israel or the
Alawites of Syria) are also among the religious people of the Midde East.

The important thing to remember is that, like the United States,
most Middle Eastern countries have diverse populations. In other
words, their citizens come from many different backgrounds. Unlike the

In what ways is the ME diverse?

3

United States, however, with its constitutional separation of church and state, in the Middle East religious identity often is more closely tied to one's social group and status.

Language. Arabic is a unifying language for many Middle Eastern countries, but there are several different kinds of Arabic. The type of language found in classic Arabic texts like the **Koran** (koh-RAN), the holy book of Islam, is not the same as the language used in today's newspapers. And newspaper Arabic is also not the same as spoken Arabic. For a comparison, think of the differences between the English used by William Shakespeare, the English used in formal lectures or research papers, and the lyrics of popular music. This will give you some idea of the different Arabic strains.

There are also different **dialects,** or varieties of a spoken language. In the Middle East, some of these are Egyptian Arabic, the Arabic of Israel, Lebanon, and Syria, the Arabic of the Persian Gulf region, Iraqi Arabic, and North African Arabic. How different are these dialects

Construction of a new building in Riyadh, Saudi Arabia. Locate Saudi Arabia on the language map on pages 6-7. What is the language spoken in Saudi Arabia?

from one another? Take the word for coffee, for example. As written, the Arabic word for coffee would be pronounced "qahwah." In Israel, Lebanon, and Syria the word is pronounced "ahwah." In the Gulf region the "q" becomes a "g." Since Arabic is written without vowels, variations in pronunciation can occur easily. Of course, there are many instances when not just the pronunciation of a letter, but the entire word is different.

Which dialect is "best"? That depends on your purpose and audience. Which is most widely understood? Since Egypt is by far the largest Arab country, as well as the center of the film industry for the Arabic-speaking world, many non-Egyptians are familiar with that dialect. So you can see that while Arabs can easily read each other's newspapers because the printed language appears the same, they may have some difficulty understanding each other's Arabic in conversation.

Languages. Arabic and Hebrew (the main language of Israel) are both **Semitic languages;** that is, they both grew out of the language of the ancient Semites, a pastoral nomadic people who originated in the Arabian peninsula. Over time, the Hebrews, who with other Semites settled in Palestine, developed their own alphabet. Although they have different alphabets, there are numerous similarities between Arabic and Hebrew words. For example, "hello," "good-bye," and "peace" are similar words in both languages. The Arabic word is *salaam*; the Hebrew word is *shalom*. When one remembers that vowels are not always written in either language, the common root of the two words is even more clearly seen.

The other two major languages of the Middle East are Persian and Turkish. Unlike Arabic and Hebrew, neither of these languages is Semitic. Persian is an **Indo-European language;** that is, it was spoken originally in an area between India and Europe. Today, Persian, or Farsi, is spoken in Iran (formerly known as Persia). Turkish is an **Altaic language** that originated somewhere in eastern Europe and Asia. It is, of course, spoken in Turkey. Persian uses the same script as Arabic, but the Turks changed to the Latin script in 1928 as part of their drive to become more European and less Asian. There are also a number of minority groups such as the Kurds of eastern Turkey, northeastern Iraq, and northwestern Iran, and the Armenians of the southern Caucasus and eastern Turkey, all of whom have their own language.

European Languages. European languages are frequently spoken in the Middle East, particularly by members of the upper class. Quite

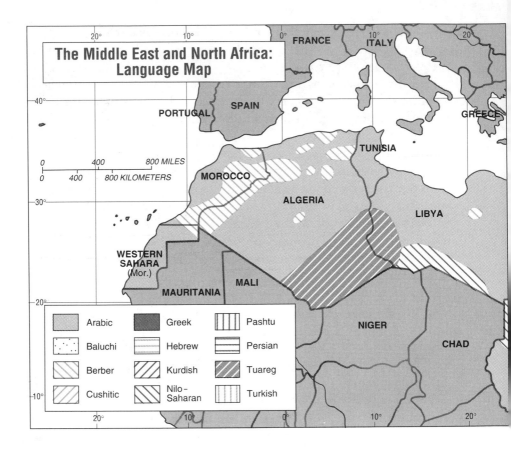

The Middle East and North Africa: Language Map

Legend:
- Arabic
- Baluchi
- Berber
- Cushitic
- Greek
- Hebrew
- Kurdish
- Nilo-Saharan
- Pashtu
- Persian
- Tuareg
- Turkish

often the choice of European language is a reflection of past European rule over a particular country. French, for example, is widely spoken in the former French colonies of North Africa and, to a lesser extent, in Lebanon. English is more commonly spoken in areas once controlled by Great Britain: Egypt, Israel, and Jordan. Today, English is widely used in the Persian Gulf states of Oman, United Arab Emirates, Qatar, Bahrain, and Kuwait. This language usage reflects their close economic ties with American and British oil companies.

The study of European languages by today's Middle Easterners should not imply that cultural borrowing has all been in one direction. Many English words have Middle Eastern origins. Among them are "cotton" (from the Arabic *qutn*), "lemon", "sugar", "sherbet", and "syrup". Others include "guitar" (from the Arabic *qitar*), "admiral", "algebra", and "alcohol". The chess term "checkmate" comes from *shah mat*, the Persian term for "the king is dead."

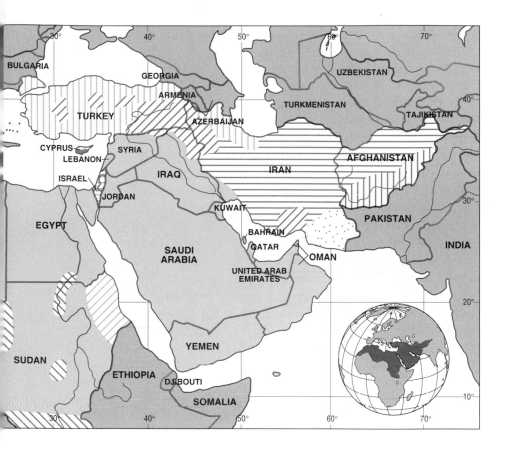

A LARGE DRY REGION

The most striking features of the Middle East's geography are that most of the area is characterized by lack of water (especially in year-round supplies), the poor quality of the soil, and sharp extremes of temperature. By no means is all of the Middle East like this. Some areas are better watered, richer, and more temperate. Thus, most people live along the coasts in mountain valleys, in river valleys, and around **oases,** fertile areas in the desert. In these places, the **population density**—the average number of people per square mile—is high. Elsewhere the land is empty of people.   uneven pop - why?

Deserts and River Valleys.   The region of the Middle East consists of several types of land formations. First, there are the vast deserts that make up most of North Africa and the Arabian Peninsula. The Sahara,

7

the world's largest desert, extends from the Atlantic coast in the west, the Atlas Mountains and the Mediterranean Sea in the north, to the Red Sea in the east. These areas are very dry. In Egypt, a large country occupying the northeast corner of Africa, about 96 percent of the land is desert. People live for the most part along the fertile banks of the Nile River. There agriculture is made possible by yearly soil-enriching floods. It was along the banks of the Nile that the ancient Egyptians developed one of the earliest civilizations. As you will read, rivers have played an important role in shaping the history and cultures of the Middle East. East of the Nile, across the Suez Canal and south of the Sinai Peninsula, is the Arabian Peninsula (see map on pages 10–11).

Bordered by the Red Sea, the Gulf of Aden, the Arabian Sea, the Gulf of Oman, and the Persian Gulf, the Arabian Peninsula consists mainly of a vast **plateau.** A plateau is a high, broad, level landform with at least one steep side. It is usually near mountains. On the Arabian Peninsula, the mountains lie along the west coast of the plateau and increase in height as one travels south. In Yemen, along the peninsula's southwest corner, the mountains reach a height of about 12,000 feet (3,658 meters). In the basin-shaped interior of the Arabian Peninsula is the Rub'al-Khali or "Empty Quarter." This uninhabited desert of 400,000 square miles (1,036,000 square kilometers) is one of the world's driest places.

North of the dry Arabian Peninsula is the Fertile Crescent, a region named for its semicircular shape and heavier rainfall. The Fertile Crescent extends along the Mediterranean coastal plain in Israel and sweeps northeast through Lebanon and Syria. Like a quarter moon, the crescent curves southward to Iraq, where it includes the Tigris and Euphrates river valleys. The Fertile Crescent is the place where many ancient civilizations began.

The Sahara. Parts of this huge desert are sandy. Other parts are rocky.

*Some of the highest mountains in the Middle East are
these in Afghanistan at the eastern edge of the region.
Other very high mountains are the Atlas Mountains in
Morocco at the western edge of the region. Find these
mountains on the map on pages 10–11.*

The Tigris and Euphrates rivers rise in the Little Caucasus mountains of Turkey and Iran (see map, pages 10–11). Flowing south through
the broad plains of Iraq, the two rivers meet at Basra to form another
river, the Shatt-Al-Arab. Unlike the more predictable floods of the Nile,
the Tigris and Euphrates rivers are more apt to flood without warning.
Also, unlike the Nile, the rivers are more difficult to navigate.

Mountains and Waterways.   Another type of land formation found in
the Middle East is the mountains. Turkey is ringed by geologically
active mountains—the Pontic Mountains facing the Black Sea and the
Taurus Mountains facing the Mediterranean Sea. Both mountain areas
are subject to earthquakes. In the middle of Turkey lies the Anatolian
Plateau, a treeless region used for <u>pastoralism,</u> or animal herding, and
dry farming. Turkey's narrow coastal regions are well watered, fertile,
and well-suited to agriculture.

Turkey lies in two continents—Europe and Asia—although the
Asian, or Anatolian, side is the larger. The two continents are separated
by several historic bodies of water. These are the Bosporus, the Sea of
Marmara, and the Dardanelles. All three waterways have had great strategic value in the past and continue to be important in shipping.

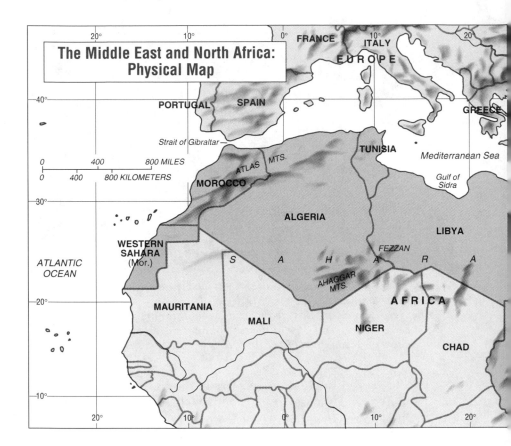

The Middle East and North Africa:
Physical Map

Southeast of Turkey lies Iran. It consists primarily of a high plateau (about 4,000 feet or 1,219 meters) situated between the Elburz Mountains in the north and the Zagros Mountains in the south. As one moves east, the land becomes drier, until it gives way to desert at the borders of Afghanistan and Pakistan.

Limited Rainfall. As the map on pages 14–15 shows, most places in the Middle East get less than 20 inches (51 centimeters) of rain each year. Much of the region is desert, due to several factors. Moisture-laden winds from the Mediterranean, Black, and Caspian seas drop their rain on the seaward side of the upland mountain slopes. Consequently, the inland areas get very little rainfall. The farther inland one goes from the mountain slopes that ring the Mediterranean, the less water one finds. The southern side of the Arabian Peninsula receives rainfall from

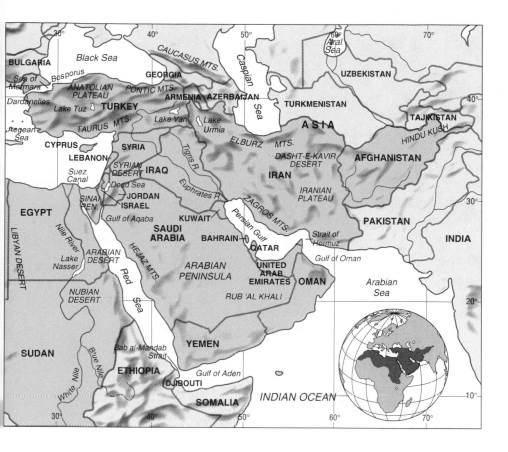

summer **monsoons** blowing from the Indian Ocean. Monsoons are winds that change direction with the seasons. Winter monsoons are generally dry, while summer monsoons are very wet. In Yemen, the amount of rainfall is sufficient to grow coffee plants. (It was through the Yemeni port of Mocha that coffee achieved worldwide popularity as a beverage.) Almost everywhere else in the region rain falls during the winter months, when the westerly winds bring moisture to the land. However, the amount and length of rainfall varies considerably from year to year. For example, one year's rainfall may be limited to two or three cloudbursts. These sudden, intense rains often produce floods that **erode,** or wear away, the soil rather than increase its fertility.

Irrigation: Help and Hindrance. Because of the dry soil and meager rainfall, nonirrigated farming is possible only in small areas of Iran,

Turkey, Lebanon, Syria, Jordan, and Israel. Wide-scale agriculture is possible only by means of irrigation. It is limited to the river valleys of the Nile and the Tigris and Euphrates. In Iran and Oman underground canals carry water from mountain streams to the plains.

However, steady irrigation can raise problems. Ground water can be completely used up. Also, there may be too much salt in the soil. When the **water table** (the ground below the surface that is saturated with water) is near the surface of the ground, salt that exists naturally in the soil is drawn upward with the water. Eventually, the amount of salt left near the surface after evaporation will spoil the soil, making it unfit for agriculture. Many acres of otherwise good farmland have had to be abandoned because of this problem.

Climate Zones.   Most areas of the Middle East generally have hot, dry summers and fairly long winters with some rain. Snow is common at higher elevations. Therefore, temperature ranges may be extreme. In most regions, spring and autumn are brief seasons. During the summer, hot, dusty winds blow inland from the south and southeast. They add to the agricultural problems by blowing away layers of top soil.

In the inland plateaus of Iran and Anatolia, winter temperatures fall below freezing, and summer temperatures can rise as high as 100°F or more. Rainfall is between 10 and 20 inches (25 to 51 centimeters). Along the coasts and the Fertile Crescent, rainfall increases up to 40 inches (102 centimeters) in Beirut, the capital of Lebanon. On the other side of the mountain ranges, Damascus, the capital of Syria, gets only 10 inches (25 centimeters) of rainfall each year. The same contrast holds true for Beersheba in Israel and Amman, the capital of Jordan. Along the Mediterranean coast, however, temperatures are very much like those of southern California.

Moving south into the desert, the land gets even drier. Even along the coast, rainfall averages only 10 inches (25 centimeters) a year. Although rain may not fall, the air may still be humid because of the closeness of the sea. This, combined with high temperatures, can make for a very uncomfortable environment. The contrast in this region is not between coastline and interior, but between desert and river valley.

It is not surprising that rivers have played an important role in the growth of civilizations in the Middle East. Egypt is "the gift of the Nile," as Herodotus, the ancient Greek historian, wrote. Summers are hot and dry; winters have little rainfall. Cairo, Egypt's capital, has an average yearly rainfall of 8 inches (20 centimeters). Baghdad, the capital of Iraq, has an annual rainfall of 6 inches (15 centimeters).

12

AGRICULTURE AND INDUSTRY

Given the land formations, availability of water, and climate found in the Middle East, **arable land,** or land suitable for farming, is severely limited. In fact, only about seven percent of all the land in the Middle East is under cultivation. But what good land is available can easily be overgrazed or overworked as farmers attempt to provide for their families. For example, hungry animal herds (particularly goats) often strip the land of its plant life. When this happens, the soil becomes even more exposed to the forces of erosion. The result is **desertification,** the process by which arable land becomes desert. Over the years, overgrazing and intense farming have caused the deserts of the Middle East to grow in size.

People have hurt the land in other ways as well. Long ago, parts of the Middle East were covered by forests. The Bible describes some of those forests, including the famous cedars of Lebanon. But for over 5,000 years, people in the region have been cutting down those wooded areas to build towns and cities and clear land for farming. Wood has long been the most prized building material in the region. The process of clearing land of forests is called **deforestation.**

Today the Middle East has very few forested areas. Just a few stands of trees grow on the slopes of the Elburz Mountains in Iran and the Lebanon Mountains. Elsewhere, the only trees that remain are those that were planted by people. They are found mainly along rivers and irrigation ditches or in cemeteries, gardens, and parks.

Trees are more than a source of building material or fuel. They prevent erosion by holding the soil in place. This is especially important in a region where most forests were in the highlands. Once those forests were gone, there was nothing to keep the soil from washing away when the spring rains came. As the hillsides eroded, flooding increased in the valleys and the plains.

Some countries, notably Israel, have started **reforestation** projects, in which they plant trees to stop erosion. The Israelis are also working to stop desertification by turning parts of the desert into farmland through irrigation. Pipelines and canals pump water from the Sea of Galilee to the Negev, Israel's desert.

Livestock: Sheep, Goats, and Camels.   It should not be surprising that herds of cattle or dairy cows are rare in the Middle East. The lush grazing land they require for survival just does not exist in sufficient amounts. Instead, people raise sheep, goats, and camels, animals which do well despite limited grazing land. Much has been written about how

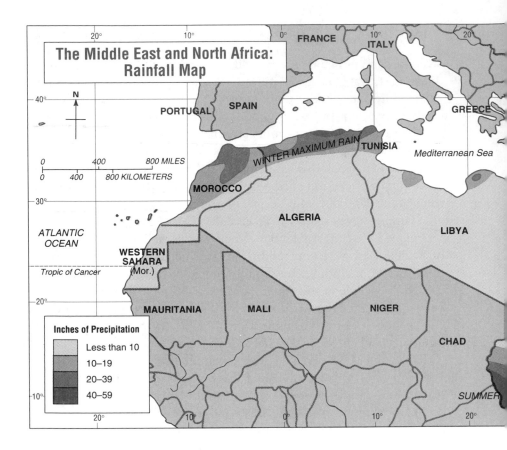

The Middle East and North Africa:
Rainfall Map

N

0   400   800 MILES
0   400   800 KILOMETERS

FRANCE
ITALY
SPAIN
PORTUGAL
GREECE
WINTER MAXIMUM RAIN
TUNISIA
Mediterranean Sea
MOROCCO
ALGERIA
LIBYA
ATLANTIC
OCEAN
WESTERN
SAHARA
(Mor.)
Tropic of Cancer
MAURITANIA   MALI   NIGER
CHAD
SUMMER

Inches of Precipitation

	Less than 10
	10–19
	20–39
	40–59

efficient the camel is in the desert environment. However, as modern technology has been introduced, the role of the camel has more and more become that of a photographic attraction for tourists.

Middle Easterners who depend solely on herding for their livelihood have become fewer and fewer in number. They probably make up less than 5 percent of the region's population. Today, it is more common for farmers to own a few field animals, which may also be used occasionally for milk and meat. In Egypt, pigeon is a common source of meat, and farmhouses have pigeon towers to attract the birds.

Agriculture. The Middle East grows a wide variety of agricultural produce. Higher rainfall along the Mediterranean coast allows farmers to grow vegetables and lush groves of fruit trees. In the past, farmers cultivated fruits and vegetables on a small scale in gardens around oases. Since World War II, however, the production of fruits and vegetables has expanded on a larger, more commercial scale. In oases and the marshlands of Iraq, dates are grown for both local consumption and

14

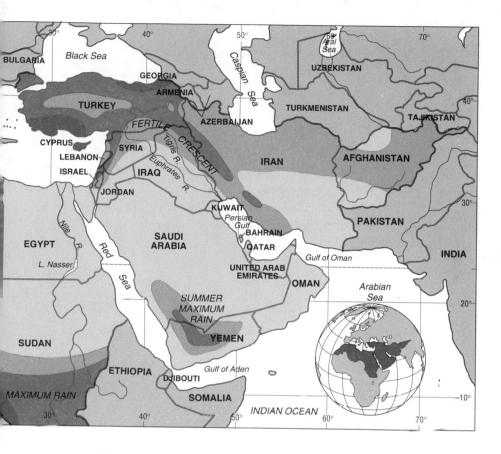

export. Crops like barley, wheat, lentils, and chickpeas are native to the Middle East and are grown wherever possible.

Commercial Agriculture.   When crops are raised to meet the needs of the local population, they are called **subsistence crops**. When they are raised to be sold, frequently for export, they are referred to as **cash crops.** Today, cash crops play an important part in Middle Eastern agriculture. Cotton is a leading cash crop of the region. By and large Middle Eastern cotton is grown under irrigation. Cotton has an ancient history and was grown by the early Egyptians for everyday use and in mummification. The expansion of cotton production in Egypt took place in response to rising demand in Europe in the 1800s. This rise in demand was related to the American Civil War, when ships carrying Southern cotton from the Confederacy to England were blockaded by the Union. A second spurt of growth in the cotton industry took place in the early 1950s. This time the response was to a world-wide shortage, which led in turn to high prices.

CASE STUDY:

From an Egyptian Village

Anwar el-Sadat was president of Egypt from 1970 until his death in 1981. He attracted worldwide attention with his visit to Israel. In 1978 he and Menachim Begin, the Israeli prime minister, won the Nobel Peace prize for their efforts to end the conflict between their countries. Sadat as a youngster had lived in a small village on the Nile called Mit Abul-Kum. He retained pleasant memories of his life there and wrote about the village in his autobiography.

Everything made me happy in Mit Abul-Kum, my quiet village in the depths of the Nile Delta, even the cold water in the winter when we had to leave at dawn for the special canal that filled to overflowing for not more than two weeks during which all land in the village had to be watered. It was obviously necessary to do it quickly and collectively. We worked together on one person's land for a whole day, then moved to another's, using any *tunbur* (Archimedean screw) that was available regardless of who owned it.

That kind of collective work—with and for other men, with no profit or any kind of individual reward in prospect—made me feel that I belonged not merely to my immediate family at home, or even to the big family of the village, but to something vaster and more significant: the land. . . .

Increasingly eager as I was for knowledge, I could never tear myself away from the life of the village. It was a series of uninterrupted pleasures. There was something different to look forward to every day: the seed-sowing season; irrigation time; the wheat harvest and the harvest celebrations; village wedding festivities; cotton harvesting, which always coincided with the harvest of dates. I remember how I used to pick enough cotton to fill the front part of my Arab dress, then run off to a woman who sold dates, and barter it all for the ripe, lush fruit. Every time I took the cattle to drink from the canal, worked our ox-drawn threshing machine, or joined the boys in picking the cotton crop, I felt I was doing so for the first time. . . .

Farmers in the Nile delta of Egypt. Farmers here used to rely on the Nile floods to water their crops. Now the fields are watered by year-round irrigation systems. The water comes from a lake created by the Aswan Dam.

This was not all I came to learn in Mit Abul-Kum. For I learned something else that has remained with me all my life: the fact that wherever I go, wherever I happen to be, I shall always know where I really am. I can never lose my way because I know that I have living roots there, deep down in the soil of my village, in that land out of which I grew, like the trees and the plants.

Adapted from Anwar el-Sadat, *In Search of Identity: An Autobiography*. New York: Harper & Row, 1977.

1. What were Anwar el-Sadat's principal memories of the years spent in his village?

2. What valuable lessons for life did he learn there?

3. What does this reading reveal about Egyptian village life?

Tobacco has been an important commercial crop in the Middle East since the 1700s. The leading growing areas are the Aegean and Black sea coasts of Turkey, the Latakia district of Syria, and parts of Jordan. Egyptian cotton is among the finest in the world. Other significant cash crops are sunflowers in Iran and Turkey and sugarcane grown under irrigation in Egypt and Iran. Israel exports a variety of fruits and vegetables, including oranges, melons, and tomatoes.

Raising cash crops is not without problems. As you have seen, cash crop farmers in the Middle East are exposed to the changing tastes and demands of the international marketplace. These are, of course, problems they share with farmers around the world, as they try to balance financial gain against economic risk.

Influences on Industrial Growth.   With the exception of oil, the Middle East has very little in the way of raw materials for an industrial base. Morocco has the world's largest **phosphate** reserves. Phosphates are a salt used as fertilizer. Tunisia is also a major producer. In the core area of the Middle East, lesser deposits of phosphate are mined around the Dead Sea in Israel and Jordan. But little other mineral resources are to be found in amounts large enough to warrant commercial investment.

Early industrialization in the region focused on the processing of such locally produced goods as cotton and flour. Cotton gins and flour mills sprang up. But competition from less expensive European manufactured goods destroyed many traditional industries and crafts. For example, Middle Eastern crafts workers could not equal the mass-produced textiles and woven cloth made in English mills in the 1800s and early 1900s. Rugmaking was a notable exception, however. Today, rugmaking is one of the outstanding traditional crafts of the Middle East. Many rugs produced in the region are regarded as works of art by collectors.

The development of heavy industry did not begin for most Middle Eastern nations until after World War II. In the late 1940s, more private **capital**, money invested in the production of goods and services, became available. In addition, newly won independence from European powers gave the nations of the Middle East a desire to build their national strength. As a result, **nationalization** of private and foreign industry took place, beginning with Egypt in 1956. When a government nationalizes an industry, it takes ownership of that industry. By taking over major industries, Middle Eastern governments hoped to bring the benefits of industrialization directly to the people. In recent years,

Modern farm equipment on irrigated land in Libya. Other Middle Eastern countries, including Israel and Saudi Arabia, also have farms largely dependent upon irrigation.

the process of nationalization has reversed itself. Joint ventures with foreign firms have been increasingly common and sought after by Middle Eastern governments. They realize help is needed in identifying and locating resources and planning future economic growth.

Industrial Development.   The course of industrial development in the Middle East has taken three paths. The first path is through light industry such as textile manufacturing and food processing. The second is through the manufacture of large consumer items such as refrigerators, televisions, and automobiles. These are frequently assembled in the region using parts imported from Europe, the United States, and Japan. The third path of development is through heavy industry such as steel plants. For their heavy industrial needs, the Middle Eastern nations must often rely on imports of raw materials.

Several obstacles stand in the way of industrial development in the Middle East. Lack of capital and skilled managers remain problems. So does illiteracy, the inability to read or write. Many adults in the region are illiterate. It is only since the 1970s that anyone who wished to go to elementary school could do so. Even today, many young people do not have a chance to go on to high school. Another problem is the low purchasing power of the consumer. The people simply do not have enough cash to spend. To generate enough sales to make a profit, businesses must frequently export their goods. That means international competition or facing other countries' trade barriers. In addition, most manufacturing plants in the Middle East are small and employ fewer than 50 people. These plants tend to be concentrated in a few areas, close to the big city markets. Finally, railroads or paved roads are often inadequate for transporting goods. These factors have held back industrial development. On the other hand, **service industries**—such as banking and finance, communications, and tourism—are very well developed.

The Importance of Oil. In 1850, world oil production was almost non-existent. Coal was then the major producer of energy for home and factory. With the beginning of wide-scale industrialization in the late 1800s and early 1900s, other sources of energy were needed. New engines had to be powered and lubricated. **Petroleum,** a liquid found beneath the surface of the earth, was capable of being burned and used as fuel for the new energy needs of modern industrial nations. Industry also found that petroleum was the base for creating many synthetic products. As demand for the energy source steadily grew, exploration for oil deposits took on great importance for industrialized countries.

Most industrialized nations of the world rely heavily on oil and natural gas for their energy needs. Most of the oil they need is produced in the Middle East. Saudi Arabia alone has 25 percent of the world's proven reserves of oil. Iran, Iraq, and Kuwait together account for another 25 percent.

Oil was first discovered in the Middle East in the 1920s by American oil engineers. Western oil companies were granted exclusive rights for developing petroleum in the years before World War II. Until the late 1960s eight Western companies controlled more than 90 percent of the oil produced in the region. Middle Eastern governments, however, have long since worked out more favorable economic arrangements with the oil companies and now control their own production rates and pricing.

In 1960 four Middle Eastern oil-producing states (Saudi Arabia, Kuwait, Iran, and Iraq) joined with Venezuela to form the Organization of Petroleum Exporting Countries (OPEC). Later they were joined by Qatar, Libya, the United Arab Emirates, Algeria, and the non-Middle Eastern states of Indonesia, Nigeria, and Ecuador. The members of OPEC hoped to coordinate petroleum policies and exercise greater control over their resource. OPEC is a **cartel,** an organization whose members work together to limit competition and maintain prices.

In 1968 OPEC recommended to its members that they look for new oil fields, buy shares in oil companies, and set prices on their products. As world demand for oil rose, the members of OPEC became more aggressive in setting their conditions and raising their prices. In the 1970s they raised oil prices sharply, causing shortages and other problems for oil-importing nations. The high cost of oil had a crippling effect on the economies of many developing countries in Africa, Asia, and Latin America. In the 1980s, however, the demand for oil leveled off. The oil-importing nations found alternative fuels and turned to conservation measures, and new oilfields were discovered—in the North Sea, for example. OPEC members now compete with each other for markets. OPEC's share has decreased from two-thirds to only one-third of the world's production. By 1986 the price of oil had fallen back to its price in the 1970s. Also, difficulties in reaching agreements on production rates and uniform pricing have reduced the power of OPEC. Yet the Persian Gulf War in 1991 revealed the continuing importance of Middle Eastern oil. It is important to note that most of the countries of the Middle East have little or no oil. Most Middle Eastern countries, therefore, face the dilemmas of all developing countries, including the high price of energy.

Problems and Promise of Oil.   As a result of their export of oil, a huge influx of money came to some of the least developed nations of the

An oil-drilling rig in Saudi Arabia. Saudi Arabia contains a fourth of the world's oil reserves.

Middle East. Many of these nations are using the money to build industry. Saudi Arabia's newest cities are centers for processing oil and producing chemicals from that oil. Oil income allows oil-rich nations to improve education and health care. Cities are transformed as mud brick dwellings give way to steel-and-glass structures. In many cases, the changes required by modernization have been too sudden and too sharp for the people to absorb. Basic social values have been brought into question as rulers try to determine what to retain of the old ways and what to adapt of the new.

As development projects were started, foreigners by the thousands entered the oil-rich countries as temporary workers. Their presence had an effect, too. The foreign workers had the skills needed in the oilfields and the development projects and were lured to the region by high-paying jobs. They earned good salaries and sent money home, thus spreading the oil wealth throughout the region and beyond. When Iraq invaded Kuwait in 1990, many people were surprised to learn that more than half of the people in Kuwait were foreigners. Most of the foreigners had come to Kuwait from other parts of the Middle East. Among them were many Palestinians and Iranians. Nearly ten percent of the foreigners were from Pakistan and other parts of South Asia.

What will happen to these countries when the oil supplies dry up? How can they best use their present money to insure future prosperity? Should they invest in the United States or Western Europe where economic and political stability will insure a safe return on their money? Or should they develop their own country or region with projects whose outcomes hold a greater risk? What industries should be developed now that will be profitable enough in 30 years to replace oil? In what areas should workers be trained and students educated? For a country like Oman, where oil exports account for 90 percent of its revenue, such questions are crucial.

PROBLEMS OF DEVELOPMENT

The oil-rich countries of the Middle East are not alone in facing crucial development questions, however. Each country in the region must determine how best to use its resources to modernize society and insure a better life for its people. Unfortunately, the best way of accomplishing these goals is not always clear.

Earlier in this chapter the problems associated with irrigation were touched upon. **Hydroelectric** projects have been developed throughout the region. Turkey and Syria have built hydroelectric projects that use water power to generate electricity. Dams have been built to generate electricity as well as for purposes of irrigation. Egypt has also developed large-scale hydroelectric projects. It completed the High Dam at Aswan in 1970. The purpose of the project was to make cultivation possible all year around, to bring new land under cultivation, and to increase electrical output. (The High Dam also created a new inland fisheries industry in the lake that formed behind it.) With such a high level of investment, the government of Egypt prefers that farmers raise valuable cash crops instead of low-priced but basic subsistence cereals. Such a policy, while making sense, has created problems. Egyptian farmers are now subject to price changes on the international market. In addition, the Egyptian government has to import food to supply local demands.

The Aswan Dam has had other effects, too. Since it prevents annual flooding by the Nile, farmers no longer get a free supply of nutrients in the flood water. Now they must purchase chemical fertilizers for their fields, which increases their production costs. Farming techniques have to be changed also. If irrigation water is not drained properly, the land may become poisoned by salt deposits. Egypt's vital tourist industry has also felt the impact of the dam project. The minerals present in the higher water levels of the Nile have increased the decay of the ancient monuments along the Nile. The High Dam was essential to Egypt's development. But these problems mean that even the most valuable projects have unexpected consequences.

The search for reliable water for plants, animals, and people is one that is shared by both the oil-rich and the oil-poor nations of the region. Water, not oil, has always been the most precious resource for the people who live in the Middle East. Today many of the oil-rich countries in the region are using their wealth to turn salt water into fresh water. That process is called **desalination**. Nearly one fourth of the more than 3,500 desalination plants in the world are located in Saudi Arabia. It also has the world's largest desalination plant. Located at Jubail, the plant produces 250 million gallons (9,500,000 kiloliters) of fresh water daily, about the size of the flow of a good-sized river. The Saudis and other Persian Gulf nations depend on desalination for most of their fresh water. Indeed, half of all the fresh water in Kuwait comes from desalination plants.

Desalination is a costly solution to the water problem. Distilling sea water, which is extremely salty, requires huge amounts of energy. That is not a problem for countries like Saudi Arabia, which has vast reserves of petroleum and natural gas. However, it is a serious problem for other

Countries of the Middle East and North Africa

COUNTRY	CAPITAL	AREA Square Miles	POPULATION Millions of People	POPULATION Density (per sq. mile)	POPULATION Growth Rate (annual %)	AGRICULTURE AND INDUSTRY
Afghanistan	Kabul	250,000	16.6	67	2.6	wheat, fruits, nuts; textiles, furniture, cement
Algeria	Algiers	919,590	26.0	28	2.7	grains, wine grapes, potatoes, dates, olives, oranges; oil, light industry, food processing
Bahrain	Manama	240	0.5	1872	2.3	fruits, vegetables; oil, oil products, gas, aluminum refining
Cyprus	Nicosia	3,570	0.7	200	1.0	grains, potatoes, citrus fruits, grapes, carob; light manufacturing
Egypt	Cairo	386,660	54.5	141	2.9	cotton, rice, beans, sugar, fruits, grains, corn, vegetables; oil, textiles, petro-chemicals, food processing, cement
Iran	Tehran	636,290	46.6	92	3.3	grains, rice, fruits, sugar beets, cotton, grapes; oil, gas, cement, sugar refining, carpets
Iraq	Baghdad	167,920	17.1	102	2.7	grains, rice, dates, cotton; oil, gas, petro-chemicals, textiles, oil refining, cement
Israel	Jerusalem	8,020	4.9	606	1.6	citrus fruits, vegetables; diamond cutting, textiles, food processing, elecrtonics, machinery
Jordan	Amman	35,480	3.4	96	4.1	grains, fruits, vegetables, olives; phosphate, textiles, cement, food processing
Kuwait	Kuwait	6,880	1.4	204	3.0	oil, natural gas
Lebanon	Beirut	4,020	3.4	843	2.1	citrus fruits, olives, tobacco, grapes, vegetables, grains; food processing, textiles, cement, oil products
Libya	Tripoli	679,360	4.4	6	3.1	wheat, barley, olives, citrus and other fruits, dates; oil, natural gas, textiles, carpets
Morocco	Rabat	172,410	26.2	152	2.5	grain, fruits, dates, grapes; phosphate, carpets, leather goods, clothing, tourism
Oman	Muscat	82,030	1.6	19	3.8	dates, fruits, vegetables, wheat, bananas; oil
Qatar	Doha	4,250	0.5	122	2.5	oil, natural gas
Saudi Arabia	Riyadh	830,000	15.5	19	3.4	wheat, barley, dates, fruits; oil, natural gas
Sudan	Khartoum	967,490	25.9	27	2.9	cotton, peanuts, sorghum, gum arabic, sesame, rice, coffee, sugar cane, wheat, dates; textiles, food processing
Syria	Damascus	71,500	12.8	179	3.8	cotton, grain, olives, fruits, vegetables, tobacco; oil products, textiles, cement, glassware, sugar refining, brassware
Tunisia	Tunis	63,170	8.4	132	2.2	grains, olives, citrus fruits, grapes, dates, figs, vegetables; oil. phosphate, textiles, food processing, construction materials
Turkey	Ankara	301,380	58.5	194	2.2	cotton, tobacco, cereals, barley, corn, fruits, potatoes, sugar beets; iron, steel, machinery, metal products, food processing
United Arab Emirates	Adu Dhabi	32,280	2.4	74	2.7	vegetables, dates, limes; oil
Yemen	Sana	203,850	10.1	49	3.5	wheat, sorghum, cotton, coffee, fruits; food processing, mining, petroleum refining

Sources: Population Reference Bureau, Inc. 1991; World Almanac, 1992

countries in the region. They are seeking other solutions to the chronic shortage of water. Syria, for example, has built a three-mile-long dam across the Euphrates River at Tabka that can store enough water to double the amount of irrigated land in that country.

Several countries, including Saudi Arabia and Israel, are carrying out work in **hydroponics.** In hydroponics, water containing fertilizer and nutrients is forced at a controlled rate through plastic pipes to the roots of individual plants. In this way, crops can be raised in record time with relatively small amounts of water and fertilizer.

Such projects reveal the importance of water to people throughout the region. No country in the Middle East has as much water as its people would like, and no country in the region completely controls its own water supplies. A dam or a pipeline in one country affects the amount of water available in a neighboring country. This has often led to sharp disagreements between the countries involved (see Chapter 9).

REVIEWING THE CHAPTER

I. Building Your Vocabulary

Match the definition with the correct term.

deforestation	dialects	desalination
population density	cash crops	plateau
desertification	culture	monsoon
nationalization	pastoralism	

1. The process of cutting down trees to make room for farms and towns
2. Relatively level land that is high in elevation
3. The varieties of a spoken language
4. The process of over-grazing or over-cultivating land
5. The process of turning saltwater into fresh water
6. The way a group of people live and work
7. The average number of people per square mile
8. Winds that change direction seasonally
9. Crops raised to be sold
10. Takeover of a major industry or industries by a government

UNDERSTANDING THE FACTS

1. What are the main religions in the Middle East? Which one do most people in the region follow?
2. What is the main language spoken in the region? Name two other languages spoken there.
3. Give an example of a Semitic language, an Indo-European language, and an Altaic language spoken in the Middle East.
4. Where do most people in the region live? Why?
5. Why is most of the Middle East not a good region for farming?

6. Name two important commercial crops in the Middle East.

7. What crops are native to the Middle East?

8. Name three obstacles to industrial development in the Middle East.

9. What countries in the region are using dams to generate electricity?

10. Name two countries in the region that have built desalination plants.

THINKING IT THROUGH

1. In some ways the Middle East is defined by language and religion as much as by geographic location.
   a. Of what significance is Islam in defining an area that reaches from Morocco in North Africa to Afghanistan on the border of Pakistan?
   b. How does Arabic unify the region? How does it divide the region?

2. List the three most striking features of the Middle East's geography. How have these factors influenced the economy of the region? Write a paragraph that discusses the impact of climate and geography on the Middle East's agriculture. You may wish to discuss the importance of limited rainfall on cultivation of certain crops, the role of irrigation, the raising of livestock, and the way geography has shaped the area's commercial activity.

3. Of what importance was the discovery of oil to the Middle East? Write a paragraph that focuses on this question. Some specifics you might consider are as follows:
   a. What rights did Western companies have in the petroleum industry until the late 1960s?
   b. How did OPEC influence world oil production and prices in the 1970s?
   c. What impact have oil profits had on the social development of the Middle East?

DEVELOPING CRITICAL THINKING SKILLS

All the statements below are false. Use the chart on page 24 to check the information and rewrite the sentences so that they are true. ·

1. The countries on the chart with the largest populations are Turkey, Egypt, and Syria.

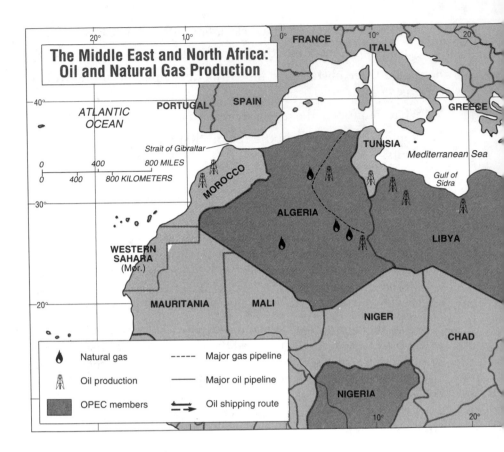

The Middle East and North Africa:
Oil and Natural Gas Production

ATLANTIC OCEAN

PORTUGAL   SPAIN   FRANCE   ITALY   GREECE

Strait of Gibraltar

0   400   800 MILES
0   400   800 KILOMETERS

MOROCCO

TUNISIA

Mediterranean Sea

Gulf of Sidra

ALGERIA

LIBYA

WESTERN SAHARA (Mor.)

MAURITANIA   MALI

NIGER

CHAD

NIGERIA

Legend	
Natural gas	Major gas pipeline
Oil production	Major oil pipeline
OPEC members	Oil shipping route

2. Libya is the second largest country in the region.

3. Machinery is a major product of Kuwait and Qatar.

4. The capital of Jordan is Jerusalem.

5. The countries with the highest population density are Bahrain and Saudi Arabia.

6. Israel is the smallest country in the region.

7. Syria, Lebanon, and Israel are sources of oil products.

8. Of the North African countries, only Morocco has a phosphate mining industry.

9. Syria has a lower population growth rate than Israel.

10. Kuwait is self sufficient in food.

28

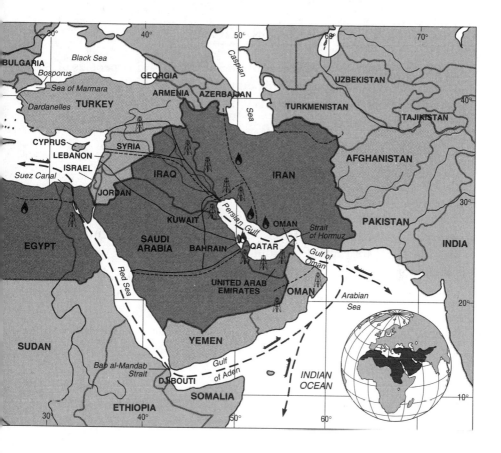

INTERPRETING A MAP

Use the map above to answer the following questions.

1. Which countries are major oil producers?
2. Which countries are major natural gas producers?
3. What country on the Arabian Peninsula has no oil or natural gas?
4. Which countries in the region are members of OPEC?
5. Which bodies of water are probably of strategic importance in the transporting of oil by ship? (Places of strategic importance are those where a military attack or a block could most easily stop the flow of oil.)

ENRICHMENT AND EXPLORATION

1. Find out more about the culture of one of the following peoples of the Middle East. Explain how its culture is similar to that of other groups in the region. What aspects of its culture are unique?

> The Berbers of North Africa
>
> The Kurds of Iran
>
> The Armenians of Turkey
>
> The Druze of Lebanon, Syria, and Israel

2. Choose a Middle Eastern city and consult an atlas to find out its average seasonal temperatures. Then describe the clothing you would choose for each of the four seasons if you lived in that city. What fabrics would your clothes be made of? Why?

2 *People and Cultures*

Life in the Middle East and North Africa varies greatly not only from country to country but also from one part of a country to another. In this chapter, you will learn more about the patterns of life in the cities and the countryside. You will read, too, about life in Israel, the only state in the region where the great majority of the people are Jewish.

The Middle East has some of the oldest inhabited cities in the world and some of the newest. Among the oldest cities are Jerusalem and Alexandria. Tel Aviv is the newest Middle Eastern city. Cities in the region serve many different functions, as you will read in this chapter.

THE CITIES

People in the Middle East located their cities near rivers or on the sea coast. Cairo is on the Nile, and Baghdad is located on the Tigris River. Alexandria, Beirut, Tel Aviv, Muscat, and Istanbul are coastal cities. As you might expect, a river location meant an available water supply. Being located on bodies of water also made the cities more accessible. Thus, they became cargo transfer points and trade centers. But inland cities like Damascus also developed into commercial centers. Located at the edge of the desert, Damascus was a centuries-old stopping point for caravans.

Cities as Political Centers. Some cities in the Middle East were founded for political reasons. A new ruler sometimes thought it desirable to have a capital that was not connected with earlier regimes. In the

A.D. 700s, the capital of the Arab Empire shifted from Damascus to the new city of Baghdad. In the 900s, a North African **dynasty,** or ruling family, conquered Egypt and founded Cairo, a name that means "the Victorious." In 1923, the new government of Turkey moved its capital to Ankara away from Istanbul, which for centuries had been the capital of the Ottoman Empire. (You will read about the Ottomans in Chapter 6.) Other cities, like Amman in Jordan and those of the Persian Gulf emirates, started as small villages or ports. These cities developed either as administrative centers for government or as economic centers.

Cities as Religious Centers.   Some cities are important as religious centers, such as Mecca, Medina, and Jerusalem. The first two are located in Saudi Arabia and are holy to Muslims because of their association with the founding of Islam. Every year millions of Muslims from all over the world converge on Mecca at once for the **hajj** (HAJ), or pilgrimage. This is a religious duty each Muslim who is able to do so should perform at least once in his or her lifetime.

Jerusalem is a city that is sacred to Jews, Christians, and Muslims. Jews come to pray at what was once the Western Wall of the Second Temple, which was destroyed by the Romans in A.D. 70. Jerusalem is also the political capital of Israel. Christian pilgrims visit the Church of the Holy Sepulchre. Muslims visit the Dome of the Rock and al-Aqsa mosque. Karbala in Iraq and Qum in Iran are two other important Muslim cities. But Mecca and Jerusalem are surely the most prominent cities with religious significance.

Cities as Social Centers.   As you have seen, Middle Eastern cities serve as economic centers, transportation hubs, political centers, and religious sites. They also act as social magnets. Middle Easterners move from their villages to the cities to attend university, look for jobs, receive health care, deal with the government, pursue leisure activities, and enjoy the excitement of city life. In recent years, however, the drawing power of the cities has had a number of unplanned consequences.

Most Middle Eastern countries have at least one large city. Most often this is the capital. Other cities are usually much smaller and lack the attractions of the capital. People move to the capital to seek a better life. Think what the United States would be like if half the population were jammed into Washington, D.C., and the other half lived in villages that had no shops or movie houses and had only recently acquired electricity, running water, and plumbing. Where would you want to live?

Ten Largest Cities in the Middle East and North Africa		
CITY	COUNTRY	POPULATION
Cairo	Egypt	6,052,836
Tehran	Iran	6,042,584
Istanbul	Turkey	5,475,982
Baghdad	Iraq	4,648,609
Alexandria	Egypt	2,917,327
Ankara	Turkey	2,235,035
Casablanca	Morocco	2,139,204
al-Jizah	Egypt	1,670,800
Beirut	Lebanon	1,500,000
Algiers	Algeria	1,507,241

Sources: Encyclopaedia Britannica, 1991 Yearbook

PROBLEMS AND PATTERNS OF CITY LIFE

There is a population imbalance between the capital city and the rest of the country. Cities are very crowded. More important, they are pressed to their limits in their ability to provide for so many people. The rate of population increase in the cities is due to a high birth rate plus the rural-to-urban migration. With a population of 13 million, Cairo is one of the most densely populated cities in the world.

The Pressure of Many People. The growth of population in the cities is so great that construction cannot keep pace with it. Many inhabitants of Middle Eastern cities live in shantytowns. Housing is either not available or too expensive. There are other problems, too. Electric circuits may be overloaded and cause power failures. The increased demand for water may lower the pressure so much that residents of a building's upper floors sometimes find that nothing comes out of their faucets. In Cairo, extra floors are periodically stacked onto buildings, which sometimes collapse.

Buses are overcrowded, traffic jams are common, and air pollution goes unchecked. Schools cannot expand fast enough and maintain quality education. Competition for jobs is fierce whatever the level of education. Still, migration from the countryside continues.

Admittedly, not all Middle Eastern cities are this badly overcrowded. Many have slums and shantytowns on their outskirts, to different degrees. But they also have their beauties. The skyline of Istanbul is dominated by heavy domes and contrastingly thin towers overlooking the Bosporus and the Golden Horn. It is one of the most beautiful sights in the world.

How Cities Are Organized.   How do people make their way in the city? The answer is simple: the same way they learned to survive drought in the village. People from the same family or from the same village join together and pool their resources. When newcomers from the countryside arrive in the city, they look up relatives or fellow-villagers who came before them. They will often share dwellings. Soon an entire city neighborhood may be identified by the name of the village from which its residents originated.

Traditionally, Middle Eastern cities were built up neighborhood by neighborhood. The walled cities of earlier times were divided into "quarters." Here, people of a particular religion or ethnic group lived together. The gates to the quarter were locked after dark, so each group was secure behind its walls. Today the gates are not locked, but people of different ethnic groups and different faiths still live apart. There have also been changes in the structure of the family that affect the way people live. Fewer people live with members of their **extended family.** An extended family is one in which grandparents, parents, children, and other relatives live together in one household. In the cities, more and more people live in **nuclear families,** consisting only of a couple and their unmarried children.

The traditional Middle Eastern city also had a **suq** (sook), or marketplace. The suq, a maze of narrow streets, was "zoned" according to the goods sold within it. Today, the suqs of Middle Eastern cities follow the same zoning pattern. Copper and brass goods are sold in one area, perfume in another, gold and jewelry in still another. Leather items (because of their strong smell) are sold far away from the center. Within many Middle Eastern cities today the suqs of the older quarters exist side by side with the plate-glass windowed shops of the city's more Westernized shopping areas.

Methods of Buying and Selling.   Shopping in the suq is always an adventure. Storeowners stand at the entrance to their shop or stall calling to passers-by and inviting them to come in. A shopper enters one of the stores, let's say one that sells clothing. Here merchandise is displayed

CASE STUDY:

Modern Cairo

Egypt, long a major center of the Arab world, is today in deep economic trouble. It gains income from its oil wells in the Sinai and from the tolls that ships pay when they pass through the Suez Canal. Yet Egypt must import most of its food and is heavily dependent on foreign aid. People from the countryside are moving into the capital, Cairo.

Egypt is perhaps the poorest Arab nation in the Middle East today. [Probably only the Sudan, Afghanistan, and Yemen have lower incomes per person.] Housing is, for the most part, aging and decrepit. Behind the Khan el Khalili section of Old Cairo, for example, there is the "City of the Dead." Here Islamic Cairenes are buried and mausoleums raised over their graves in honor of the dead. When I visited the graveyard I found it to be occupied by living creatures—450,000 of them. They were squatters who had illegally occupied the edifices in the City of the Dead because there was no housing for them in Cairo. Most of these men, women, and children are recent immigrants from Egypt's villages, and they come to Cairo for better jobs, for better shelter. And more keep coming every month.

Present-day Egypt is a country of startling contrasts. In Cairo, there is the Khan el Khalili section, with some buildings nearly 1,000 years old. Not far away is the affluent Garden City section and the island of Zamalik. These are enclaves for the very rich, whose possession of luxury goods is constantly on display. Ox-carts and shiny Mercedes cars struggle together through incredibly crowded and narrow streets.

The economic challenges that face Egypt's government are immense. Egypt now has a shortage of at least 1.1 million housing units in Cairo alone. . . . Unless one is very rich, it is virtually impossible to obtain decent housing in Cairo.

Adapted from United Nations pamphlet, "Fund for Population Activities."

1. What is a major urban problem for Egypt?
2. What are some of the contrasts one sees in Cairo?

Shoppers in Arab cities buy their food and other goods in marketplaces, or suqs, like this one.

on pegs, hanging from the beams, or piled high on the shelves or floor. Rarely is merchandise marked with a price tag.

If the shopper expresses an interest in an embroidered dress or shirt, for example, the storeowner places the goods in front of the potential buyer. The customer looks through the colors and sizes until he or she finds one that is desirable. The customer inquires as to price and the shopkeeper (usually a man) responds. Then follows a ritual-like bargaining process. The customer may point out flaws in the garment and then make a counteroffer, usually much below the shopkeeper's price. The shop boy arrives with a coffee tray. The customer sips the drink while looking at other goods. The bargaining continues. As the customer prepares to leave, a final offer is made and accepted. The customer departs with the purchase—having split the difference in price with the shopkeeper.

Haggling, or bargaining, is characteristic especially of the buying and selling of expensive items, such as rugs. For smaller purchases there are usually fixed prices.

The typical buying and selling technique in the suq provides valuable lessons about doing business in the Middle East. Middle Easterners take time to know their business partners before discussing terms; they do not expect to make a quick deal. Negotiating skills are highly valued in Middle Eastern society.

The Mosque—The Muslim Place of Worship. In Islam, the place of ritual prayer is a religious building called a **mosque**. "Mosque" comes from the Arabic word *masjid*. The word means place of prostration, one of the postures used by Muslims in prayer. Each Middle Eastern city usually has a giant or central mosque that is big enough to hold all the people of the community for group prayers, with men and women praying in separate parts of the mosque.

Worshippers and visitors show respect for the mosque as a place of worship by removing their shoes upon entering. There is a fountain in front of the entrance for the ritual washing of hands, face, and feet that takes place before prayer. The interior of the mosque consists of much open space. There is no seating, because of the movements that accompany Muslim prayer. Instead, there are floor coverings that range from simple reed mats to elaborately woven rugs.

Mosques vary in size, building material, and decoration. But they usually have three elements: **mihrab, minbar,** and **minaret.** The mihrab is a niche in the wall that indicates the direction of Mecca, since part of Muslim ritual is to face Mecca while praying. The minbar is the pulpit from which sermons are preached. The minaret is the tower from which the call to prayer is made five times daily. (However, a poor village may

Handcrafted Persian rug. Rugmaking is considered an art. Crafts workers of the Middle East produce many beautiful examples of this traditional craft.

still have a mosque without a minaret or an elaborate pulpit. The direction of Mecca in such a mosque may be a simple wall hanging.) Today, the voice of the **muezzin** (myoo-EZ-uhn), the one who gives the call to prayer, is usually amplified by a loudspeaker. Muslims need not be in a mosque to heed the call to prayer. People can lay down their prayer rugs at work or on the street, pray, and then return to business.

The walls of the mosque may be whitewashed or covered with beautiful tile work. Many mosques have verses from the Koran in beautiful **calligraphy,** or script, on the walls in patterns. Frequently, the writing is

An intricate page from the Koran. Muslims believe the Koran to be the word of God as it was revealed to Muhammad.

Contrasts in architecture in Baghdad. This ancient city, now the capital of modern Iraq, is located on the banks of the Tigris River. What is the tower on the mosque called?

so intricate that it is impossible to read. Since many Muslims have memorized the entire Koran, it rarely matters if the verses cannot be read. Other decorative elements in the mosque may include elaborate woodcarving, metalwork, and beautiful glass lamps or chandeliers. Mosaics in abstract or geometrical forms are widely used in mosque decoration. Human or animal figures are not permitted to be shown in Islamic art.

In large cities, mosques are sometimes part of a complex that includes a school and dormitory, a hospital, a soup kitchen, baths, and tombs. Frequently, these institutions are gifts to the community from a wealthy patron.

Schools. In many ways, schools in the Middle East are like those in the United States. Most countries have a system of education that extends over a twelve-year period. Children attend primary school for six years, then move on to preparatory and high school levels.

Until the mid-twentieth century, education in the Middle East was reserved for a small, privileged part of the population. Colonial rule usually did not favor widespread education. People learned to read with the

Chemistry class at the University of Constantine, Algeria.

Koran as both holy book and reading primer. With the wars of independence and, in some cases, the arrival of oil wealth, elementary and secondary school education became available to most children. The government often runs the schools, but some are privately owned.

Children study the basics—reading, writing, arithmetic, social studies. They are taught in the official language of the country—Arabic, Farsi, Turkish, Hebrew. In Iraq's Kurdish areas, school is taught in Kurdish. And many students study a second language; English and French are the most popular. Sometimes parents send their children to special schools to study religion. In places where people observe religion most strictly, it is taught in public schools as well.

Education is usually free but not required by law in every country. In Saudi Arabia, for example, elementary, secondary, and higher education is free but not compulsory. In addition, the Saudi government provides scholarships for college and university students. In Israel, free compulsory education is provided for all children between 5 and 16 years of age. In the Middle East today, an elementary education is available to all boys and most girls. Over half will go on to high school. Most of these educational opportunities have come since the 1970s. The growth of education has led to a dramatic increase in literacy. Just 50 years ago, only 10 percent of the people in the region could read or write. Today over 65 percent can do so.

There is a wide selection of universities in the Middle East. These range from the American University of Beirut to the Technion in Haifa to al-Azhar in Cairo. The last is a one-thousand-year old university that attracts students from across the Muslim world. The universities use many English-language textbooks, particularly in engineering and the sciences. Middle Eastern students are eager to keep pace with the latest advancements in the West.

University social life differs widely according to campus. In Israel, campus life is very similar to that of American colleges. In other countries, campus social life may be more restricted. In conservative Saudi Arabia, for example, female students are taught separately from male students. There is no dating. Women have their own classrooms and are taught via closed-circuit television if instructors are male. In less conservative Muslim nations, men and women go to school together.

Students' dress depends on local custom, social class, and religious attitudes. Western-style clothing is common on many campuses. More traditional dress, for example, ankle-length shirts and cloth headdresses for men, is worn in the countries of the Arabian peninsula. This type of clothing is far more comfortable to wear in a desert climate than jeans. On other campuses, women wear Western-style dresses of various lengths, while others wear long-sleeved dresses over matching slacks. In recent years, a new form of dress has developed among the more religiously observant women. They wear a loose-fitting, long coat and head scarf so that only their hands and face are exposed in public.

Health Care and Social Welfare. The level of health care is a problem in the Middle East. In most countries, diseases which are no longer widespread in the United States are still common. Many children and adults suffer from malnutrition, diseases due to contaminated water, parasites, and malaria because of the shortage of doctors and hospitals. Public services, such as water, garbage collection, and sewers vary from country to country. There are modern hospitals in most countries, but people have to pay for their health care, which not many can afford.

The health of the people varies greatly from country to country. It can also be very different in the cities from what it is in the rural areas. One broad level of comparison is the average **life expectancy.** This is the average number of years that a newborn baby can be expected to live. (See table on page 42.) For example, the average life expectancy in the Middle East as a whole is about 63 years. In Egypt it is about 66 years. People in Israel can expect to live 76 years on average, the longest in the region. Another measure of the health of people is the **infant mortality rate.** (See table on page 42.) That is the number of babies who die before reaching the age of one year, per thousand live births. The average for the region in 1989 was 77 deaths per thousand live births. That means about eight babies out of every hundred died before the age of one. In Syria, the infant mortality rate was 56. The lowest rate is in Israel, where it was 14.

Wealth from oil has made it possible for some countries in the region to provide free medicine and medical care for all citizens. Saudi Arabia is one such country. By 1983, there were 78 hospitals in Saudi Arabia and over 1,000 health centers. Today the King Faisal Medical Center near Riyadh has a reputation for being one of the most technically advanced in the world. In the United Arab Emirates, the government operates a system of social welfare benefits.

Of all the nations in the region, Israel has the most highly advanced system of social welfare. The state provides for people injured in industrial accidents and there are also maternity payments. The Ministry of Social Welfare provides for general assistance, relief grants, child care, and other social services.

Life in the Middle East and North Africa

COUNTRY	AVERAGE INCOME per Person (in dollars)	LIFE EXPECTANCY at Birth (in years)	INFANT MORTALITY RATE	LITERACY RATE (percent)	COLLEGE AND UNIVERSITY STUDENTS per 1,000 Inhabitants
Algeria	2,170	64	74	52	4.8
Egypt	630	57	73	44	14.2
Iran	1,800	65	43	48	3.6
Iraq	1,950	64	69	70	8.6
Israel	9,750	76	10	92	24.5
Jordan	1,730	71	38	71	20.4
Libya	5,410	67	64	60	8.1
Morocco	900	62	75	35	5.3
Saudi Arabia	6,230	63	71	c. 50	8.0
Syria	1,020	69	37	c. 50	15.2
Turkey	1,360	64	62	90	6.9

Sources: Population Reference Bureau, Inc., 1991; World Almanac, 1992; World Facts and Figures, 1989; World Book

POPULATION TRENDS

Three important trends characterize the population of the Middle East. One is that the population is growing rapidly. There are more people in the region than ever before, and they are competing for a limited number of jobs and resources. The second trend is increasing migration. Many Middle Easterners are moving to new homes in the region. Others are moving out of the region in search of jobs. The third trend is **urbanization**, the movement of people to cities from the countryside. Most people in the region now live in cities and towns and have jobs in mining, manufacturing, and service industries.

A Rapidly Growing Region.   Fifty years ago, the Middle East had about 52 million people. Today it is home to over 210 million people. Most of the growth is due to a falling death rate. People throughout the region are living longer. The infant mortality rate, in particular, has dropped sharply as a result of improved medical care. Supplying food for the increased population, however, is a major problem, for there is no more farmland on which to grow food crops today than there was half a century ago.

Migration.   Fifty years ago, most Middle Easterners rarely left their hometown or village. Today millions of people in the region live far from home. Some are **refugees.** They have had to flee their country for political reasons. Among the region's refugees are Palestinians, Lebanese, Kurds, and thousands of other victims of wars in the region.

Many migrants have left home to find work. Skilled workers in large numbers have migrated to the oil-rich countries of the Persian Gulf region to take high-paying jobs. Palestinians, for example, hold various jobs in the Gulf countries and throughout the Muslim world as well. These jobs range from construction work to positions in government. Large numbers of men from Egypt and Yemen can also be found working in other Middle Eastern countries. Some Middle Easterners—including thousands of Turks, Moroccans, and Algerians—have taken jobs in Western Europe.

As a result of migration, many countries in the region have lost some of their most educated and energetic people. These countries have, however, gained "breathing room," as fewer people clamor for jobs. Also, many migrants are men whose families remain at home. These migrants send back millions of dollars of their earnings to their parents, wives, and children. That money helps the local economy.

Urbanization.   The third trend in the region is urbanization. About 50 years ago, only 20 percent of the people in the Middle East lived in large cities. No city in the region had as many as a million people. As you can see from the table on page 33, there are now many cities with populations of well over a million. By 1968, a third of the people in the Middle East lived in cities. Today well over 50 percent make their homes in urban areas. In many large cities in the region, one third to one half of the population is made up of recent arrivals.

THE VILLAGES

While cities in the Middle East grow as newcomers stream in from towns and villages, many people in the region still live in small settlements. Their way of life is **traditional.** That is, they still live and work much as their ancestors did. In the past, there were few changes from one generation to the next. Today, however, changes are taking place more quickly.

Making a Living.   In the past, most village farmers rented the land they worked and paid the owner a share of their harvest. Many villagers rarely saw the owner of the land their families had worked for generations. Rich landowners could afford to live in the cities. Many of these absentee landowners had no concern for the welfare of the peasants who worked their land. The peasants often lived in poverty, tied to the land by debts and other obligations.

   A number of governments have tried to help poor village families in recent years. Much of this help has taken the shape of land reform. In 1961, Egypt passed a law limiting the amount of land a person could own to 100 acres (40 hectares). Special programs have made it possible for some landless peasants to buy the land that then became available.

How Villages Are Governed.   In rural areas village **headmen** are the leaders. They may be chosen by the local heads of households or appointed by the central government. The power of the headman varies from village to village. One factor that might influence a headman's power is the strength of the local government. The existence of a rival source of power in the village could be another factor. Village headmen are usually members of important families. Therefore, they often represent authority in the village, rather than the rights of the villagers. In Middle Eastern countries with strong one-party systems, such as Iraq

In recent years most Middle Eastern countries have switched from being rural societies to being urban ones. The only Middle Eastern countries where the majority of people are still farmers are Afghanistan, Morocco, Yemen, Oman, Saudi Arabia, Sudan, and Turkey.

and Syria, the head of the village is usually a prominent party member. In other words, power is located at the top of the social pyramid and not at the base, where most of the people are.

Family Life. How are individual households organized? The typical household consists of a man, his wife, their grown sons, and the sons' wives and children. As sons marry and have families, rooms are added on to the father's house. When the father dies, the sons may decide to stay together. If this happens, the eldest son is recognized as the head of the household. More often, however, the sons separate, as each is eager to become the head of his own household with all the status and responsibility of that position.

Married daughters usually live with their husband's family. But daughters keep their family names even after marriage. Since daughters may eventually live in other households and add to *that* household's income with their labor, sons are preferred to daughters. Sons give a family prestige and their labor adds to its wealth. Also, sons can be counted upon to support their parents in their old age.

Middle Eastern peasant families tend to be large. In the past, when many infants died from either disease or poor diet, peasants had many children to insure that at least one or two sons would survive. These sons were their economic security for their later years. Today, health care has improved and more children are surviving to adulthood. But the birth rate remains high. The growing population has meant greater pressure on the land and, as a result, greater numbers of people are moving to the crowded cities.

The Status of Women.   In rural areas, Muslim women do not have equal status with men. They have status of their own, nevertheless, in their households. Here, they supervise their daughters-in-law and grand-children and work in the fields. Unlike some urban women in the Middle East, rural women are less secluded, partly because of their heavy work load and the demands placed upon them.

Village women tend to marry relatives—particularly cousins on their father's side of the family. (By marrying cousins, the family insures that property stays within the family.) Although married women move to separate households, their parents and brothers and sisters generally live close by. Even after a woman is married, her family retains close ties with her. Her behavior reflects on her family of origin. If the husband is cruel to his wife, he risks a beating from his wife's brothers. When relatives marry, there is a tendency for the whole family to become involved if the couple has marital problems.

Women can inherit property under Islamic law, although their portion is half of what a male receives since men are expected to support their wives. This practice may not always be honored since there is a resistance to dividing up the land into too many pieces. However, once ownership is established, a woman's property or wealth is hers to do with as she pleases. No matter how wealthy she may be, however, her husband is still obligated to support her. In practice, women sell their jewelry and property if the men have trouble providing for the family.

Problems of Rural People in an Urban Setting.   The strong network of family ties within the village is in strong contrast to the individualism associated with modern city life. People who move from villages to the cities often suffer severe shocks to their way of living, working, and thinking. For example, in the city, peasants have no way to use their traditional skills. Also, they miss the emotional and financial support that is part of village family life. It is difficult to imagine what it must take to force a peasant to move to the city. But many have and continue to do so. Because so many peasants have moved to the cities in past years, social scientists now speak of the **ruralization** of the cities. They use this term to suggest how peasants have brought their village ways to the city. Instead of adapting to the modern ways and life-styles of the city, they are overwhelming the cities with their large numbers while keeping their traditional ways.

Nomads. There is still another group in Middle Eastern society. Only one percent of the population, it consists of people who migrate with their animal herds in the deserts and mountains. These people are **nomads.** Nomads who live in the deserts of the Middle East are known as **Bedouins** (BED-oo-winz). Traditionally, the nomads' life has been hard, with very few material possessions and constant exposure to the elements. Today's nomads live with change, just as villagers and city dwellers do. It is not unusual these days, for example, to see a Bedouin bring his animals to market in a pickup truck.

ISRAEL

Israel is a unique nation not only in the Middle East but also in the world. Its culture, like that of other countries in the region, goes back thousands of years. But it is the only state in the world where Jews are a majority of the population and thus is the only non-Muslim state in the Middle East. It is also the most culturally diverse country in the region.

The Return to Palestine. Until about 2,000 years ago, most Jews lived in the land of Judah. Their land was conquered first by the Babylonians in 586 B.C. and then by the Romans in A.D. 70. To punish a Jewish uprising, the Romans changed the name of Judah to Palestine. In the centuries that followed, Jews built communities all over the world. Only a small group remained in Palestine.

In the late 1800s, a number of European Jews began to plan for a mass return to Palestine. They were prompted by acts of persecution and discrimination against Jews in country after country. These men and women called themselves **Zionists,** after Mount Zion in Jerusalem. They bought land and built small settlements in Palestine. Then in 1933, Adolf Hitler came to power in Germany. He set out to destroy all the Jews of Europe. As his armies swept over one European country after another during World War II, Jews were herded into concentration camps, where six million were killed. When the war ended, many of the survivors fled to Palestine. There they helped Israel become an independent nation in 1948.

A Jewish State.   Although about 17 percent of the population of Israel is Muslim and many Christians also live in the country, Israel is a Jewish state. Jewish law affects many aspects of public life. For example, government offices, banks, movie theaters, and many stores are closed on Saturday, the Jewish Sabbath. Hebrew, a language once used mainly in prayer, is now the language of everyday life for most Israeli Jews. Many older Israelis, who came from Eastern Europe, speak Yiddish, the language of the Jewish communities of that region. Jewish religious leaders have much political influence in Israel, as Muslim leaders do in neighboring countries. Yet Israel is a democracy. All adult citizens over the age of 18—men and women, Jews and non-Jews—have the right to vote. Anyone can become a citizen, but Jews have special privileges. In 1950, Israel passed the **Law of Return.** It stated that any Jew, anywhere in the world, has the right to come to Israel and immediately become a citizen.

Immigration.   Even before the law was passed, thousands of immigrants were pouring into the country. Between 1948 and 1951, Israel's population more than doubled. The newcomers came to Israel not only from Europe but also from such countries as Australia, Mexico, the United States, India, and Argentina. The vast majority, however, were from Eastern Europe and from Arab countries in the Middle East. Over 500,000 Jews from other parts of the Middle East and North Africa have settled in Israel.

By 1992, nearly 75 percent of Israel's Jews were born in the country or in other parts of the Middle East, and immigration continued. Beginning in the mid-1980s, for the first time the Soviet Union allowed large numbers of Jews to emigrate. Since then, 300,000 Russian Jews have settled in Israel. In the same period, the entire community of Ethiopian Jews—about 18,000 people in all—has come to Israel.

Uniting a Nation.   Although almost all of Israel's recent immigrants have been Jews, they have come from many different cultures. Today's Israelis have their roots in more than 100 different countries, each with its own language, customs, and traditions. Many immigrants from the former Soviet Union, which discouraged all religious activity, do not practice the religion of Judaism. On the other hand, the Ethiopians are deeply religious. Whatever their religious practices, these recent Israeli immigrants all share the dream of building a new life in their own nation.

From the start of its existence as a state, Israel insisted that newcomers become citizens and share in all aspects of Israeli life. The gov-

Jews of all ages praying at the Wailing Wall in Jerusalem. One of the holiest Jewish shrines, it is only a few yards from the Dome of the Rock, one of Islam's most revered places.

ernment set up hundreds of centers where the immigrants could learn Hebrew. There, Russian Jews have learned to communicate with Ethiopian Jews, South African Jews, Jews from the United States, and other immigrant groups. They are brought together in other ways, too. Their children attend the same schools, and eventually almost all the young people will serve in the army.

Israeli Life. Most Israelis live in cities and towns, where the typical Israeli house is not a house at all but a small apartment. About one fourth of the Israeli people live in the three largest cities, Jerusalem, Tel Aviv, and Haifa. Some Israeli cities look much like those in other parts of the region. Others resemble European or American cities. Most are a blend of both Middle Eastern and Western traditions. In large cities, immigrants often choose to live together in a neighborhood. Some band together to buy or build an apartment house. There is comfort in living among people who share your customs and beliefs. Only ten percent of all Israelis live in rural communities. Yet even these are a blend of old and new.

For about 100,000 Israelis, home is a **kibbutz** (kih-BOOTS). A kibbutz is a community owned jointly by the people who live there. Most kibbutzes are farming communities. Members work the land together and share the profits. In recent years, many kibbutzim have placed more emphasis on developing industries and hotels.

The vast majority of Israel's farmers make their homes in a type of cooperative community known as a **moshav** (moh-SHAHV). There each family owns its own land and its own house, though farmers work their land cooperatively. They share expensive tools and equipment. They also sell their harvest as a group. Many immigrants were attracted to the idea of a moshav because it resembled villages they had left behind in their native lands.

Although Israel is a Jewish state, it allows all groups—Jewish and non-Jewish—the freedom to practice their religions. Among the Jews, the so-called Orthodox Jews are the ones who adhere most closely to the ancient principles of Judaism in their daily lives. They make up about a fifth of the Jewish population of Israel. Orthodox Jews are similar to believers in Islam in that they maintain that religion and government are closely related. Most Israeli Jews, however, feel that religion and government should be separate, as it is in most Western countries.

Arab Israelis.   Most of Israel's Arabs live apart from the Jews, in their own villages or in Arab urban neighborhoods. Many Israeli Arabs are torn between loyalty to other Palestinian Arabs and Israel. The fact that they are a minority in the country partly accounts for this. In addition, they are uneasy with the Western character of much of Israeli's culture. Although Israeli Arabs are better off economically than Arabs in other Middle Eastern countries, many feel that they are discriminated against in job and educational opportunities. The Israeli government, on its side, is concerned that the primary loyalty of many Israeli Arabs is not to Israel but to the Palestinian goal of the creation of their own state. You will read more about the animosity between Israelis and Arabs in Chapters 7 and 8.

REVIEWING THE CHAPTER

I. Building Your Vocabulary

Choose the word or phrase that best completes the following sentences.

suq	infant mortality rate	dynasty
nuclear family	extended family	nomads
refugees	traditional	moshav
life expectancy	minaret	mosque

1. A ruling family that maintains its position over a considerable amount of time is a _____.

2. Shoppers and storekeepers bargain in a Middle Eastern market place called a(n) _____.

3. The place Muslims gather for prayer is a religious building known as a(n) _____.

4. The number of babies who die before the age of one per 1,000 births is called the _____.

5. A household that consists of a couple and its unmarried children is called a(n) _____.

6. The name for a family of three or more generations who live together is a(n) _____.

7. People who move from place to place with their animals are known as _____.

8. People who flee their country for political reasons are _____.

9. A way of life marked by little change from one generation to the next is considered _____.

10. A village in Israel where individuals own their own land but work it cooperatively is called a _____.

II. Understanding the Facts

Choose the best answer.

1. What do Alexandria, Beirut, Tel Aviv, and Istanbul have in common?
   a. They are all coastal cities.   b. They are all national capitals.
   c. They are all major financial centers.

2. Which of the following does *not* apply to Jerusalem?
   a. religious center   b. capital city   c. seaport

3. Which of the following is a political center?
   a. Mecca   b. Qum   c. Ankara

4. Which of the following is the most densely populated?
   a. Amman   b. Cairo   c. Damascus

5. In which country is college life most like college life in the United States?
   a. Israel   b. Saudi Arabia   c. Iraq

6. What is a life expectancy rate?
   a. how long people live   b. how long people hope to live
   c. the average number of years a newborn can be expected to live

7. Where do most Middle Easterners live?
   a. in the desert   b. in towns and cities   c. in villages

8. What percentage of Middle Easterners are nomadic herders?
   a. about 1 percent   b. 35 percent   c. about 10 percent

9. From what parts of the world did most Israeli immigrants come?
   a. North America and Western Europe
   b. the Middle East and Eastern Europe
   c. North America and Eastern Europe

10. What is the official language of Israel?
    a. Hebrew   b. Yiddish   c. English

III. Thinking It Through

1. a. What are the three main population trends in the Middle East?
   b. How does each affect life in the region?

2. How is education changing life in the Middle East today?

3. How have the lives of many Middle Easterners been affected by modernization?

4. a. Name three ways Israel is like its Muslim neighbors.

   b. Name three ways it is unique.

BUILDING CRITICAL THINKING SKILLS

1. Name one cause of population growth in the Middle East and one effect of population growth on cities in the region.

2. Name one cause for Israel's Law of Return and one effect of this law.

INTERPRETING A CHART

Study the chart on the next page. Then answer these questions.

1. Which country in the region has the largest population?

2. Which country has the largest percentage of its people living in urban areas? In towns and cities?

3. Which country on the chart has the largest percentage of people living in rural areas?

4. a. Which country on the chart has the largest percentage of its workers in agriculture?

   b. Which country has the largest percentage of its work force in industry?

   c. Which country has the largest percentage of its workers in service industries?

5. What conclusions can you reach about life in the Middle East from the information on the chart?

Population Facts

COUNTRY	POPULATION (millions of people)	URBAN (percent)	RURAL (percent)	DISTRIBUTION OF WORK FORCE (in percentages)		
				AGRICULTURE	INDUSTRY	SERVICES
Algeria	26.0	43	57	14	25	36
Egypt	54.5	45	55	43	21	36
Iran	46.6	54	46	25	22	36
Iraq	17.1	73	27	13	17	61
Israel	4.9	90	10	4	27	64
Jordan	3.4	70	30	6	18	76
Libya	4.4	70	30	17	39	38
Morocco	26.2	46	54	40	24	27
Saudi Arabia	15.5	73	27	14	34	52
Syria	12.8	50	50	30	30	42
Turkey	58.5	60	40	45	19	28

Sources: Population Reference Bureau, Inc., 1991;
Enclopaedia Britannica, 1991 Yearbook.

ENRICHMENT AND EXPLORATION

1. Choose one Middle Eastern city and write a research report that focuses on its role as a social center. What role does it play in education, social services, and as a population magnet? Organize your report around some of the themes of this chapter.

2. Find a map of an old city in the Middle East in an atlas or in a travel guide. Compare the oldest part of the city to newer sections. How is the new section laid out? How were older parts of the city laid out? Where are tourist attractions? Businesses? Factories? Prepare what you learned as a report. Then compare your findings to those of classmates who researched other cities. What conclusions can you draw?

3 People of the Ancient Middle East (c. 10,000 B.C.–A.D. 600)

Stone tablets and other written records suggest that the peoples of the Middle East were building **civilizations,** or complex cultures, over 6,000 years ago. These civilizations were among the first in the world. The marks of a civilization are a large settled population, food production through agriculture, an established government, a developed religion, specialized crafts, long-distance trade, and, often, a system of writing. Civilizations do not develop overnight. They develop slowly over many, many centuries. The development of a civilization is a process made up of thousands of small changes, most of which individually do not make much difference in the lives of the people. Yet together they result in a new way of life.

THE PROCESS OF CHANGE

Why was the Middle East home to the world's earliest civilizations? There is no single answer to this question. A variety of factors promoted cultural changes there and spurred the inventions and ideas that led to the growth of civilizations.

Responding to Natural Changes.   Necessity often leads to changes in culture. Hunting and gathering was a successful way of life in the Middle East for a long time. Then about 15,000 years ago, people there began to feel the effects of climatic changes. The climate became warmer than it had been. Some plants and animals became harder to find. At the same time, the number of people living in the region increased sharply.

PEOPLE OF THE ANCIENT MIDDLE EAST
c. 10,000 B.C.–A.D. 600

10,000–3,500 B.C.	Neolithic Age in the Middle East. Farming begins; villages appear.
7750 B.C.	Jericho is founded.
c. 4000–2450 B.C.	Sumerians build a civilization in the Tigris-Euphrates valley.
3500 B.C.	Sumerians develop a system of writing.
c. 3500–30 B.C.	Egyptian empire
2500–1500 B.C.	*Indus Valley civilization*
2000 B.C.	Babylonian Empire emerges.
1025 B.C.	Israelites set up the kingdom of Israel.
722 B.C.	Assyrians conquer the northern kingdom of Israel.
586 B.C.	Babylonia conquers the southern kingdom of Judea; destruction of the Jewish temple; beginning of Jewish Diaspora.
509–49 B.C.	*Ancient Roman republic*
499–479 B.C.	Persian Empire battles Greek city-states.
461–429 B.C.	*Golden Age of Athens*
332–30 B.C.	Greek Empire in the Middle East
146 B.C.	Rome conquers Carthage.
30 B.C.	Egypt becomes a Roman province.
31 B.C.–A.D. 180	*Pax Romana*
A.D. 70	Rome sacks Jerusalem and destroys the second Jewish temple.
A.D. 313	Constantine recognizes Christianity.
A.D. 400	*Christianity becomes the Roman Empire's official religion.*
A.D. 330–1453	Byzantine Empire
A.D. 451	Council of Chalcedon leads to first major division among Christians.
c. A.D. 600	Middle East is divided between Persian and Byzantine empires.

Different groups of people responded to shortages of food in different ways. Some left the region. Others tried to secure a more dependable food supply by **domesticating,** or managing, herds of sheep, gazelles, and other animals. Still others paid more attention to food plants. Together, without realizing it, they brought about a new age known as the **Neolithic Age.** It was marked by the growth in the size of herds of goats, sheep, and other domesticated animals, the planting of wheat fields, and the development of permanent villages. For much of the Middle East, the Neolithic Age began about 12,000 years ago and lasted for about 6,500 years.

Archaeologists, the scientists who study the lives of early peoples, generally agree that nomadic people knew how to grow crops and herd animals long before they finally settled down and became farmers. As it became harder to find food, producing one's own food became more important. Groups began to stay in one place for longer periods of time. In about 7750 B.C., one such group started a permanent settlement at Jericho, near the Dead Sea. Others built their villages in river valleys.

There is no way of knowing when people stopped regarding agriculture as only a temporary solution to their need for food and began to consider it the basis of their food supply. In the Middle East, people reached that point some time between 6000 B.C. and 4000 B.C.

Changes Have Unexpected Effects. Once people of the Middle East settled in one place, they were confronted with new challenges and new opportunities. Many farmers were attracted to **Mesopotamia,** the land between the Tigris and Euphrates rivers. They were drawn there by the plentiful supply of water and by the lack of stones and trees that had to be cleared before planting. The newcomers soon found that the green valley's rich soil returned large yields, sometimes equal to 50 to 100 times the amount of grain they sowed. The only problem was how to use and control the two rivers. Every spring, melting snows from the mountains caused the Tigris and the Euphrates to overflow their banks.

Farmers learned to build dams on rivers to prevent floods and store water for use during the long, hot, dry summers. They dug irrigation canals to bring the water directly to their fields. Their efforts paid off. Crop yields improved to the point that some villages had a surplus of food. As a result, not everyone had to farm for a living. A village could support potters, weavers, and other artisans. As crafts developed, so did trade. Villages grew slowly into towns and a few became large enough to be called cities. The story was much the same along the Nile and other river valleys throughout the Middle East.

When people built dams, they expected them to protect their fields. No one dreamed they would result in new kinds of jobs or even spur the growth of cities. Yet more often than not, that is exactly what happened. One change slowly led to many others.

Cultural Exchange in the Middle East.   Cultural changes often occur as a result of meetings between people of different cultures. The Middle East has long been a center for such cultural exchanges. The growth of farming increased the number and frequency of those exchanges. Carts, boats, and other inventions made it easier to transport goods and people. Also, people now had more reason than ever to trade.

Archaeologists have found evidence of trade high in the Zagros Mountains. Nearby are springs of **bitumen** (bih-TOO-muhn), a natural asphalt. Bitumen was the first commercially important product of Middle Eastern oil fields. For at least 8,000 years, people have been using bitumen to fasten flint blades to handles, waterproof their baskets and roofs, build boats, and caulk hulls. Jericho's early growth may have been partly a result of its location near the bitumen springs of the Dead Sea. Another important trade object was **obsidian** (uhb-SID-ee-uhn). Trade in obsidian is at least as old as trade in bitumen. Obsidian is a hard glass that forms when molten lava from a volcano cools rapidly. It can be fashioned into razor-sharp knives. Like bitumen, obsidian was found in the Zagros Mountains, near the headwaters of the Tigris River. The river was one of many trading routes in the region along which people moved the obsidian. Villages and then towns grew up along those routes. People gathered there to trade grains and pottery for obsidian and bitumen and later for copper, silver, and other metals. As groups traded, they shared knowledge and ideas. People then adapted those ideas to their own needs, spurring still more changes.

War is another process by which cultural exchange takes place. Over the centuries, many groups have invaded the Middle East, in search of food or farmland. Each invasion brought changes. Victory by one group of people did not necessarily result in the disappearance of the defeated people and their culture. Often, the victors and the defeated lived side by side, each influencing the other's way of life. Slowly a new culture developed that was a blending of both, yet different from either.

A Crossroads of Civilization.   Long after the rise of civilizations in other parts of the world, the Middle East continued to be a major crossroad of culture and trade. With land and sea routes passing through the area, geography worked in its favor. It was not until the A.D. 1400s that advances in navigation made long ocean voyages possible. Only then did it become cheaper and faster to travel by ship around the southern coast of Africa to Asia.

The Middle East was not, however, simply a stopping point on a route between east and west or north and south. It was also an important center of international trade. Cloth, pottery, artwork, foods, and raw materials produced in the Middle East were valued all over the world.

The area was also the birthplace of an idea that transformed the world. People there were the first to develop **monotheism**—the worship of one God. Three monotheistic religions, Judaism, Christianity, and Islam, all started in the Middle East. Places holy to all three religions have long attracted pilgrims from distant places to sites in modern Israel and Saudi Arabia.

Trade, war, and even foreign visitors can bring changes to a region. History is the story of those changes and how people responded to them. History also recounts how people responded to natural changes such as as drought or flooding. These too can alter the course of history.

THE ANCIENT WORLD (4,000 B.C.–500 B.C.)

Some time after 4000 B.C., agricultural settlements appeared in the lower part of the Tigris-Euphrates valley.

Civilizations Develop. The Middle East produced several centers of civilization: on the Anatolian plateau, in the Tigris-Euphrates River valley, and in the Nile River valley. Another center arose in the area extending south from Anatolia, or modern Turkey, into Syria and Palestine along the Mediterranean (see map below). This region developed rapidly through contacts among the peoples of the river valleys.

Early centers of civilization were organized around a city or a group of cities and the surrounding countryside. Sometimes the city-states formed alliances for protection against a common enemy. Sometimes, through conquest, a strong city became the center of a new empire.

The Sumerians of the Tigris-Euphrates Valley. Not much is known about the origins of the Sumerians. But historians believe they moved into the southern part of the Tigris-Euphrates valley some time before 4000 B.C. (See the time line on page 61.) They were responsible for a series of developments that provided the base upon which other people-who came after them built.

In Sumerian society, the temple-community was the center of life. Gradually it developed into the **city-state.** A city-state is an independent town or city and the surrounding countryside. The chief Sumerian city-states were Ur, the center of cultural life, Erech, and Kish. Priests were the leaders of the community. They collected taxes, stored grain for future use, maintained the irrigation canals, and directed building projects. A ruling group gradually emerged from among these priests.

The ancient Sumerians worshiped many gods, believing them responsible for causing natural events. They believed it was important to please the gods to ensure good harvests, prosperity, and general good fortune. Because Sumerian religious leaders interpreted the events caused by the gods, it was not unusual for the temple of the gods to become the most important building in each city-state. These terraced temples were called **ziggurats,** and they functioned as administrative as well as religious centers.

Labor in ancient Sumer was specialized. The ziggurat served as a workshop center in which crafts workers trained. Social differences in

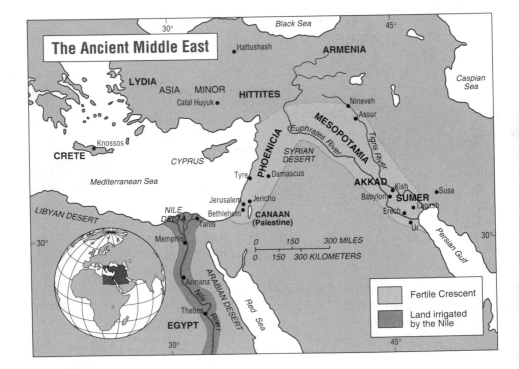

the community began to widen. The priestly ruling class lived on the surplus of what the peasant farmers produced.

As Sumerian society became more complex, the need for accurate records emerged. This need gradually led to the development of writing after 3500 B.C. The writing took the form of wedgelike symbols on stone tablets and is called **cuneiform** (kyoo-NAY-uh-form), from the Latin word *cuneus,* or wedge. What appears on the vast majority of these tablets are commercial notes, but some preserve temple records or fragments of Sumerian literature. Mathematics also evolved, making it possible to construct canals and public buildings.

Ur-Nammu, a Sumerian king, established a legal code and set down its rules in writing. Previously there had been only an oral law. Other contributions of the Sumerians included business contracts, a seed planter, epic poems, and medical remedies. The Sumerians passed on to later civilizations their knowledge of the arch as a device in building and their system of mathematical measurements in units of 60. Today we have 60 seconds in a minute, 60 minutes in an hour, and 360 degrees in a circle.

The Sumerians were not the only people to build city-states in Mesopotamia. The fertile land between the Tigris and Euphrates rivers was home to many city-states.

Invaders Bring New Influences.   As population expanded and as city-states multiplied, arguments arose over the ownership of land and water resources. These conflicts resulted in periods of continuous warfare among the Sumerian city-states.

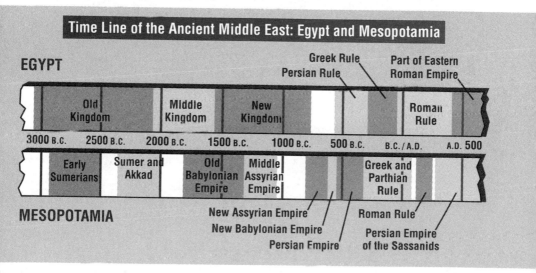

Time Line of the Ancient Middle East: Egypt and Mesopotamia

At about the same time, people living on the northern fringes of the river valley began to move south. Since the river valley could be easily reached, the small, settled agricultural communities attracted raiders and invaders.

Between 2500 B.C. and 500 B.C. various peoples moved into the Tigris-Euphrates valley. The Akkadians were the first to invade. They were followed by the Babylonians, Assyrians, and Chaldeans. All of the conquerors settled in the region and influenced the people they ruled. They were in turn changed by contact with the area and were finally conquered by other peoples. The ease of invading Mesopotamia encouraged new conquerors to dominate larger areas. While the Sumerians controlled only the southern part of the river, the later Assyrians and Chaldeans ruled over most of the Tigris-Euphrates valley. Throughout this period of invasion, laws were written down, trade increased, the arts developed, population expanded, and society became more complex.

After the fall of the Sumerian city of Ur in about 2000 B.C., a new empire in Mesopotamia arose farther north, in the city of Babylon. One king of the Babylonians, Hammurabi (1792–1750 B.C.), is remembered for his famous law code: the Code of Hammurabi. The goal of its 300 laws was to bring justice to the world, to prevent the powerful from destroying the weak. To some extent slaves and citizens of low status were protected by these laws. But commoners clearly did not possess the rights enjoyed by nobles, nor did they receive equal protection under the law. The surviving code is written in cuneiform on a stone slab. It is arranged in specific categories, beginning with the administration of justice and ending with laws concerning the purchase of slaves abroad.

Some of the most interesting laws in the Code of Hammurabi concern the protection of women:

If a man . . . leaves his wife without proper maintenance and she then goes to live with another man, she need not return to her first husband if and when he returns.

If a man wishes to divorce his first wife because she is unable to bear him children, he must give her the cash value of her bridal gift and make good the dowry she has brought from her father's house before he can divorce her.

If a man's wife becomes crippled (with rheumatism, arthritis, etc.) and he decides to marry another woman, he may do so. But [he] cannot divorce his first wife, who shall continue to live in the same house and to be cared for for the rest of her life.

Hammurabi of Babylonia receiving the law from the seated sun god. Below this scene are the laws carved in cuneiform. Hammurabi revised and expanded earlier Sumerian and other laws.

THE EGYPTIANS OF THE NILE VALLEY

Historians know little of the origins of the early settlers in the Nile River valley. But they do know that the Nile valley was quite different from Mesopotamia. While the settlers in the Tigris-Euphrates valley were open to attack from all sides, the Nile valley was protected by surrounding deserts.

Farming along the Nile. The Nile valley differed from the Tigris-Euphrates valley in another important way. The Nile was more predictable in its flooding. The following ancient agricultural calendar shows the stages of the Nile floods and the farming activities that accompanied each stage:

June	Rise of the Nile begins. Harvesting of cereal crops ends, threshing continues.
July	The Nile, accelerating its rise, enters the flood state. Threshing ends.
August	The Nile approaches full flood. The vintage picking of grapes begins.
September	The Nile flood peaks and begins to fall. The vintage is completed. Dates are picked.
October	The Nile flood is past. Sowing of cereal crops begins. Olives are gathered. The harvest of dates is at its peak.
November	Sowing of cereals continues, cultivation begins. Olives and dates are gathered.
December	Cultivation continues. Olives are gathered.
January	The olive harvest ends. The new growing season of vines and olives begins.
February	Preparations are begun for the grain harvest.
March	Preparations continue.
April	The grain harvest begins.
May	Harvesting continues, threshing begins.

The fertile river banks of the Nile were ideal for raising crops. Of these, wheat for making bread and barley for beer were the most important. Thus, settlements were concentrated along the banks of the Nile rather than in cities. Yet, as happened in the Tigris-Euphrates valley, large numbers of people living together required the development of political, economic, and social systems.

Organized societies appeared later in the Nile valley than in Mesopotamia. But once the Egyptians were joined together into one state by King Menes (MEE-neez), some time around 3200 B.C., Egypt became a unified country. During this long time, however, there were frequent civil wars between the **dynasty,** or ruling family, and other noble families. There were also invasions. Among the invaders were the Kushites, who lived in what is now Sudan.

The Hyksos, an Asiatic people who moved through Palestine and Syria, also conquered Egypt at a time when it was weakened by civil war (about 1720–1570 B.C.). Using cavalry and chariots, the Hyksos caught the Egyptians unprepared. The Hyksos dominated Egypt for 150 years. After they were driven out in 1570 B.C., Egypt expanded beyond the Nile valley in the hope of protecting itself from attack on its eastern frontier. Thus the "New Kingdom" began.

Daily Life in Ancient Egypt.   To the ancient Egyptians, the **pharaoh,** or ruler, was believed to be a god. The whole of Egyptian society was organized to serve the pharaoh both in life and after death. Peasants farmed the land to supply bread and cotton for the pharaoh's bureaucrats, priests, and soldiers. Soldiers conquered territory in order to bring back booty, slaves, and new luxuries. Scribes developed **hieroglyphics** (heye-ruh-GLIF-iks), a form of picture writing, to record the goods stored in the royal warehouses and to write about religion. Artisans and laborers formed armies of workers to build huge temples, statues, and the pyramids—the great massive tombs for the pharaoh and his family. Building the pyramids required great engineering and mathematical skills. The Egyptians also used mathematics, especially the mathematical principle later known as the Pythagorean Theorem, to measure land flooded every year by the Nile. The Egyptians passed on to other civilizations these and other important scientific ideas.

The Egyptians believed that the souls of the dead lived on after death. The pharaohs built the pyramids in which they placed everything they would need in the afterlife. Frescoes painted on the walls of the tombs show how people baked bread, repaired tools, hunted wildlife, sailed boats, and built the pyramids. From these paintings and from artifacts such as jewelry, weapons, and models of boats, we know much about everyday life in ancient Egypt. We know that physicians performed surgery and that slavery was legal.

Throughout its history, Egypt has had great impact on the Middle East. As leaders of a powerful empire, the ancient Egyptians controlled

A photograph of Egypt's pyramids and the Great Sphinx taken in the early 1900s. The Great Sphinx represented a god who was supposed to guard tombs.

trade throughout the eastern Mediterranean. They received gold, ivory, and slaves from central Africa, spices from Arabia, wood and dyed cloth from the coast of Syria and Palestine, and beautifully decorated pottery from Crete. Egypt would later become an important province of the Roman Empire, an important center of Islamic learning, and a cultural center of the Arab world.

ANATOLIA AND THE MEDITERRANEAN COAST

Outside the two river valleys the regions lying along the Mediterranean and Aegean seas produced people who made important contributions to civilization. These were the Hebrews, Canaanites, Phoenicians, Aramaeans, Hittites, and Lydians. As the large empires of Egypt and Mesopotamia underwent internal struggles, these smaller groups and city-states became powerful. When the large empires regained their

66

strength, they reconquered the less numerous peoples. From about 1300 B.C. to 500 B.C. the people of the Anatolian and Mediterranean coasts came into contact with the great river-valley civilizations.

The Phoenicians were highly skilled sailors and traders. They founded many colonies along the shores of the Mediterranean and thus spread civilization throughout the area. They settled as far west as Spain and even traded as far north as England. The major Phoenician contribution to civilization was the development of a phonetic alphabet of 22 consonants to which the Greeks later added vowels. The Romans in turn adapted this alphabet. It is the Roman alphabet that is the foundation of the writing systems of English and most European languages.

In Turkey the Hittites found a way to smelt iron. The Lydian people of western Turkey developed a system of money. Soon coins began to replace the barter of goods as the system of commerce.

The Hebrews, who had come from Mesopotamia to Canaan (Palestine), adopted and transmitted the idea of monotheism. According to their beliefs, God is a caring ethical god, a god of mercy as well as justice. Their history is recorded in the Hebrew Bible, which Christians call the Old Testament.

When famine struck the area, the Israelites, as they were called, migrated to Egypt, where they were enslaved. During the reign of one of the pharaohs, perhaps Ramses II (1304–1237 B.C.), the Israelite leader Moses led the Twelve Tribes of Israel through the Sinai Desert, back to Palestine. According to their beliefs, Moses received from God at Mt. Sinai the Ten Commandments, a set of religious and moral laws which became the basic precepts of Judaism and, later, Christianity.

Israelites settled in Canaan, conquered the Philistines and other peoples, and, about 1025 B.C., set up the kingdom of Israel. The kingdom became powerful during the reigns of the Hebrew kings Saul and David. David built Jerusalem, and his son, Solomon, began the construction of the first temple there. Solomon imported cedar from Lebanon and other luxurious materials for it. It was the religious center for Judaism. Solomon made diplomatic alliances with the neighboring rulers and formed a trading partnership with the Phoenicians.

But Solomon's successors were weak, and the Israelite kingdom split into two. The northern kingdom of Israel, made up of ten tribes, was conquered in 722 B.C. by Assyrians from northern Mesopotamia. In 586 B.C. the Babylonian king Nebuchadnezzar conquered the southern tribes of Judea, destroyed the temple, and exiled many Jews to Babylonia (Mesopotamia). The year 586 B.C. marks the beginning of the **Diaspora** (deye-AS-puh-ruh), or the settling of Jews outside Judea and Israel.

CASE STUDY:

The Book of Ruth

The Bible describes much about life in ancient Palestine. The Book of Ruth is from the Hebrew Scriptures, the Old Testament. The story of Ruth gives us a picture of everyday Jewish life in a humble agricultural village. After the death of her husband, Ruth and her mother-in-law, Naomi, have returned penniless to Bethlehem at harvest time.

One day Ruth said to Naomi, "Let me go to the fields to gather the grain that the harvest workers leave. I am sure to find someone who will let me work with him. . . .

So Ruth went out to the field and walked behind the workers, picking up the heads of grain which they left. It so happened that she was in a field that belonged to Boaz.

Boaz said to Ruth, "Let me give you some advice. Don't gather grain anywhere except in this field. Work with the women here; watch them to see where they are reaping and stay with them. I have ordered my men not to molest you. And whenever you are thirsty, go and drink from the water jars."

Ruth bowed down with her face touching the ground and said to Boaz, "Why should you be so concerned about me? Why should you be so kind to a foreigner?"

Boaz answered, "I have heard about everything that you have done for your mother-in-law since your husband died. I know how you left your father and mother and your own country and how you came to live among a people you had never known before. May the Lord reward you for what you have done."

At mealtime Boaz said to Ruth, "Come and have a piece of bread, and dip it in the sauce." So she sat with the workers, and Boaz passed some roasted grain to her. She ate until she was satisfied, and she still had some food left over. After she had left to go and gather grain, Boaz ordered the workers, "Let her gather grain even where the bundles are lying, and don't say anything to stop her. Besides that, pull out some heads of grain from the bundles and leave them for her to pick up."

So Ruth gathered grain in the field until evening, and when she had beaten it out, she found she had nearly twenty-five pounds (11 kilograms). She took the grain back into town and showed her mother-in-law how much she had gathered. She also gave her the food left over from the meal.

Naomi asked her, "Where did you gather all this grain today? Whose field have you been working in? May God bless the man who took an interest in you."

So Ruth told Naomi that she had been working in a field belonging to a man named Boaz. Naomi said to Ruth, "Yes, my daughter, it will be better for you to work with the women in Boaz's field. You might be molested if you went to someone else's field." So Ruth worked with them and gathered grain until all the barley and wheat had been harvested. And she continued to live with her mother-in-law.

Abridged from *The Good News Bible*, American Bible Society, 1976.

1. From this description, what can you learn about agricultural life in ancient Palestine?

2. Why did Boaz tell Ruth to take the grain from his fields? What did he admire about Ruth?

3. According to the story, how were the poor provided for?

Sheep graze in a field outside the ancient biblical city of Jericho, about 20 miles (32 kilometers) northeast of Bethlehem.

PERSIA, GREECE, AND ROME RULE
THE MIDDLE EAST (500 B.C.–A.D. 500)

During the 1,000 years from about 500 B.C. to A.D. 500, three great empires successively held large areas of the Middle East as part of their territories: the Persians, the Greeks, and the Romans.

The Persians. The Persians conquered and united the peoples of the Fertile Crescent and invaded Egypt. But each time they tried to extend the Persian Empire northward into present-day Europe, the Greeks fought them off and pushed them back into Asia. In the Persian Wars (499–479 B.C.), King Darius of Persia was defeated by an alliance of Greek city-states in the battle of Marathon (490 B.C.). His successor, Xerxes (ZERK-seez), was forced to retreat after the battle of Thermopylae (thur-MAHP-uh-lee) (480 B.C.) and the battle of Salamis (480 B.C.).

Alexander Spreads Greek Culture. The Greeks struck a fatal blow at the Persian Empire 150 years later under the leadership of Alexander the Great (356–323 B.C.). Alexander led Greek armies into Asia, crushed the Persians, and then marched his troops all the way to India. From this victory the Greek Empire in the Middle East emerged. The event proved revolutionary in the history of East-West relations. Not since Xerxes had anyone tried to unify the Greek and Persian worlds.

Alexander was only 33 when he died in the city of Babylon in Mesopotamia. Upon his death his generals divided the empire, founding new dynasties in Egypt, the Fertile Crescent, Asia Minor, and Greece. Thus Greek ideas, education, and literature spread through the Middle East and mixed with local traditions. Out of this mixture came a new culture known as Hellenistic civilization. Cities such as Alexandria in Egypt and Persepolis in Persia became major centers of culture.

Greek control over the area lasted for about 300 years, from 332 B.C. to 30 B.C., at which time a new empire had appeared. Centered in Rome, it soon spread its power toward the Middle East. But Greeks remained an important cultural influence, especially in art, philosophy, and navigation, even during the Roman Empire.

The Roman Empire and the Middle East. In 146 B.C. the Romans conquered the city-state of Carthage, in what is now Tunisia, and the city-state of Corinth in Greece. Roman armies moved across the

Persepolis, the capital of the Persian Empire. Thirteen huge columns still stand amid the ruins of the Persian kings' palace.

Dardanelles into Asia Minor, then south through Turkey. They reached Syria by the year 64 B.C. At about the same time, Roman power spread across North Africa toward Egypt. Egypt became a Roman province after 30 B.C.

The Romans set out to bring order to a vast empire that stretched from the Atlantic Ocean to the Tigris-Euphrates rivers. As rulers, the Romans borrowed law, religion, and culture from the conquered peoples. Latin, the language of the Roman Empire, carried the more advanced ideas of the Middle East to people who lived in western Europe.

The period between 31 B.C. until the death of the Roman emperor Marcus Aurelius in A.D. 180 is known as the **Pax Romana** or "Roman Peace." During this time the Romans fought few outside enemies. People could travel from one end of the empire to the other without fear.

Nevertheless, there were revolts in various parts of the Roman Empire in the Middle East. One such revolt took place in Judea in A.D. 66. The Romans had appointed Herod, a half-Jewish Roman citizen, to be king of Judea. But the Jews opposed Herod's rule. After the massacre of a small Roman garrison in Jerusalem, the Romans placed the city under their direct control. In August, A.D. 70, Roman legions sacked Jerusalem and destroyed the temple. At Masada, a fortress in the desert, a small band of Jews withstood the Roman army for three years (A.D. 70–73). When defeat was certain, they committed suicide rather than be taken alive by the Romans. In the twentieth century, their deaths became a rallying cry for Israel's survival.

After the death of Marcus Aurelius, the Roman Empire passed through turmoil. Unrest was brought about by invaders, rebellion within the empire, and the rise of a new Persian empire to the east.

The Byzantine Empire.   To run the empire more efficiently, the Roman emperor Diocletian (A.D. 284–305) divided the Roman Empire into two parts. The western part continued to decline until the last quarter of the fifth century, when it disappeared completely. The Eastern Roman Empire, however, held off invaders from the south as well as from the north and managed to survive for a thousand years. One of the strongest Roman emperors, Constantine, dedicated a new capital, in A.D. 330, and named it Constantinople—in honor of himself. Strategically located on the Bosporus, which divides Asia from Europe, the city served as the capital of the Eastern Roman, later the Byzantine, Empire. A major center of Christianity, Constantinople fell to the Ottoman Turks in 1453. Today it is the Turkish city of Istanbul.

Carvings on an arch of triumph built by the Roman emperor Titus to celebrate his conquest of Jerusalem. The seven-branched candlestick and other sacred objects were looted from the Jews' Second Temple by the Romans.

A Byzantine painting of Mary and Jesus in the Church of the Annunciation in Nazareth, Israel. Byzantine artisans told the story of Jesus's life in paints and brilliantly colored mosaics.

JUDAISM AND CHRISTIANITY

Over a period of 1,400 years, roughly from 700 B.C. to A.D. 700, the world produced individuals who founded most of the great religions and philosophies. Confucius, Buddha, Zoroaster, Socrates, Plato, Aristotle, Jesus, and Muhammad all lived within this period. Three religions originated in the Middle East: Judaism, Christianity, and Islam. All are widely practiced today. Each religion produced a written text that is a guide to the beliefs of that faith and a history of its birth. The books are the Bible, or Old Testament, the New Testament, and the Koran (also spelled Quran). None of these was written exactly at the time when the events described in it were happening.

The Growth of Judaism. Judaism is the oldest monotheistic religion. Jews believe that there is only one God who is above all and who created everything. They believe that God created the Jewish people to live according to the **Torah.** The Torah (TOH-ruh), the first five books of the Hebrew Scriptures (or Old Testament), is a blueprint of laws for a moral way of life. By accepting the Ten Commandments at Mt. Sinai, the Jews formed a **covenant,** or pact, with God. It was their belief that if they observed God's laws, God would protect them.

The Torah is also a history of the Jewish people. It describes the story of the patriarchs and Moses and the giving of the Law. The rest of the Bible illustrates the rule of the judges and kings and the activities and words of the **prophets,** great religious thinkers and teachers. The later prophets, such as Isaiah, Jeremiah, and Ezekiel passed judgment on the people of Israel and reminded them of their promise to God.

When the Babylonians destroyed Jerusalem and the first temple in 586 B.C., many Jews were exiled to Babylonia. The Jews lived there as a community, waiting for the day of their return to Jerusalem. Within about 50 years, the Persian Empire conquered Babylonia. The new ruler permitted Jews to return to Jerusalem. There the returned Jews rebuilt the temple. Yet many Jews remained in Babylonia. For centuries most Jews in Babylonia and Persia engaged in farming, though many lived in towns and cities. In Babylonia, Jewish scholars prepared an edition of the **Talmud** (TAHL-muhd) in about A.D. 500. Another version had been compiled in Palestine one hundred years earlier. The Talmud is composed of many legal interpretations of Jewish law.

The Jews who had returned to Jerusalem and Judea had periods of self-rule and rule by foreign powers. Then the Romans conquered the region. The Romans tried to govern the Jews indirectly by appointing governors from among the local people. But revolts continued and Palestine was placed under direct Roman rule. During a four-year revolt that ended in A.D. 70, the great temple was destroyed once again. One wall of the temple survives today, however. Called the Western Wall, it is one of the most sacred places in the world to Jews. Many Jews were forced to become slaves in lands as far away as Spain. Others joined Jewish communities in other parts of the world.

Thus the date A.D. 70 also marks a growth of the Diaspora, or the dispersion of the Jews from Judea. The Romans renamed the province Palastina, or Palestine. Even before the temple's destruction, Jews had built many **synagogues** (SIN-uh-gahgs) abroad. Now these houses of prayer, assembly, and study became centers of Jewish religious life.

The Beginning of Christianity. Jesus was born in Bethlehem, a village in southern Palestine, during the early period of Roman rule. He grew up in Nazareth in the Galilee, the northern part of what is now modern Israel. As a Jew, Jesus took up the cause of the common people and preached social reform to his fellow Jews. The first Christians were Jews, as was Jesus. Jesus's apostles, or disciples, spread his teachings first in Palestine and later, after his death in Jerusalem, throughout the rest of the Roman Empire.

Christians believe that Jesus was the **Messiah.** The word *messiah* comes from ancient Hebrew and Aramaic. It means "anointed." *Christ* comes from the Greek word that also means "anointed." The arrival of the Messiah was foretold in the Old Testament. Jews believed that the event would usher in a new era of peace and love among people. The Roman rulers of Judea, fearing another revolt, had Jesus executed by crucifixion. Christians believe that Jesus rose from the dead and will return to usher in the Messianic Age of peace. They also believe that Jesus is the Son of God whom God sent to atone for the sins of all people. This latter point differentiates Christians from Jews and Muslims, who do not believe that Jesus was divine.

After the death of Jesus, his disciples continued to spread the new faith of Christianity. The apostle Paul taught that anyone could become a Christian if he or she accepted Jesus as the Messiah. He also taught that a person did not need to accept all of the Jewish laws to be a follower of Jesus. Peoples of many different faiths and backgrounds were attracted to and accepted Christianity. The lower classes and slaves were offered hope of justice in this world and eternal salvation after death. When more and more people in their empire accepted the new faith, the Roman emperors felt threatened and began to persecute Christians.

By the A.D. 300s, Christianity enjoyed a large following from all social classes. When the emperor Constantine recognized Christianity in 313, he began a movement for its adoption throughout the empire. By the end of the century, Christianity became the Roman Empire's official religion.

Christians accept the Hebrew Scriptures, or Old Testament. They accept its ethical teachings and believe that it foretells the coming of Jesus as the Messiah. Biographies of Jesus's life and teachings became part of the New Testament. Like Jews and Muslims, Christians believe there is one God, the creator of heaven, earth, and all things. Jews, Christians, and Muslims believe that all people are created by God and that God judges each person by his or her conduct on earth. In addition, Christians believe that Jesus is the Divine Son of God and that people should follow his teachings and love God. To Christians, Jesus was the Messiah. Some Jews regard Jesus as a Jewish reformer, and Muslims believe that Jesus was one of God's prophets.

The Jewish and Christian Dating Systems.   The dating systems used by Jews, Christians, and Muslims vary. The Jewish calendar in use today is that dated from the year of the Creation according to Jewish tradition. You may therefore see the initials A.M. for *anno mundi*, Latin for "in the year of the world," with dates. For example, the year 1990 may be referred to as A.M. 5751 for Jewish religious purposes. The ancient Romans, on the other hand, developed a different dating system. Then, about 1,400 years ago, the Roman calendar was adjusted, based on counting the years from the birth of Jesus. Today the calendar in general use worldwide is based on a readjustment of the earlier Christian calendar. Dates representing years before Jesus's birth are labeled B.C. (before Christ). Dates after his birth are dated A.D. (*anno domini*, "in the year of our Lord"). For the same dates as on the Christian calendar, Jewish scholars sometimes use the initials B.C.E. ("before the Common Era") instead of B.C. And they may use C.E. ("in the Common Era") instead of A.D. In the next chapter, you will learn about the numbering system of the Muslim calendar.

Divisions Among Christians.   Gradually, because of differences in the language of prayer, customs, and disputes over religious teachings, major divisions developed between Christians in the Middle East. The first major split occurred in the fifth century A.D. The disagreement concerned what religious leaders declared about the nature of Jesus. At the Council of Chalcedon in Turkey in A.D. 451, church leaders confirmed the dual nature of Jesus—that his nature is divine and that he retains his full humanity so that people may follow his example and gain salvation. (This is the position held today by the Roman Catholic, the Greek Orthodox, and the Protestant churches.) However, many believers rejected this decision. They believed Jesus is of a single nature, which is divine.

Those not accepting the Council of Chalcedon formed four major churches. The largest in about A.D. 600 was the Ancient Church of the East, often called the Nestorian Church. Its members are called Assyrians or Nestorians. Prayer and worship are conducted in Aramaic. Edessa in Greece was a very important city for them. Other Christian churches that rejected the Council of Chalcedon are called the Oriental Orthodox or Ancient Eastern Churches. One of these is the Coptic Orthodox

Church, which is centered in Egypt. A second Oriental Orthodox Church is the Syrian Orthodox Church. Its members are called Jacobites after a sixth-century bishop, Jacob Baradaeus. A third Orthodox Church is the Armenian Orthodox Church. All four of these Christian groups continue to have members in the Middle East today. Another Christian group, the Maronite Church, claimed not to have rejected the decisions of the Council of Chalcedon. It traces its origins back to Lebanon in the late fourth and early fifth centuries A.D. The Maronites form one of the largest Christian churches in the Middle East.

Other Religions and Empires.   Communities of Jews were now scattered throughout the Middle East: in Mesopotamia, in Egypt, and throughout the Roman Empire. There were even Jews in Arabia. The Jews managed to keep their faith and their identity as a people even though many now lived thousands of miles from Palestine. They were able to do so partly because Judaism is more than a religion; it is also a way of life. Everywhere the Jews settled, they built a synagogue and started a school. Although communities were scattered and travel was difficult, the Jews continued to look to the Middle East for leadership. At first, scholars in Babylonia provided the leadership. There and later in Palestine, Jewish scholars continued to study and interpret the Bible. In doing so, they helped to unite the Jewish people and keep their faith alive.

There were also peoples of other religions. Some believed in the ancient religions of the Roman Empire. In Iran, the religion of Zoroaster, Zoroastrianism, became the state religion of the Persians. Zoroastrians believe in the constant struggle between good and evil.

Politically, the Middle East was divided between the Byzantine Empire and the Persian Empire. Around A.D. 600, the border between the two empires was somewhere in the Syrian Desert. In the desert lived nomadic tribes who allied themselves with one or another of the empires. Often the tribes changed sides when it suited them.

The Byzantines and the Persians fought each other many times during the 500s and early 600s. These military campaigns achieved little for either side, as each pushed the other back and forth across the Fertile Crescent. The peoples living in this areas were taxed repeatedly to pay for the cost of maintaining the warring armies.

As the two empires fought for control of the Fertile Crescent a new power was emerging in Arabia, that of the Arabs. And they were uniting around a new religion that would change the character of the entire Middle East—Islam.

REVIEWING THE CHAPTER

I. Building Your Vocabulary

Match the definition with the correct term.

civilization   monotheism   Mesopotamia
Diaspora   Pax Romana   covenant

1. the land between the Tigris and Euphrates rivers
2. dispersion of Jews
3. period of peace during the first century A.D.
4. a complex culture
5. belief in one God

II. Understanding the Facts

Write the letter that best completes the following sentences or answers the following questions.

1. The Neolithic Age was marked by the growth of
   a. farming.   b. hunting and gathering.   c. cities.

2. Wedge-like symbols on stone or metal tablets were called
   a. cuneiform.   b. bitumen.   c. pyramids.

3. Which of the following people did not invade the Middle East between 2500 B.C. and 500 B.C.?
   a. the Assyrians   b. the Chaldeans   c. the Romans

4. Hammurabi was an ancient king of the
   a. Assyrians.   b. Babylonians.   c. Egyptians.

5. The Asian peoples who used horses and chariots to invade Egypt in the 1600s B.C. were the
   a. Hyksos.   b. Greeks.   c. Persians.

6. The Roman alphabet was adapted from the writing system of the
   a. Phoenicians.   b. Hebrews.   c. Persians.

7. Hellenistic civilization was a mixture of which of these two cultures?
   a. Greek and Persian   b. Latin and Egyptian
   c. Turkish and Christian

8. The capital of the Byzantine Empire was located at
   a. Rome.   b. Constantinople.   c. Alexandria.

9. Of which religion is the Talmud a sacred text?
   a. Islam   b. Christianity   c. Judaism

10. In A.D. 313, the Emperor Constantine recognized which of the following religions?
    a. Judaism   b. Christianity   c. Islam

III. Thinking It Through

1. How did the growth of agriculture influence the growth of civilization? What was the relationship between the growth of civilization and the rise of early Middle Eastern cities?

2. How would you distinguish between the terms *culture* and *civilization*?

3. Egypt has been called "the gift of the Nile." Why?

4. Why was Alexander the Great's conquest of the Persian Empire a key event in the history of East-West relations?

5. Compare and contrast Judaism and Christianity. What do they have in common? How do they differ?

DEVELOPING CRITICAL THINKING SKILLS

Explain the relationship between each of the following pairs of statements. Tell which is the cause and which the effect.

1. a. People settled in one place and built permanent housing.
   b. People discovered they could grow plants for food.

2. a. The need for accurate records developed.
   b. Sumerian society became more complex.

3. a. The Nile overflowed its banks every spring.
   b. The Egyptians built a civilization.

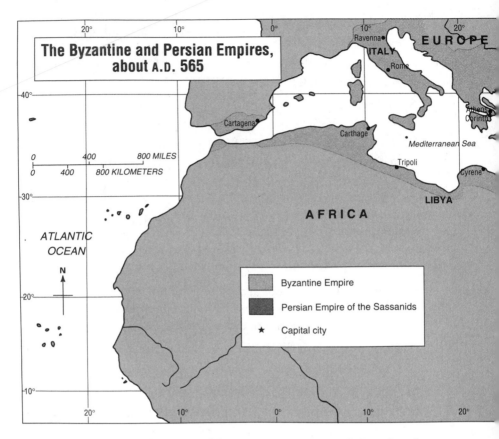

The Byzantine and Persian Empires, about A.D. 565

20°   10°   0°   10°   20°

Ravenna
EUROPE
ITALY
Rome

40°

Cartagena

Carthage

Mediterranean Sea

Athens
Corinth

Tripoli

Cyrene

0   400   800 MILES
0   400   800 KILOMETERS

30°

LIBYA

AFRICA

ATLANTIC
OCEAN

N

20°

Byzantine Empire

Persian Empire of the Sassanids

★   Capital city

10°

20°   10°   0°   10°   20°

4. **a.** Alexander the Great and his successors spread Greek culture throughout the Middle East.

   b. A new culture known as Hellenistic civilization developed.

5. **a.** Christianity split into two parts, along the lines of the ancient Roman Empire.

   b. Within Christianity differences in the language of prayer, customs, and religious teachings gradually developed.

INTERPRETING A MAP

Study the map above. Then answer the following questions.

1. Which empire controlled the waterway between the Mediterranean and the Black seas?

2. Which empire controlled Egypt?

   What was the capital city of the Persian Empire of the Sassanids?

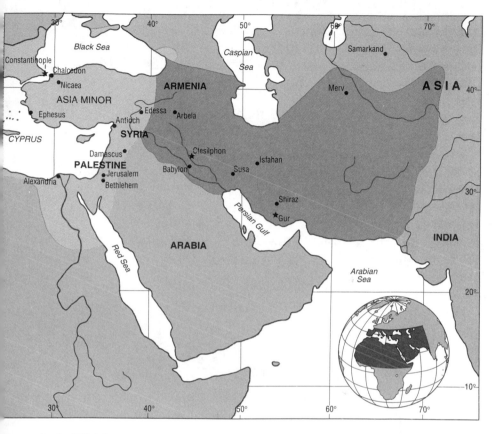

4. Which empire controlled the fertile lands between the Tigris and Euphrates rivers?

5. Which people lived on the peninsula southeast of Egypt and southwest of the Persian Empire of the Sassanids?

ENRICHMENT AND EXPLORATION

1. Do research on one of the following groups: the Phoenicians, the Assyrians, the Chaldeans, the Babylonians, the Persians. Prepare a report on your research. In your report answer these questions: What did they learn from earlier civilizations? What impact did they have on those that followed?

2. What does the word synthesis mean? Think about this word in relation to your reading of the chapter. Write a short essay explaining how Hellenistic civilization was a synthesis of all that came before it. Was Roman civilization also a synthesis? Explain.

MUHAMMAD AND THE EMERGENCE OF ISLAM
A.D. 500–1000

A.D. 570	Muhammad born in Mecca.
622	Muhammad's flight from Mecca; beginning of Muslim calendar; Islam becomes a religion.
630	Muslims conquer Mecca.
632	Muhammad's death; Abu Bakr becomes the Prophet's first successor.
635	Muslims conquer Syria.
640	Muslims control the Tigris–Euphrates valley.
642	Muslims control Egypt.
650	Persia is under Muslim control.
656	Islam is divided between Shiites and Sunnites.
656–710	Muslims conquer North Africa.
661–750	Umayyad caliphs rule.
711	Muslims invade Spain.
732	The Frankish leader Charles Martel defeats the Muslims at the battle of Tours.
744	Abbasids replace the Umayyads as rulers of the Muslims in the East; Umayyads rule Spain.
751	Muslims defeat the Chinese at the battle of Talas.
768–814	*Reign of Charlemagne*
800–1000	*African kingdom of Ghana*

4 Muhammad and the Emergence of Islam (A.D. 500–1000)

By the beginning of the seventh century, the powerful empires in the Middle East found themselves exhausted from fighting each other on and off for more than 300 years. Each empire's established state religion was unique. The Persians, centered in present-day Iran, had adopted Zoroastrianism. The Byzantines, who ruled most of the area stretching from Turkey south into Egypt, were Christians. The peoples in the border regions of western Iraq, Syria, and Palestine were ruled at times by the Byzantines, at times by the Persians. They were taxed by both, forced to fight by both, and sometimes persecuted because of their religious beliefs. When the armies of a new empire began to move north from the Arabian Peninsula, the peoples of the Middle East welcomed them.

What is significant about this new empire is that it came out of an area not traditionally involved in the region's power struggle. And it sent an army to conquer in order to spread a belief, a new religion. This belief was called **Islam**, which in Arabic means service or submission to the will of God. The followers of Islam were called **Muslims**, people who submitted themselves to the will of God.

The Arabs were the first Muslims. They were led by the Prophet Muhammad, the "Messenger of God," and his successors, who united the tribes of Arabia. Under the green flag of Islam, the Muslims spread their faith first throughout Arabia, then to Iraq, Palestine, and Syria. In little more than a hundred years after the death of Muhammad, Muslims carried their rule and their religion as far as China in the east, to the Taurus Mountains in the north, and westward across North Africa into Spain.

Today, with well over 900 million practicing Muslims, Islam is one of the world's great religions—and also one of the fastest-growing. This is especially true in certain parts of sub-Saharan Africa. Most Muslims now live outside the Middle East. Indonesia, India, and Pakistan have large Muslim populations. There are major Muslim communities in the Central Asian republics of Turkmenistan, Uzbekistan, Kazakhstan, Kyrgyzstan, and Tajikstan; the Balkan peninsula in southeastern Europe; and in China. Islam is also growing rapidly in the United States.

In this chapter you will study the rise of Islam and some of the beliefs and practices of Islam.

THE FOUNDING OF ISLAM

In many ways Islam is similar to Judaism and Christianity. It is monotheistic; that is, Muslims believe that there is only one God. (*Allah* is the Arabic word for God.) Muslims everywhere consider the Old and New Testaments of the Bible as revelations coming from God. Many of the same ethical rules of conduct in the Bible are to be found in the teachings of the Prophet Muhammad. There are, however, significant differences. Muslims do not believe Jesus is the Son of God. Rather, they consider Jesus a great prophet. For them, Muhammad is the last and most complete of God's prophets. It is Muhammad, therefore, who occupies a special place in the hearts and minds of all Muslims. Muslims believe Muhammad's revelations to be the most perfect expression of God's teachings. According to Islam, these teachings, revealed in Arabic directly from God through the angel Gabriel, were collected in the **Koran** (koh-RAHN).

Muhammad.   Muhammad was born in Mecca, a city that is now in Saudi Arabia, around A.D. 570. His father, Abdallah, died before Muhammad was born, and his mother died when he was six years old. At first Muhammad lived with his grandfather. Later, when his grandfather died, Muhammad went to live with an uncle. At the time of Muhammad's birth, Mecca was both a religious and a trading center. The desert tribes of the Arabian peninsula came to worship at the **Kaaba** (KAH-buh) located in the city. The Kaaba, a large cube-shaped structure, housed dozens of shrines of the pagan Arabs, including a black stone that remains sacred to Muslims. Mecca was also a key stop on the route of the incense traders who traveled from Yemen north to Damascus in Syria. (See map on pages 100–101.)

The Kaaba, the holiest shrine of Islam. It is the small cube-shaped building near the center of the Great Mosque, in Mecca, Saudi Arabia. The sacred Black Stone is in the eastern wall of the Kaaba. The Kaaba is draped in special black cloth.

Mecca was an international crossroads of ideas as well as goods. Jews in Arabia and Syria in the 500s and 600s had many contacts with Arab merchants. At the same time, Christianity had become an important religion both in Syria and in Egypt. As a young man, Muhammad often traveled with his uncle's caravan into Syria and Palestine. As a result of these trips, he came into contact with the ideas of educated Christians and Jews. It is probable that these contacts had much to do with the development of his religious thought.

When he was 25 years old, Muhammad married a wealthy widow named Khadijah. Muhammad's first revelation came in 611, when he was about 40 years old. According to tradition, he was meditating alone in a cave outside of Mecca in the lunar month of Ramadan. Muhammad heard the voice of the angel Gabriel and began to receive the teachings which later were written down in the Koran. His revelations continued throughout his life.

Muhammad preached the oneness of God, the evil of worshipping idols, and the coming of Judgment Day. At first he had few followers:

only his wife, several relatives, and some poor people. As he continued to preach publicly, however, he gained a larger following. But Muhammad's early success earned him the hatred of the powerful of Mecca. Opposition came from the wealthy merchants and town leaders. They feared his new religion might put an end to their profitable trade with the tribes that came to worship at the Kaaba.

Muslims believe that during this period in his life, Muhammad went on a night journey that carried him from Mecca to the Dome of the Rock in Jerusalem. From there, they claim, he rose to heaven. This site, according to Biblical and Islamic tradition, was where God had tested Abraham by asking him to sacrifice his son. According to some Jews, it is also the site of the Holy of Holies, the most sacred part of the Temple.

The Hijra.   In A.D. 622, because of growing threats against his life, Muhammad fled from Mecca. He went to Yathrib, called Medina, also a sophisticated town and trading center. This historic flight is called in Arabic the **hijra** (HIJ-rah). (The hijra is also called the **hejira** in English.)

Some of the religion's new converts had invited Muhammad to Medina, where they wanted him to help settle quarrels among tribes that lived around the oasis. Most of the people in the area were Arabic-speaking Jews and non-believing Arabs. The move to Medina proved to be a critical one in the development of Islam. In Medina, Muhammad's revelations changed. Islam as a religion became a community and a state. Muhammad became the supreme judge, ruler, and commander in chief.

The Muslim Calendar

The Muslim calendar begins from 622, the year that Muhammad fled from Mecca to Medina. This was the year of the hijra. The caliph Umar reckoned the year 622 as the beginning of a new era for Muslims and for humankind in general, and, therefore, as the Year One of the Islamic calendar. According to the Islamic calendar, therefore, the year 1992 in the Western calendar is 1413. Based on the moon, the Islamic calendar divides the year into six months of 29 days, and six months of 30 days. This lunar calendar has 354 days. The Islamic calendar adopted 11 leap years within every 30-year period, losing a little over three years during the course of one Christian century. Islamic years are marked "A.H.", meaning "after the hijra."

The Growth of the Muslim Community. Muhammad continued to live in Medina, where he preached and gained followers. He organized local affairs based on the teachings of his new religion. As the community grew, Muhammad began to lead raids against the caravans from Mecca, interrupting the flow of trade and wealth to that city. In 624, at the battle of Badr, southwest of Medina, the Prophet led a band of only 300 troops against a caravan with 1,000 guards. He defeated them completely, thereby gaining control of the important caravan routes to the north. Muhammad's followers saw the victory as a sign of God's support.

Muhammad soon established a reputation as a disciplined military, political, and religious leader. His followers were the tribes of Arabia, mostly desert nomads, although the townspeople of Mecca were also identified according to families. As Islam grew, tribes allied themselves with the Prophet. Muhammad came to blows with several Arabic-speaking Jewish tribes, who supported him or remained neutral at first but then opposed him.

In 630, Muhammad conquered Mecca, from which he had fled only eight years before. As his first act in Mecca, Muhammad smashed the idols in and around the Kaaba. (Today the Kaaba is the most sacred place in Islam and marks the direction towards which Muslims pray.) Following the capture of Mecca, many more tribes joined the growing group of Muslims. Muhammad became the clear leader of the Hijaz (hih-JAZ), the area on the coast of the Red Sea where Mecca and Medina are located. Mecca, Medina, and Jerusalem remain Islam's holiest cities because of their connections with Muhammad's life and events described in the Koran.

Muhammad spent the last two years of his life, from 630 to 632, encouraging distant tribes to recognize him as the Prophet of God. For their guidance, he set down rules of behavior. Tribes were not to attack fellow Muslims, and were required to give charity to those in need. These rules became part of the new religion. Before we look at how Islam spread throughout the Middle East, we will examine the religion's beliefs and practices.

ISLAM: THE RELIGION

Islam, like Judaism, is at the same time a religion and a total way of life. This means that, like other religions, Islam has certain beliefs and a system of worship. In addition, it provides its believers with specific rules for proper conduct. These range from instructions about government and finance to, among other things, rules governing family life, food, etiquette, business, dress, and personal hygiene. Islam is a system in which the sacred, or holy, is not separated from the secular. The Western concept of the separation of church and state is not part of the ideal of traditional Islamic practice. With the rise of Islam a new set of religious practices and writing emerged. These made the new faith distinct from other monotheistic religions.

The Five Pillars of Islam. Islam is based on five main duties, known as the "Five Pillars of Islam." These are the things that a religious Muslim is supposed to do. Thay are given in order of importance. The first, and most important pillar, or *Shahada,* is a statement of faith. Muslims declare that "There is no God but God, and Muhammad is the messenger of God." This is the most basic principle of Islamic faith, like the first of the Ten Commandments, or the Covenant, in Judaism and Christianity.

The second pillar is *Salat,* or prayer. All Muslims are required to pray at five different times of the day while facing Mecca as they kneel. Although Muslims are advised to go to a mosque for the main prayer at mid-day on Friday, they may pray wherever they are. As you read in

Praying at Tehran University, Iran. During prayer, in what direction do Muslims face?

Chapter 2, Muslims are reminded that it is the time to pray by a muezzin, who calls the faithful to prayer. The muezzin climbs up the minaret of the mosque to announce the times of prayer during the day. The sound of the voices of muezzin from many different mosques calling the people to prayer is a distinctive feature of Middle Eastern cities.

Many Muslims pray at their places of work or at home. Bedouins or travelers stop by the road to pray. As they face Mecca, Muslims perform a series of recitations and kneeling, prostrating, and standing movements. If not in a mosque, a Muslim will pray on a special rug or mat used only for prayer, or in a clean place.

The third pillar is *Sawm*, or fasting. The Islamic month of Ramadan is celebrated as the month in which God revealed himself to Muhammad. Throughout Ramadan, Muslims fast from dawn to dusk. At night there are great meals where friends and family exchange gifts, and at the end of the month there is a large festive holiday.

The fourth pillar is *Zakat*, or charity. Islam accepts the fact that some individuals will be wealthier than others and those less fortunate must be helped. Muslims are supposed to give a percentage of their income to charity.

The fifth pillar is the *hajj*, or pilgrimage. Once in his or her lifetime, every Muslim who is able to is supposed to go on a pilgrimage to Mecca. Each year, at a particular time, about a million Muslims travel to Mecca from all over the world. The hajj is a very important religious event, lasting several days. Often very old people go on the hajj not expecting to return to their homes. The hajj is also an occasion to meet Muslims from many different countries. In earlier times, great caravans wound their way toward Mecca, growing along the route as they gathered more and more people in each town they passed. Rulers sent elaborate gifts to Mecca in honor of the pilgrimage. People also took advantage of this massive gathering to trade with those from far away. The hajj also became an important place for the exchange of ideas.

Here is a fifteenth-century account of the entrance of pilgrims to Mecca:

> It was the month of Dhu'l Hijja. People were preparing to enter the city, and the [leader] of Mecca . . . came out to meet the caravans. It is the custom of the pilgrims when they enter Mecca and Medina to drape their. . . litters with beautiful covers of gold-braided silk, colored draperies, and the like. They adorn their camels with gold and silver bracelets on their feet, put helmets of silver mail on their brows, and display great pomp and splendor.

This gladdens souls and fills hearts with joy. Praise be to God for the glory and greatness of Islam.

Today, the ruling family of Saudi Arabia is the guardian of the holy cities of Mecca and Medina. Modern pilgrims arrive by jet at the King Abdul Azziz International Airport near Jedda, on the Red Sea coast. Stretching for 35 square miles (91 square kilometers), the airport is larger than the international airports of New York, Chicago, or Paris. The Hajj terminal is constructed of a space-age fabric that reflects the sun's heat and retains light. The fabric makes the terminal look like two huge tents suspended from cables and steel pylons. The terminal can process 5,000 pilgrims each hour, or about one million pilgrims annually during the hajj season.

Once in Mecca, Muslims circle the Kaaba seven times and perform other rituals. Rich and poor, kings and peasants, people of all races and countries are dressed alike, in white. The pilgrimage reminds Muslims that all are equal under God.

Koran. The Koran is Islam's holy book, the collection of Muhammad's revelations. Muslims believe the Koran to be the word of God revealed to Muhammad through the angel Gabriel. These teachings were not written down while Muhammad was alive, but memorized and recited. After his death, Muhammad's followers became concerned that some of the teachings might be lost or incorrectly recalled.

Zayd ibn Thabit, who had been Muhammad's secretary, was given the task of gathering the teachings. He said: ". . . I sought out and collected the parts of the Koran, whether written on palm leaves or flat stones or in the hearts of men." This collection was organized into the Koran in about 652.

Koran in Arabic means "recite," which was God's first command to Muhammad. It is the word of Allah as it was revealed to Muhammad, his prophet. Traditionally, the Koran has been recited by specially trained people who memorize the text and, using a particular chant, tell it to others.

The Koran is organized into 114 *suras*, or chapters. The opening *sura* of the Koran is often called the "essence of the Koran." No contract or business transaction between Muslims is made without reciting this prayer. The first line is found at the beginning of every book, on the walls of houses or shops, in cars and many other places. It is called *al-Fatiha:*

IN THE NAME OF GOD
THE COMPASSIONATE
THE MERCIFUL

Praise be to God, Lord of the Creation,
The Compassionate
The Merciful
King of the Late Judgment!
You alone we worship, and to You alone
we pray for help.
Guide us to the straight path,
The path of these whom You have favored,
Not of these who have incurred Your wrath,
Nor of those who have gone astray.

Other Writings. Muslims do not study only the Koran. There are many non-holy works that are used as guides for the Islamic community. They are known as *hadith*.

When the Arabs had conquered a huge empire, the problems of governing these lands led them to look for answers that could not be solved through the teachings in the Koran. In this way, they collected a set of traditional interpretations of practices by looking back to see how the Prophet acted in certain situations. These practices and statements are usually presented in the form of "I heard from . . . who heard from . . . who heard from . . . who heard from the Prophet say . . ."

An Egyptian studying the Koran.

CASE STUDY:

The Example of the Prophet

Muslims everywhere look to the example of the life of Muhammad for instruction on how to live. This Saudi Arabian magazine excerpt describes modern observance of the holy month of Ramadan.

Ramadan, the month of fasting, is observed by Muslims all over the world with great care and devotion. In Ramadan they abstain from eating food between sunrise and sunset. They may also offer an additional congregational prayer during the night. Muslims are reminded of the fact that it was in the month of Ramadan that the Koran was revealed to the Prophet Muhammad.

The Prophet Muhammad used to be very meticulous in observing fasting and other religious obligations during the month of Ramadan. He used to spend all he had on the needy and the poor. Most of his time was devoted to offering prayers and remembering God. Abu Huraira reported the Prophet as saying, "Fasting is a shield. When any one of you is fasting on a day he should neither indulge in obscene language nor raise his voice. If anyone reviles [scolds, uses improper language against] him or tries to quarrel with him he should say, "I am a person fasting."

During the month of Ramadan the Prophet used to spend the last ten days staying in a mosque. During this period [the observer] disassociates [separates] himself from all worldly affairs and spends his time in prayers. One of the nights in the last ten days is said to be the *Lail-il-Qadr*. The word *lail* means "night" and *qadr* means "measure." But it is also translated as the "night of grandeur and majesty." During this night the Prophet, along with his family, used to offer night-long prayers and seek God's forgiveness and mercy.

Adapted from *Arabia: The Islamic World*, Review IV (46), June 1985.

1. What are the important observances during the month of Ramadan?
2. What is the origin of these observances?
3. How does Muhammad serve as an example for people today?

Within a few generations after Muhammad's death these *hadith* become a part of the Muslim tradition. Each one had to be **authenticated**, that is, the transmitters of each tradition had to be checked and declared reliable. Once a *hadith* was declared authentic, people looked upon it as a guide in cases where the Koran had nothing to say.

As Islam developed, many books were written as commentaries on or explanations of the Koran and the *hadith*. From the beginning, Islam attracted scholars who studied and discussed the Koran and the teachings of Muhammad. Their commentaries on the holy law, which filled many volumes, is called the **Shari'a**. *Shari'a* means "the straight path." It was the scholars' role to try to understand how to do things for which the Prophet had not given specific guidance.

In the Middle East today, administration of the *Shari'a*, Islamic law, is on a country-by-country basis. Each Muslim country has its own experts on Islamic law, called **ulema** (oo-luh-MAH). The ulema are scholars who have attended an Islamic school, called a *madrassa*, and then a religious college. There they learn the Koran, *hadith*, commentaries on Islamic law, theology, philosophy, Arabic, and other courses of Islamic study.

The *ulema* advise the ruler and decide on questions on the basis of Islamic law. They analyze past tradition and reach an agreement on how law is to be applied in contemporary circumstances.

There is no central authority for interpreting or enforcing Islamic law. A local religious leader, the **imam** (ih-MAHM), is responsible for pursuing the ideals for Islam, for presiding over prayers, funerals, and festivals. But he is not a priest. He does not serve as an intermediary between the people and God because each Muslim prays directly to God. Not all Muslims agree with this view. According to the Shiites, there have been only 12 imams throughout history. The twelfth or "hidden imam" was forced into hiding by Sunnites. The Shiites believe he will emerge as the messiah on the day of the last divine command.

Even though Islam allows for local variations in customs and traditions, there is a single worldwide community of believers, the *ummah*, who are bound to accept the roles and traditions of their religion. Thus, Islam is a total guide for each individual and for society.

ISLAM AND THE INDIVIDUAL

In addition to the "Five Pillars of Islam," Muslims are expected to be moderate and humane. Eating and drinking too much are frowned upon, while cleanliness is a religious duty. An observant Muslim may not drink alcoholic beverages, eat pork, or gamble. Muslims are not permitted to draw or sculpt images that might be worshipped as idols. For this reason, calligraphy, or beautiful script, became an art form in itself in the Islamic world. The curves and the dots in Arabic script lend themselves to organization in decorative patterns.

Hospitality is a great virtue in Islam. Travelers, in their accounts of journeys through the Middle East, report being overwhelmed at the lengths Muslim hosts would go in preparing feasts in their honor. Respect for the elderly is also highly regarded. Women also have legal rights in Islam, and it is considered the duty of men to protect and provide for them.

One of the customs sanctioned by the Koran is the guarding of the women in the family by men. Although techniques of guarding vary depending on ethnic group and environment, the most common method is seclusion in the home, or **purdah.** In some areas of the Middle East, women veil themselves when they are outside the home. (Rural women required to work in the fields do not wear the veil.) However, in some Muslim countries, such as Tunisia and Turkey, it is rare to see veiled women. And the demands of city living continue to dissolve the traditional roles demanded of women by strict Islamic law. Still, women who pursue careers and lives outside the home remain in the minority throughout the Middle East.

Women on their way to work in the port city of Jidda, Saudi Arabia.

Engineers in Baghdad, Iraq. In what way does this woman differ in customs from the women in the photograph on page 94?

As you read in Chapter 2, marriage in Islam is carried out by means of a contract. The rights and duties of each partner are often negotiated and then spelled out in detail. They are approved by each party before witnesses. The contract usually involves the bridegroom (or his family) promising money, animals, or goods to the bride and her family. Other agreements are made to care for him in return for her joining his family and raising their children.

According to Islamic law, a husband must offer his wife freedom from their marriage contract if he marries a second wife or if he stays away from home too long. In addition, Islam grants women the right to own and inherit property (at one-half the amount received by the sons). Theoretically men receive more because they are obliged to provide for their women.

As in other societies, all major events in a person's life, from birth to death, are part of the religious and social system. For example, the birth and naming of a son, when he is a week old, is a festive occasion. Often the celebration is a dinner with family and friends, including a recitation from the Koran.

Boys and girls are encouraged to memorize the Koran as part of their religious upbringing. (The popular Egyptian singer Um Kulthum was famous for her clear pronunciation of poetry. When she was a girl, she was a skilled Koran reciter.) Chanting of the Koran is also a part of the funeral ceremony. Muslims are buried in white shrouds covered in green cloth, embroidered with verses from the Koran. Their bodies are placed in graves on their sides, facing Mecca.

A village wedding dance in the Zagros Mountains of Iran. Notice that the women wear traditional costumes but the men wear Western-style clothing.

ISLAM AS AN INSTITUTION

From its very beginning, Islam was the most important **institution** in Islamic society. An institution is defined as the organization of people for some common purpose. An example of a political institution is a government, whereas the family is a social institution and an industrial corporation is an economic one. In all of these, people join together to accomplish what they could not do alone.

A religion may also be a social institution in which people group together to achieve certain goals. Their religious objectives may be communion with God, the salvation of the soul, the development of moral codes, or the maintenance of ancient and respected traditions. Islam regulates not only the roles of men and women as individuals. It also regulates the political, social, and economic institutions.

In Islam, public life and private behavior are simply different aspects of "living the right life." Iran and Saudi Arabia, for example, have legal systems based on Islamic religious laws. However, most Muslim nations with secular constitutions incorporate some but not all religious laws in the constitutions. Turkey is the only Muslim country in the Middle East whose secular laws are separate from its religious laws.

96

Muhammad's Successors. With Muhammad's sudden death in 632, the question of who was to lead the Arab tribes arose. Traditionally, the tribal chief was elected. But Muhammad had changed the traditional tribal system of government by exercising both spiritual and secular authority.

Furthermore, Muhammad had left no clearly designated successor. He had declared himself the last of the prophets and proclaimed that his mission would end with his death. Thus there was no need for a spiritual heir. Yet someone had to assume his role as commander in chief and lawgiver. The years following his death witnessed a bitter power struggle among several rival factions, each claiming the right to choose a successor. Out of this struggle two great divisions developed within the Islamic religion, about which you will read later.

Abu Bakr, Muhammad's father-in-law, was recognized as the Prophet's first successor. He was called the *Khalifa*, or **caliph**. Upon Muhammad's death Abu Bakr had told the Prophet's followers, "Oh believers, if you believed in Muhammad, Muhammad is dead! But if you believe in God, God is alive and will never die. *La ilah illallah wa Muhammad rasul allah* ('There is no deity but God, and Muhammad is the Messenger of God.") Thus, by taking spiritual and worldly leadership, Abu Bakr prevented the breakup of the Islamic community.

Abu Bakr was followed as caliph by Umar and then by Uthman, a son-in-law of Muhammad. All three caliphs had known Muhammad and were his companions during his lifetime. Their leadership saved Islam and opened the way for a period of expansion which has few parallels in recorded history.

The caliphs after Muhammad ruled over a rapidly growing community. Raids northward by the tribes became wars of conquest, as the weak Byzantine and Persian armies failed to match the strength of the Muslim fighters. Faith in Islam served to bind the tribes of Arabia together, while a war of conquest outside of Arabia further united the tribes.

The Division of Islam: Shiites and Sunnites. Uthman, Muhammad's third successor, was murdered in 656 by discontented Muslims. He was succeeded by Ali, who was the cousin of Muhammad and who had married Muhammad's daughter, Fatima. Many people believed that Ali should have been the first caliph and that his heirs should have succeeded him.

Others opposed Ali's succession to Uthman. Ali had criticized Uthman's policies and accused him of practices that were not in agreement with Muhammad's teachings.

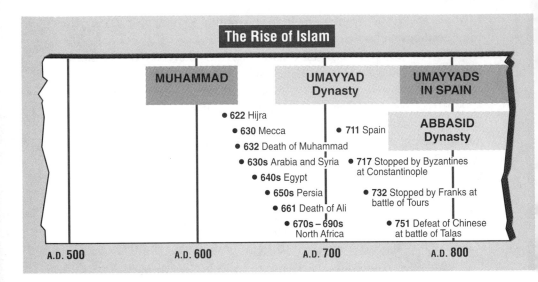

The Rise of Islam

MUHAMMAD

UMAYYAD Dynasty

UMAYYADS IN SPAIN

ABBASID Dynasty

- **622** Hijra
- **630** Mecca
- **632** Death of Muhammad
- **630s** Arabia and Syria
- **640s** Egypt
- **650s** Persia
- **661** Death of Ali
- **670s – 690s** North Africa
- **711** Spain
- **717** Stopped by Byzantines at Constantinople
- **732** Stopped by Franks at battle of Tours
- **751** Defeat of Chinese at battle of Talas

A.D. **500**   A.D. **600**   A.D. **700**   A.D. **800**

Uthman's nephew, Mu'awiya, commander of the Muslim army in Syria, demanded justice for his uncle's murder. Those who supported Ali were called *Shi'at Ali*, or the party of Ali. The name **Shiite** (SHE-eyet) derived from this group name. Mu'awiya's supporters came to be called **Sunnites** (SOO-neyets). The Shiites and Sunnites clashed repeatedly until 661, when Ali was murdered. At that time, Ali's son Hasan yielded to Mu'awiya. In a later revolt of Ali's followers in 680, his other son, Husayn, was killed in a massacre at Karbala in Iraq.

The division of Muslims into Shiites and Sunnites was at first more political than religious. It was not as important in the early Islamic period as it later became. Several other schools of belief also existed in Islam, although the Shiah and Sunni were the main ones. Today the Shiites still believe that the leadership of the Islamic community belongs to Ali and his descendants. They observe the anniversary of Husayn's death at Karbala as an occasion of mourning and revere him as a martyr. Shiites believe that the descendants of Ali and Husayn, who are known as imams, hold the highest authority in Shiite life. Some believe that there were imams who followed after the death of Husayn until the twelfth imam, who mysteriously disappeared. This "hidden imam," they believe, will be like a messiah. Another Shiite group, the Ismailis or Seveners, believes that the seventh imam, Ismail, will be a messiah. They attach mystical significance to the number seven.

In Shiite Islam, the ulema carry on a tradition of the *Shari'a* as it was handed down from Ali through the imams. In Iran today, the highest-ranking members of the Shiite ulema are known as **ayatollahs** (eye-uh-TOH-luh). Ayatollahs lead the Shiite community during the temporary absence of the "hidden imam."

Throughout history, while Shiites were ruled by Sunni rulers, they did not recognize the legality of Sunni rule. They developed their own code of law. To the Sunnites, therefore, the Shiites represented opposition to the state and Sunni law. Today, there are large populations of Shiites in Iraq, Lebanon, and Bahrein. Iran is the largest Shiite nation, while the Shiite holy cities of an-Najaf and Karbala are located in Iraq.

The Umayyads. Mu'awiya became the first of a family of caliphs called the **Umayyads** (OO-meye-adz). Their base was in Damascus. From there, the caliphs continued to spread Islam to other peoples. At the same time, they tightened their control over the vast areas already conquered.

Under the Umayyads, the caliphs governed efficiently and expanded Muslim authority. They stressed the political and economic aspects of government and ruled more like monarchs than religious leaders. They organized tax collection, maintained a postal service, minted coins, and checked weights and measures. They supervised the Arab soldiers who fought for Islam. In this way the whole of Islamic life was brought under the direction of the religious leader.

Abd al-Malik, who was caliph from 685 to 705, imposed Arabic as the official language of bureaucracy and government in the conquered lands. He began to mint coins in the name of the Islamic empire. Earlier, people had used Greek and Persian coins. Abd al-Malik also set up a postal system based on horse relays and generally increased Arab and Islamic control over the existing administration and bureaucracy.

In the beginning of their conquests, the Arabs left old governmental systems in place. They sought to have their territories continue to be productive, not upset by new systems. Tax collectors remained in their jobs, to make certain that money went to the conquerors instead of to the former Byzantine or Persian rulers. Gradually, as we shall see later, the influence of Arab custom and Islamic law was felt. The Umayyads faced problems of popular unrest because the tribes were unaccustomed to and resentful of the new authority of the state. In addition, tribes fought among themselves. There were still those who disputed the Umayyads' right to rule and supported Ali's followers. And there were also the enormous number of newly conquered peoples, many of whom were neither Muslim nor Arab. Jews and Christians had limited legal rights, almost complete religious freedom, exemption from military service, and fixed taxes.

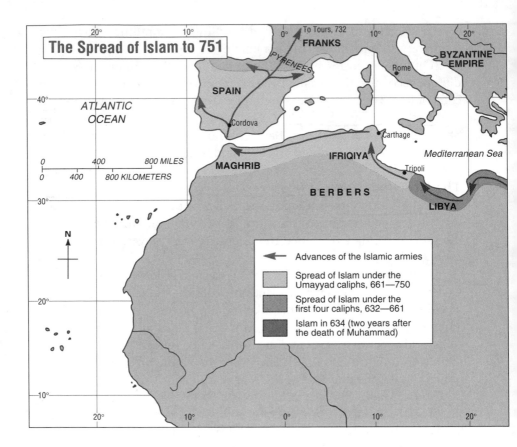

The Spread of Islam to 751

ATLANTIC OCEAN

| 0 | 400 | 800 MILES |
| 0 | 400 | 800 KILOMETERS |

SPAIN
Cordova

FRANKS
To Tours, 732
PYRENEES

BYZANTINE EMPIRE

Rome

Carthage

Mediterranean Sea

MAGHRIB

IFRIQIYA
Tripoli

BERBERS

LIBYA

N

→ Advances of the Islamic armies

Spread of Islam under the Umayyad caliphs, 661—750

Spread of Islam under the first four caliphs, 632—661

Islam in 634 (two years after the death of Muhammad)

THE EXPANSION OF ISLAM

The Arab Conquests.   One of the main features of the rise of Islam was the speed with which the Muslim Arabs conquered vast territories. This was partly due to their own skill, partly due to the weakness of the Persian and Byzantine empires, and partly due to the sympathy of the people they conquered. The Arabs fought successful campaigns one after the other as they spread east, north, and west.

After the death of the Prophet in 632, Arabs moved out of the desert regions of Arabia toward the rich lands in the north. By 635, Arabs were in Syria. Within five years, they had conquered most of the land around the Tigris-Euphrates valley. Arab tribes captured Alexandria in 642, and, as a result, all of Egypt fell to them. By 650 most of Persia was under Arab control. Having conquered most of the heartland of the Middle East, they began to move east and west.

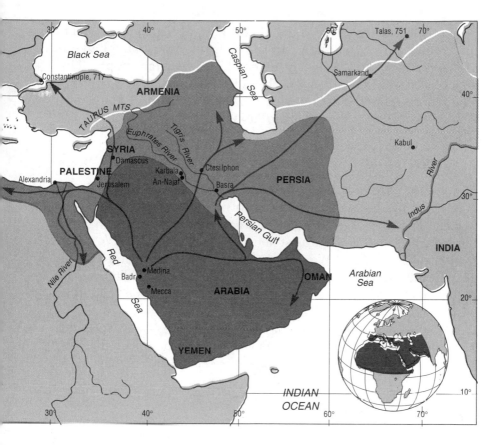

Within 60 years Arab armies swept west across North Africa to Morocco. From there they spread northward across the Strait of Gibraltar, invading Spain in 711. Crossing the Pyrenees, in hopes of further European conquests, the Arab armies were stopped by the Franks. These were a powerful Germanic people who ruled in the land that would become France. In 732 the Frankish leader, Charles Martel, defeated the Arabs at the battle of Tours, only one hundred miles from Paris.

As some Arab armies were driving west across North Africa, others were moving rapidly eastward across present-day Iran and Afghanistan into northern India. There they were met by Chinese troops of the Tang Dynasty. Like the Arabs, the Chinese under the Tang rulers were expanding into parts of Central Asia. In 751 the Arabs defeated the Chinese at the battle of Talas. As a result of this victory, Islam spread throughout the Indus River valley. It took hold across northern India in what is now Bangladesh, and eastward into Indonesia.

101

In the northern regions of the Middle East, Muslim armies went as far as the Taurus Mountains. In the 660s the Arabs launched one of many attacks on the Byzantine capital of Constantinople. This attack failed, as did an attempted blockade of the capital. The border of Islam in the Middle East remained in the Taurus Mountains until Constantinople fell to the Ottoman Turks in 1453.

Jihad. For Muslims all of these campaigns were part of one war, the holy war, or **jihad** (ji-HAHD). *(Jihad* means "striving" or "contending.")* While still in Medina struggling against the forces of Mecca, the Muslims had been urged to fight their pagan enemies. Thus jihad was the name given to the war against non-Muslims, the *Dar al-Harb*. *Dar al-Harb* means "House of War" and referred to the lands and peoples beyond Muslim control. The part of the world where Islam rules is called the *Dar al-Islam*, the "Abode of Islam." Although the Arab tribes were small, they were united by their faith in Islam.

Jihad sometimes—but not always—took the form of war. According to Islam, jihad against nonbelievers was sacred. Those who died in a jihad were assured of going to Paradise. A second and perhaps more important meaning of jihad was that of a struggle against one's innermost selfish tendencies. The "Greater Jihad" was therefore the perfection of one's own spirit.

The Abbasids. Discontent under the Umayyads became open revolt after the death of the Caliph Hisham in 744. Followers of Ali ibn al-Abbas were the focus of a revolution that put a new line of caliphs, the Abbasids (uh-BAS-idz), at the head of the Muslim state. Under the Abbasids, the direction and leadership of the Islamic Empire was moved from the Arabian peninsula. The Abbasids established a new capital city, Baghdad, in the heartland of the Middle East. Thus, in less than 100 years after the death of Muhammad, the entire ancient Middle East and areas beyond came under Muslim rule. Areas where Greek and Roman culture had flourished, and where Buddhist and Hindu beliefs dominated, were to be transformed into centers of Islamic civilization. As a result, Islam became a universal religion, one for all peoples. In the next chapter you will see how this new civilization spread.

REVIEWING THE CHAPTER

I. **Building Your Vocabulary**

Write the letter that best answers each of the following questions.

1. What is Muhammad's historic flight from Mecca to Medina called in Arabic?
   a. hijra   **b.** the hajj   **c.** jihad

2. What is the pilgrimage to Mecca required of Muslims known as?
   a. hijra   **b.** the hajj   **c.** jihad

3. What are interpretations of Islamic law that are not explained in the Koran called?
   a. suras   **b.** ulema   **c.** hadith

4. The Sunnites make up one major division of Islam; what are followers of the other major division known as?
   a. Shiites   **b.** ulema   **c.** Abassids

5. What is another name for the part of the world where Islam rules, known in Arabic as Dar al-Islam?
   a. hajj   **b.** the Abode of Islam   **c.** the Muslim Empire

II. **Understanding the Facts**

1. What does the word *Islam* mean?

2. Who controlled Palestine just before the Arab conquests of the seventh century?

3. Before the spread of Islam, what were the religious beliefs of most Bedouin Arabs?

4. How do the Muslims regard Jesus?

5. In what modern country are both Mecca and Medina located?

6. What does the Muslim holiday of Ramadan commemorate?

7. Among Sunni Muslims who is responsible for presiding over prayers, funerals, and festivals?

8. What was the outcome of the battle of Tours?

9. What was the outcome of the battle of Talas?

10. Where did the Abbasids build a new capital city?

III. Thinking It Through

1. How did Muhammad's early contacts with Jews and Christians influence his religious thought? Give examples.

2. In what way is Islam both a religious and a secular institution?

3. How did Muhammad's move to Medina alter the development of Islam?

4. Why did Muhammad's death bring on a political crisis in Islam?

5. What was Abu Bakr's contribution to Islam?

6. What are the "Five Pillars of Islam"? Why might they appeal to Arab Bedouins and contribute to the spread of Islam?

7. What contributions did the Umayyads make to the consolidation of early Islam?

8. Of what importance was war in the spread of Islam in the seventh and eighth centuries?

9. How did the battles of Tours and Talas alter the course of world history?

10. What were the political implications of the disagreements between the Sunnites and the Shiites?

DEVELOPING CRITICAL THINKING SKILLS

1. List facts that support the following generalization: The Western concept of the separation of church and state has no place in traditional Islamic practice.

2. List facts from Chapters 3 and 4 to support the following generalization: In ancient times the Middle East was a crossroads of competing civilizations.

ANALYZING A MAP

Use the map on pages 100 and 101 to analyze the following paragraph. Then answer the questions that follow.

> In 717 the Byzantine Empire succeeded in checking the Arabs at Constantinople. Fifteen years later, in 732, a Frankish army at Tours blocked the Arab advance into western Europe. Of these two dates 732 is far more famous, but 717 is probably just as important. Had the Arabs succeeded in seizing the great fortress city of Constantinople from the Byzantines, they probably would have conquered the weaker West as well. As a result all of Europe may have come under Arab military, cultural, and religious control.

1. Do you agree with this assessment? Why or why not?

2. How does the map suggest that the Mediterranean would have become an Arab lake with the conquest of Constantinople?

3. Which countries under Arab control in the eighth century are still Islamic? Which are not? (Use the map on pages 2–3 to help you.)

ENRICHMENT AND EXPLORATION

1. Find a modern translation of the Koran. Read an early chapter and compare it to the book of Genesis in the Old Testament. What themes are common to both holy books?

2. What does the word *crusade* mean? How were the Arabs of the seventh and eighth centuries crusaders in the name of Islam?

3. Find out more about the origins and development of the Shiite movement and its impact on modern Islam. Research basic themes and problems.

AN ISLAMIC CIVILIZATION
750–1400

750–1265	The Abbasids rule the Islamic empire.
756–1031	Umayyad emirate in Spain
825	al-Khawarazmi publishes a book on the mathematical system developed by the Hindus.
850	Arabs complete translations of major works from all parts of the Middle East into Arabic.
900–1048	Battani, al-Biruni, and other Arab scientists develop complex astronomical tables.
969	Fatamids found Cairo.
1000–c. 1150	The Seljuk Empire
1054	Disputes lead to a division of the Christian Church into the Roman Catholic church and the Eastern Orthodox Church.
1071	The Seljuks take over some Byzantine lands in modern Turkey and move into Iraq, Syria, and Egypt.
1172	Islamic Berbers from North Africa take over Islamic Spain.
1095–1290	The Crusades
1200–1450	*African empire of Mali*
1215	*Magna Carta signed in England.*
1241	Mongols conquer much of Russia.
1258	Mongols invade the Middle East and capture Baghdad.
1260	Mamelukes defeat the Mongols in battle.
1260–1294	*Kublai Khan rules China.*
1347	*Black Death strikes Western Europe.*
1359	Mongols overthrown in Persia; Turks take control.

5 The Development of an Islamic Civilization (750–1400)

Unlike other invaders who destroyed whatever they found in their path, the Muslims kept much of what they conquered. They met peoples with advanced technologies which they adapted to their new culture. They also took over established ideas, skills, and ways of governing and used these for their own benefit. This blend of old and new in the Middle East resulted in the creation of Islamic civilization. A civilization consists of many things. These include the ways of living, art, customs, beliefs, technology, and government of a complex society that depends upon cities.

As the capital shifted from Mecca and Medina to Damascus and later Baghdad, local peoples gradually gained a more important role in governing the empire. They added to the development of what was to become an international Islamic culture.

By the year 1000, new conquerors were invading the region. Turkish-speaking nomads on horseback moved west from Central Asia. They took control of large areas of the Middle East, Russia, and Europe. In the Middle East, these tribal people adopted Islam. But they added bits of their own cultures to what they found. Thus, despite many invasions and the collapse of Arab rule in the Middle East, the Islamic empire endured.

BRINGING TOGETHER AN EMPIRE

As you read in the last chapter, the Umayyads built up a powerful Arab state. They faced many problems, however. Fiercely independent Arab tribes fought one another and resisted the new centralizing authority of the state. And there were still those who opposed the

Umayyads' right to rule. These opponents supported Ali's Shiite follow-ers instead. There was also the problem of governing vast numbers of newly conquered peoples. Many of these peoples were neither Muslim nor Arab.

The Abbasids (750–1256).   After the death of the Umayyad caliph Hisham in 744, growing internal conflict became a full-scale revolt. The followers of Ali ibn al-Abbas (from Muhammad's tribe, but not a direct descendant) led the revolt. They put a new line of caliphs, the **Abbasids** (uh-BAS-idz), at the head of the Muslim state. The Abbasid caliphs were in power by 750. Once in power, they moved the capital of the Islamic empire from Damascus east to Iraq. There they built a new capital city, Baghdad.

Here is a late ninth-century description of the building of the city:

> The caliph gave orders to [bring together] engineers . . . and specialists . . . to lay out the plan of his city. He [called for] masons, laborers, and craftsmen who were carpenters, smiths, and diggers.
>
> He laid out the plan in the month of Rabi' I of the year 141 [July–August 758]. He made of it a round city, the only round city known in the world. He laid the foundations at the moment chosen by the astronomer . . . . He provided the city with four gates . . . . Each of the four gates had arcades. Over each of the gates of the city at the main wall there was a great vaulted gilded dome, around which were places to sit and lean, where one could sit and look down on all that was happening below. [Entrance] to these domes was by a ramp over the vaulting . . . . The ramp, on which one could ride, was fitted with doors which could be closed.

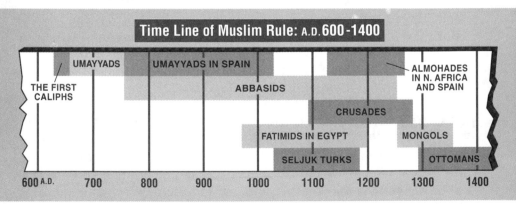

Fig109

With the Abbasids in power, Persian influence on government, learning, and art increased. The defeat of the Sassanid Persians placed Iran and Iraq firmly under Muslim control. As the great wars of conquest ended, Islamic caliphs focused more on developing the empire. And they had the power to do it. The caliph was no longer merely a tribal **sheikh** (SHAYK), or chief. He was the supreme ruler of an empire. He led a huge army and headed a large bureaucracy.

The Growth of Trade. The Abbasid revolution brought major changes to the Middle East. Economic life flourished and agricultural output increased. The Abbasids spent money on irrigation projects. One of these projects drained the swamps in southern Iraq. The Abbasids also eased taxes on the peasants. Resources such as metals, wood, and precious stones were plentiful. These were fashioned into beautiful handcrafted items. The textile industry expanded. Brilliant carpets and elegant tapestries, cloth, and silk were traded all over the empire.

Security and order within the Islamic lands grew under the Abbasids. During the early years of the Islamic empire, the situation in the countryside was unsettled. Roads were dangerous. Bedouin tribes attacked caravans. Travelers passed through the countryside at their own risk. Under the rule of the Abbasids, a great trade network developed. In the period from about 750 to 1500, Islam was the main civilization in the Eastern Hemisphere outside East Asia. It carried its culture to isolated peoples and brought innovations from one society to another. For example, Chinese inventions like the compass reached Europe through Arab traders. European inventions like artillery passed through the same hands.

Seaborne trade from the Persian Gulf became more active under the Abbasids. After 700 a Muslim trading colony in Ceylon (modern Sri Lanka) became prominent. Gulf traders began to travel to China at this time. They took advantage of the monsoon winds to sail from Persia to the southern tip of India, across the Bay of Bengal to the South China Sea. Given time for repairs, a ship could make a round-trip voyage every two years. On land, travelers journeyed over the Silk Road from China to the Middle East. Muslim traders brought silk from China, furs from Russia, and gold and precious stones from Central Asia. Spices came from the East Indies and black slaves from Africa. Investors in the cities supplied camel caravans, which could be gone for years. These caravans stopped at desert inns called *caravanserais* (kar-uh-VAN-suh-reez), which provided them with food, rest, and company during the long journeys.

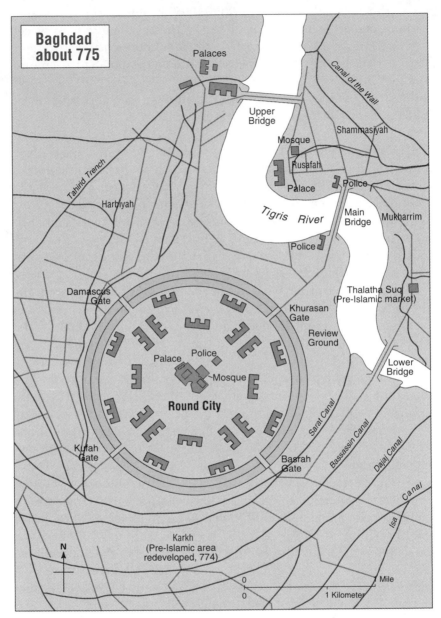

Baghdad about 775

Palaces

Canal of the Wall

Upper Bridge

Shammasiyah

Mosque

Rusafah

Palace

Police

Tigris River

Main Bridge

Mukharrim

Police

Tahirid Trench

Harbiyah

Damascus Gate

Khurasan Gate

Thalatha Suq (Pre-Islamic market)

Review Ground

Lower Bridge

Palace

Police

Mosque

Round City

Sarat Canal

Bassassin Canal

Dajaj Canal

Kufah Gate

Basrah Gate

Isa Canal

N

Karkh (Pre-Islamic area redeveloped, 774)

0   Mile

0   1 Kilometer

The circular city of Baghdad was started in 762 by the Abasid caliph al-Mansur as the capital of the new dynasty. Within 50 years, Baghdad had over a million people and was the center of one of the golden ages of Islamic culture.

Islamic glassware from the 800s through the 1300s. The large vase in the center is from Damascus or Aleppo in Syria. What other kinds of products were carried along the Muslim trade routes during this period?

New roads and canals made trade and travel easier. Roads spread out from Baghdad in all directions. Bridges were built across the Tigris and Euphrates rivers, and the two rivers were joined by a canal. Muslim trade moved from Spain to India without the restrictions placed upon it by different states. Arabic words such as "traffic," "tariff," "magazine," "caravan," and "bazaar" all date from this period.

Starting in the 800s, a number of new products moved between Asia and Europe by way of the Middle East. The orange tree was brought from India to Arabia. From there, it became known as far west as Spain. Sugar came from India and papermaking passed from Asia into the Middle East. In time, the technique of papermaking was brought to Europe. The Middle East also produced world-famous goods of its own. Mosul (in Iraq) was known for its cotton muslin, Damascus for its linen damask and steel, Mocha (in Yemen) for its coffee, and Baghdad for its pottery. Some of the world's finest glass came from the cities of Tyre and Sidon.

Baghdad at Its Peak.   Baghdad became a major center of world trade. Wealth from the booty of warfare, taxes, and commerce poured in. Baghdad became famous as a capital of luxury.

> On its flanks flow two great rivers, the Tigris and the Euphrates. Thus goods and foodstuffs come to it by land and by water with the greatest ease. Every kind of merchandise is completely available, from east and west, from Muslim and non-Muslim lands. Goods are brought from India, Sind, China, Tibet, the lands of the Turks, the Daylam, the Khazars, the Ethiopians, and others to such an extent that the products of the countries are more plentiful in Baghdad than in the countries from which they come.

The Abbasid court took on the splendid trappings of the earlier Persian Empire. The caliphs lived in magnificent palaces, attended by slaves, palace guards, and officials. There, they were surrounded by elaborate pageantry and ceremony. The stories of *The Thousand and One Nights* come from this period. During the reign of the legendary Harun al-Rashid (786–809), the Abbasid caliphate reached its peak.

The Caliphate in Spain.   During the Abbasid revolution one of the Umayyads, Abd-al-Rahman, managed to flee to Spain. With the support of the strongest Arab faction in Spain, he defeated the forces of the governor outside Córdoba. He then founded an independent Umayyad emirate. Like the Eastern Abbasid, it was based on "true justice" and toleration for all religious and ethnic groups but it allowed those groups more freedom. This position strengthened his standing among Spain's different peoples. He ruled as Abd-al-Rahman I from 756 to 788. His successors were to rule in Spain until 1031. (But other Muslims continued to rule there until 1492. In that year the last Muslims were expelled by the Christians from a reduced kingdom in southern Spain. The centuries-long struggle is known as the Reconquista.)

By the tenth century, an efficient Muslim state system had developed in Spain. It became the best organized administration to be found anywhere in western Europe at this time. But the real strength of Muslim Spain lay in its cities. The cities had strong economies and skilled workers. In addition, they were centers of technology and learning. Spanish cities were famous for textiles, leather goods, ceramics, weapons, and fine steelworking. Spanish seaports on the Mediterranean coast grew rich from trade with Italy and France. At the court of Caliph Abd-al-Rahman III (912–961), writers, poets, and musicians were encouraged.

The Golden Mosque, Baghdad, Iraq.

Spain became a great center of learning. To a great extent it was in Spain that ancient Greek and Roman learning was kept alive and later carried to the rest of Europe.

The Spanish Umayyads ruled most of Spain and the western part of North Africa. Today, this region is made up of Morocco, Tunisia, and Algeria. But in the tenth century it was known in Arabic as the **Maghrib** (MU-gruhb), meaning in Arabic place of the setting sun, or West. Both Spain and the Maghrib followed the same Islamic legal tradition and even developed their own forms of Arabic script. In the Maghrib, most of the people gave up their old religions and became Muslims. The Moroccan city of Fez became a center of trade and culture.

The Organization of the Empire. In the early years of Muslim expansion, the caliph Umar set up military garrisons to control the surrounding lands. The men who lived in these garrisons owed loyalty to the caliph or his local representative. But the collection of taxes and the administration of government were often left in the hands of local officials. So long as they followed orders, the local people could run their own laws.

In order to pay the troops and the government officials, the Muslim rulers collected a poll tax (that is, a tax of a fixed amount per adult) from non-Muslims. This tax was called the *jizya* (JIZ-yuh). Non-Muslims also paid additional land taxes. All of these taxes helped to fill the treasury of the new Muslim state.

It is difficult to say how many people converted to Islam. Despite popular belief, Muslims did not ride through their conquered lands, offering people the choice of conversion or death. Particularly under the Umayyads, they did little to change the religion of the people in the areas they conquered.

Certain non-Muslims had a special status in the Islamic world. Jews, Christians, and Zoroastrians were called "People of the Book" by the Muslims. This was because each had a sacred religious text. Known as *dhimmis*, (THIM-eez), these non-Muslims were protected under Islamic law by a special document, the *dhimma*. *Dhimmis* had to pay the *jizya* and the land tax. They were not allowed to carry weapons. Often they had to wear special clothing or badges. These "People of the Book" were not often allowed to build new houses of worship. At certain periods of history in the Islamic world, they were not permitted to build homes higher than Muslim ones. At the same time, they were allowed to practice their faiths, organize their own communities, and take part in economic and political life. Later, when Jews were persecuted in Christian lands, they found a safe home in Muslim territory.

There was a flowering of Jewish culture at the very time that Islamic civilization was reaching a peak. From leading a basically agricultural life, Jews entered more into businesses, crafts, medicine, sciences, trade, and sometimes government. Both Muslims and non-Muslims could take part in a relatively free society. Outright persecution of Jews was not common, although it sometimes did happen. When the Abbasids moved their capital to Iraq (ancient Babylonia), they moved the center of their empire to an area already the leading center of Jewish life. There, Jews not only achieved importance in trade. The scholars at their two Babylonian academies gained greater authority as teachers of the Babylonian Talmud. (See page 74.) Jews in all parts of the world looked to these teachers for religious leadership.

Outside Iraq, the three most important Jewish communities were in North Africa in what is now Tunisia, in Egypt, and in Spain. In North

Africa and Egypt, Jews developed careers in trade. In Egypt, especially, Jews were able to gain positions in government at times. Most Jews spoke Arabic. In Spain, Jews under Islamic government enjoyed freedom and prosperity for several centuries. Many were peasants; some owned farms and vineyards. Others were artisans and crafts workers, making leather goods such as shoes and saddles. Jewish crafts workers also made luxury goods such as fine textiles and jewelry. Hasdai ibn Shaprut was a leading physician, diplomat, and statesman in Spain. Judah ha-Levi became the most famous writer of Hebrew poetry in centuries.

By 1172, however, most of Islamic Spain came under the control of Islamic Berbers from North Africa. The new rulers tolerated neither Jews nor Christians. Many Jews converted or fled either to Christian parts of Spain or to the more tolerant Muslim Egypt. The greatest Jewish philosopher of the period was Moses Maimonides (my-MON-uh-deez). He left Spain in 1148 and 17 years later settled in Egypt. Maimonides became the rabbi of Cairo and physician to the sultan of Egypt. In Hebrew, he wrote a famous work that arranged traditional Jewish teachings according to subject matter. It was a systematic summary of the legal rules of the Talmud and other religious writings. His most famous work was *Guide to the Perplexed,* written in Arabic. It tried to harmonize the teachings of Judaism with the Greek philosophy of Aristotle. Aristotle was accepted by most Arab scholars of the time. The *Guide* created controversy. However, it influenced many Jewish, Muslim, and Christian philosophers.

As you have read, a major split among Christians had already led to several new Christian groups in the Middle East before the rise of Islam. (See page 76.) When Muslims gained power, the Nestorians and the members of the Oriental Orthodox churches were treated as *dhimmis.* Thus, most of the time, they too were guaranteed their lives, their property, and the right to worship as they chose. As Muslim power spread toward Christian parts of Europe and toward the Byzantine Empire, a second major split in Christianity occurred. Major disputes in the 800s led to the break in 1054. Much of southern and western Europe looked to the pope in Rome for leadership. These Roman Catholics prayed in Latin. In the Byzantine Empire, services and prayers were in Greek. The head of the Eastern Orthodox church was the patriarch in Constantinople.

More and more people in the conquered lands were attracted by the new religion and did convert to Islam. Many wanted to escape the extra

CASE STUDY:

A Day in the Life of a Court Physician

In the eleventh and twelfth centuries Egypt had a sizable Jewish population. One of the most respected members of the community was Moses ben Maimon, also known as Maimonides. He was not only one of the most important Jewish scholars, but also physician to the sultan.

I live in Fustat and the king lives in Cairo. Between the two places there is a distance of two Sabbath days' journey [about 1.5 miles or 2.4 kilometers]. With the king I have a heavy program. It is impossible for me not to see him first thing every day. If he suffers any indisposition, or if any of his sons or [wives] falls sick, I cannot leave Cairo, and I spend most of my day in the palace. It may also happen that one or two of his officers fall sick, and I must attend to them. In short, I go to Cairo early every morning, and if there is no mishap and nothing new, I return to Fustat in the afternoon, and certainly not before then. . . . I find the anterooms all filled with people. There are Gentiles and Jews, great and small, judges and bailiffs, friends and enemies, a mixed multitude, who await the moment of my return. I dismount from my beast and wash my hands and go to them to soothe them and placate them. . . . I go out to treat them and write prescriptions and instructions for their illnesses. They come and go without a break until night, and sometimes until two hours of the night or more. . . . By nightfall I am so worn out that I cannot speak. Finally, no Jew can speak to me or keep company with me or have private conversation with me except on the Sabbath. Then all or most of the congregation come to me after prayers, and I instruct the community on what they should do throughout the week. They read for a while until noon, and then they go their way. Some of them return and read again between the afternoon and evening prayers.

This is how I spend the day.

Abridged from Bernard Lewis, *Islam From the Prophet Muhammad to the Capture of Constantinople. Book II. Religion and Society.* New York: Harper & Row, 1974.

1. Whom did Maimonides treat in Cairo?
2. How did he spend the Sabbath?

taxes that fell on non-Muslims. They also sought to become full citizens. In fact, part of the conflict during the Abbasid revolution grew from the complaint of new Muslims that they were treated as inferior by the Arabs. Most slaves occupied the bottom of the social ladder. These were mostly Greeks, Turks, Spaniards, Berbers, Kurds, Armenians, and blacks. The institution of slavery had a major impact on Islamic society. Economically, the slave trade was a profitable business. Socially, through the institution of the harem, slavery played an important role. Politically, individual slaves had influence as bodyguards and favorites.

ISLAMIC CIVILIZATION (750–1000)

The Islamic religion and empire were not born in a vacuum. Muslim faith and law as well as literature, art, and philosophy drew upon elements of the civilizations that existed at the time of the rise of Islam.

The Creation of a New Civilization.   Islam did not spread only by conquest. Missionaries and traders carried Islam into new lands such as Central Asia. More than military might is needed to explain why the peoples of the Middle East—who had thrown off the Phoenician, Roman, and Byzantine invaders—came to accept the Arabic language and Islamic religion. It is also worth noting that Indonesia, although geographically distant from the Arab world and speaking a non-Arab language, has the largest Muslim population in the world. Interestingly, it is a country the Arabs never conquered.

Religion played an important role in bringing together the Middle East. Belief in one God, in the message of the Prophet Muhammad, in personal salvation, in the equality of individuals before God, and in rules of moral conduct helped to hold the Middle East together. An intense cultural life existed in the area from Afghanistan to Spain— the extent of the Muslim empire. Another story was taking place in Europe at this time, however. The Europeans were undergoing constant invasion and suffering economic decline. Learning had almost ceased, and the knowledge and traditions of ancient Greece and Rome were nearly forgotten. The Islamic world, on the other hand, remained a center of civilization.

Islamic Education.   Although most boys were expected to work from an early age, opportunities for education were available for them and a few were able to go to school. Those who did so studied mainly religious texts. Such a student might begin his studies of the Koran at the age of six or seven. If he was gifted or his family had great wealth, he might continue to study in a nearby city. There, in a large mosque, he studied the Koran, hadith, and Islamic law. In addition, he learned Arabic grammar. An exceptional student might then go on to study with a famous judge in Baghdad. He might also go to Egypt, where he could attend the oldest university in the world, al-Azhar. After a student there received a letter from his professor stating that he had completed his studies, he could set up his own school. For an intelligent and well-to-do young man an Islamic education created great opportunities to advance. He could join the ulema or serve in the government.

The Life of the People.   Local conditions determined what people ate and what they wore. Wheat was the basic grain and it was prepared in different ways. It could be ground and baked into the flat pita bread we know today, cooked as bulgur (cracked wheat), or eaten as porridge. Cheese, butter, and yogurt were provided from the milk of sheep, goats, camels, water buffaloes, and cows. Lamb was the most common meat. Alcohol was forbidden by Muslim law, but the rule was sometimes disregarded. There were many kinds of fruit juice and sherbet. This dessert was originally prepared from snow mixed with rose water or fruit syrup.

People wore linen and cotton clothes in summer and woolen garments in winter. Muslims were required to dress modestly, and they preferred loose-fitting robes to trousers. Horsemen wore baggy pants. Women covered their hair but did not always wear a veil. Men covered their heads with different types of brimless headgear. (A brim would get in the way of prayer.) Headgear often served to identify a person. For example, a green turban identified the wearer as one who had made the hajj to Mecca. Bedouins wore the **kufiyah**. This is a headcloth held in place by a headband.

Islamic society was basically **patriarchal**, that is, ruled by men. Although a few upper-class women wrote poetry and took part in government, most Muslim women in cities stayed at home and cared for the children. In some rural areas women worked with their husbands in the fields and took part in crafts. Children were expected to obey their parents, women their husbands and, after marriage, their in-laws.

The wealthy had the time to read and to appreciate art. Princes called for beautifully decorated Korans. Scribes copied these by hand in elaborate Arabic script. Then, they decorated the borders with gold leaf.

118

Stories of ancient Persian heroes were written down and illustrated with miniature paintings of intense detail. Writers set down the deeds of Muslim heroes and translated ancient Greek and Roman texts into Arabic. The Muslim preservation of these works on medicine, poetry, philosophy, and literature was of lasting importance. Centuries later the Europeans studied them during the Renaissance.

Scientific Achievements of the Islamic World. Perhaps the Muslims' greatest achievements were in the sciences. In the field of medicine especially, the Muslims made outstanding original contributions to human knowledge.

As you have read, Muslim scholars translated Greek texts on science, mathematics, and philosophy. Caliph al-Mamun (813–833) set up his famous "House of Wisdom" at Baghdad. Here, Greek, Persian, and Sanskrit works were translated into Arabic. The "House of Wisdom" was also a scientific academy, observatory, and public library. A similar institution was started in Damascus. The major task of translating books from all parts of the Middle East was largely completed by 850. Later, Indian astronomical records were translated into Arabic.

Mathematics. It was perhaps through these translations that the Arabs first came into contact with what are now called Hindu-Arabic numerals. In the early 800s al-Khawarazmi went to India. There, he learned about the mathematical system used by the Hindus. Returning to the Middle East, he published a book in 825 on the numerals of the Indians. In this book the principles of the decimal system were discussed. At the same time al-Khawarazmi introduced the concept of zero into the Arab world. The Muslims called the little circle that stood for zero *sifr,* or empty. It is from this word that the English word *cipher* evolved.

Al-Khawarazmi also added to the science of algebra (from the Arabic, *al-jabr*). Algebra had been begun by the Greek Diaophantus in the third century A.D. By applying Arabic numerals to the science of algebra, al-Khawarazmi simplified and advanced the development of the modern mathematical sciences. Arabic scholars also developed trigonometry.

Astronomy and Geography. As you have read, an observatory was part of Caliph Mamun's "House of Wisdom" at Baghdad. Here, Arab astronomers increased their knowledge of geography and astronomy. This effort arose in part out of the needs of the Islamic faith. Muslims, you will recall, were obliged to pray in the direction of Mecca. They were also required to know the precise times for sunrise and sunset, in order to observe the fasts during the holy month of Ramadan. Moreover, from all over the Islamic Empire, devout Muslims needed to plot the hajj, the journey of pilgrimage to Mecca. These needs led to the search for accurate measurements.

By the ninth and tenth centuries, Arab scientists such as Battani (858–929) and al-Biruni (973–1048) had developed complex astronomical tables. These were widely used in Europe until the fourteenth century. Muslim astronomers were able to measure with some accuracy the size of the earth. They also measured one degree at 45 ⅔ miles (73 kilometers), a measure that is within half a mile of the correct calculation. Thus, they were able to set standards for longitude and latitude. And Muslim observations of heavenly bodies were very precise. Their records served as useful guides to modern astronomers.

In addition, Arab scientists improved other instruments of measurement. By their efforts, remarkably accurate results were achieved. They also improved the **astrolabe,** the instrument that made navigation on the high seas possible. This was done by fixing approximate positions of the stars at a particular moment. Thus, by the 1200s astronomers and geographers of many nations and religions were flocking to the Middle East. There they joined the Muslims in search of scientific knowledge.

Chemistry. In this period the Arabs were almost alone in creating the science of chemistry. As you have read, they knew the writings of the ancient Greeks on scientific subjects. The Arabs had been studying chemistry as early as the seventh century. By the 700s a number of scholars were investigating chemical reactions. These scholars were soon able to tell the difference between acids and alkalis. Arab scientists were convinced that all metals were made of the same basic substance. They could, therefore, be transformed into other metals and alloys. Modern atomic physics, to a large degree, has justified their beliefs.

One of the most famous of the Arab scientists was Jabir ibn Hayyan. In the West he was known as Geber. Living and working in Kufa, Iraq, in the eighth century, Jabir stressed the importance of experiments. He said, "He who performs not practical work nor makes experiments will never [reach] the least degree of mastery." The discoveries of a number of important chemical compounds are credited to him. Among these was the preparation of nitric acid.

Jabir also made great contributions in the practical applications of chemistry. He explained the processes for refining steel and other metals. He described methods of dyeing cloth and leather and of waterproofing cloth by varnishing it. One of his inventions was a "golden" ink

Islamic astronomers like these made many important contributions to the study of the heavens. This painting is a miniature, a small painting used to illustrate manuscripts and books.

that replaced costly inks made from real gold. This ink was used to decorate books and paintings.

Another famous chemist, Muhammad ibn Zakariya al-Razi, continued Jabir's work. Al-Razi was also a physician. He was the first to classify his observations regarding chemical substances. From the fourth to the twelfth centuries, Arabic texts were translated into Latin and used in Europe. In translating these Arab texts, the translators tried to make the technical explanations clear. As a result, they often kept the Arabic terms for some substances but used European spelling. Thus, some chemical names we use today are close to their Arabic originals: camphor, borax, elixir, talc, and saffron.

Medicine. Of chief interest to the Muslims was medicine. Their contribution to knowledge and treatment of disease was unique for its time. By preserving and studying ancient texts, Arab Muslim scholars were able to bring to the medieval world the work of the Greek scholars Hippocrates and Galen.

Great medical institutions dotted the Muslim world. The first **bimarastan,** a combined hospital and medical school, was built at Baghdad in the mid-700s. Under the Abbasids, hospitals and medical facilities continued to be built throughout the empire. By the year 1000 there were about 6,000 medical students in Baghdad alone.

Students at the *bimarastans* took courses in diseases, chemistry, and medical theory. They observed surgery and had practical experience in clinics. This is very much like the studies of medical interns today. Moreover, the Arabs believed that physicians should be "well rounded." Therefore, the schools taught music, mathematics, astronomy, and other courses.

Arabic medical books remained the most widely accepted works on disease until the end of the eighteenth century. Al-Razi, about whom you have already read, produced one of the world's most important series of medical studies. His *Treatise on Smallpox and Measles* remained a reference book in England into the 1800s. Al-Razi wrote more than two hundred scientific books. These included a medical encyclopedia that remained in wide use in Europe until the late 1400s. An even more famous contributor to medical knowledge was Abu Ali al-Husayn ibn Sina (980–1037). He was known to Europeans as Avicenna. Well known as a philosopher and mathematician while still in his teens, Avicenna also became famous as a physician. Like al-Razi, he put together an encyclopedia of diseases. In this work, Avicenna also gave the appropriate treatments and medications for each disease. This work was translated into Latin and Hebrew and served as the medical text-book in many European universities for several centuries.

Arabic doctors were highly skilled in the uses of drugs and therapy. Juleps, rose water, camphor, and myrrh were produced by Arab pharmacists. Doctors also used steam baths to cure fevers and had a form of anesthesia hundreds of years before the West.

Major developments in medicine also arose out of the Islamic communities in Spain. Doctors there developed new techniques in surgery and in the treatment of wounds. They also learned more about the nature of contagious diseases. Outbreaks of smallpox, cholera, and bubonic plague had recently spread to Europe, and Muslim physicians were able to help the sick with their knowledge about the nature of these diseases.

Doctors with a sick patient. The patient's son stands behind his father's pillow. What were some of the Muslim achievements in the field of medicine and public health?

Philosophy, Literature, and the Arts (800s–1000s). Throughout this period the Middle East produced some great scholars. Like European Christianity during the Renaissance, Islam faced the problem of trying to join its faith with human reason. To this purpose the Muslims used Greek learning in an effort to explain their religious ideas. One such thinker was the famous Spanish Arab philosopher and physician Abu al-Walid Muhammad ibn Rushd (1126–1198), called Averroës (uh-VER-uh-weez) by Europeans. But in this period Islam also produced a group of scholars who were almost entirely concerned with pure philosophy. Two such individuals were al-Biruni and ibn Sina (Avicenna). As you have read, al-Biruni specialized in astronomy, mathematics, and physics. But he also did major work in philosophy, poetry, and history. Much the same can be said of ibn Sina.

Literature. *The Thousand and One Nights* is perhaps the most widely read work of Middle Eastern literature. Among the best known stories in the series are those of Ali Baba, Sinbad, and Aladdin. In the area of poetry Omar Khayyam, a Persian mathematician who lived in the eleventh century, made an outstanding contribution in his famous Persian-language work, the *Rubaiyat*. *Rubaiyat* means "four-line verses." In addition, the impact of Arabic poetry on the West has been widely debated by historians. Many scholars point to the contact between Islamic Spain and southern France. Because of this contact, historians view Islamic poetry as a chief source for the medieval troubadours and poets of the courtly love tradition that entered Europe.

Music. Arabic became the literary language of the Islamic world. Poets were held in high regard. Music developed and combined with poetry to provide the Muslims with tales of love, war, and heroism. The lute, the lyre, and the flute were used by Arabic musicians. They also used horns, castanets, drums, cymbals, and tambourines.

Architecture. Art and architecture made rapid progress. At first, the Arab Muslims took on Byzantine, Egyptian, Syrian, Mesopotamian, and Indian art forms. One of the most important pieces of knowledge was the method of building the dome. This architectural element appeared over and over in Muslim mosques. The design theme was seen in Europe by the early twelfth century. Another Muslim architectural form was the minaret. This thin, high tower provides a balance with heavy-domed prayer rooms in a way that is very pleasing to the eye.

Later, Islamic art used new techniques in art and architecture. For example, the horseshoe arch and the pointed arch were used in the great mosques in Damascus and Cairo. The mosques had huge central spaces, with arcades and colonnades. Ribbed vaulted ceilings arched

The Alhambra Palace in Granada in southern Spain. The Court of Lions and the rooms around it were built in the period from 1354 to 1391.

over the entire structure. Graceful open grilles made of wood or stone covered the outer walls. Other structures such as the Alhambra in Spain and the famous Taj Mahal in India are outstanding examples of different Islamic building styles.

Decoration was not limited to the outside of the Islamic mosque. Inside, brilliant combinations of mosaic tiles and beautifully colored glass covered the walls. Arabic script taken from the Koran ran around the upper parts of the walls. Marble decorated the lower portions of the walls, and rich, finely detailed rugs and carpets were laid on the floors. Delicate carvings in ivory or wood gave the finishing touches to the interior doors, cornices, and mihrab, the traditional niche that faces Mecca.

125

INVASION AND DECLINE

The Islamic Empire began to break down as differences threatened the unity of the Middle Eastern world. Some of these differences were religious in nature. **Sufism** (SOO-fiz-uhm) began to make gains. This mystical movement places great emphasis on individual worship and piety. Holy men attracted bands of followers and went beyond what was permitted in the Koran. According to strict Muslim teaching, the good Muslim could only reach a perfect state through the teachings of the Prophet Muhammad.

At the same time, a group of Muslims known as **Ismailis** began to interpret the Koran differently. The Ismailis are members of the Shiite sect. In the Ismaili view, the Koran was a general guide rather than an exact statement of religious beliefs. An Ismaili movement brought about revolts in the western part of the empire. These led to the rise of the Fatamid dynasty in Egypt and North Africa. The Fatamids claimed descent from Fatima, Muhammad's daughter.

Abbasid power was weakened by the rise of city dynasties. One of these was the sharifs of Mecca. (*Sharif* means descendant of the Prophet Muhammad through Fatima, the prophet's daughter.) In Egypt, the Fatamids founded Cairo in 969. They made it the center of a powerful and rich state with European trading contacts. In Spain, as you have read, the breakdown of the empire began as early as the mid-700s. In Syria, Arabia, and even in Iraq itself, independent dynasties came into being. With the caliphs thus weakened, and strict Islam challenged by Sufism, the entire empire was open to change. This change came with Seljuk Turks, a group of peoples that had entered Persia in the beginning of the eleventh century.

The Seljuk Turks. The Seljuk Turks were nomads on horseback from the steppes of Central Asia. They were the first of a series of Turkish-speaking tribes to move into the region. Some time around the year 1000, several tribes moved across the Anatolian plateau. At the same time, others traveled across Persia. As this movement took time, the tribes slowly adopted Islam. The Seljuk Empire stretched across Persia, Kurdistan, and Iraq. Despite its loose organization, the Seljuk Empire lasted until the mid-twelfth century.

At first the Abbasid caliphs of Baghdad used the Turkish tribes as **mercenaries,** or paid professional soldiers, to protect them from others trying to found new dynasties. As Abbasid power declined, however, the

Turks began to use their growing influence. The Seljuks fought the Byzantines in 1071 and took over some Byzantine lands in what is now modern Turkey. (But at this time the Turks did not move dramatically into Byzantine lands.) Under their leader, Saladin (1169–1193), Turkish tribes brought Iraq, Egypt, and Syria under Seljuk control.

The Crusades (1095–1290). In the meantime other events were taking place. From Europe came the famous Crusaders. These were European nobles like King Richard the Lion-Hearted of England. The Crusaders wanted to free the Holy Land (Palestine) from Muslim control. They were called to this mission by the pope. In the name of the Christian religion, the Crusaders invaded the Middle East. The wars that followed lasted for over two hundred years. They came to be known to history as the Crusades.

Once in the Middle East, the Crusaders tried to set up kingdoms of their own. Soldiers of the crusading armies, however, were often more guided by a desire for wealth and glory than religion. They robbed land and goods, killed Muslims and Jews, and were finally driven out.

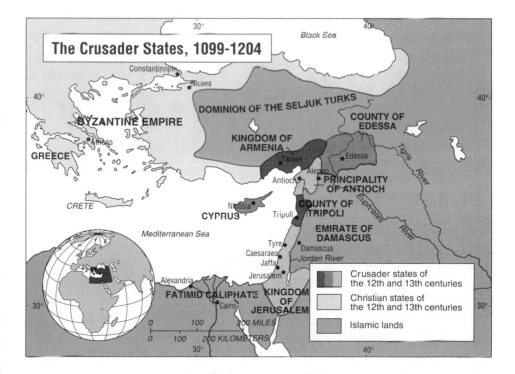

The Crusader States, 1099-1204

The First Crusade (1095–1099) took place almost one hundred years before Saladin came to power. The Third Crusade (1189–1192) was the strongest attempt to spread European influence in the Middle East. To Muslims, however, the Crusades were just another series of battles to maintain and expand the power of Islam.

Though the Crusaders were driven out of the Holy Land, their meeting with Islamic culture had an important impact on Europe. The Europeans met Muslims who had a higher degree of civilization than their own. Also, Europeans tasted new foods and wore clothes of new and comfortable materials. Europeans and the people of the Middle East increased their trade. And, once trade was carried out on a regular basis, ideas between the two regions began to move more freely.

Those who came after Saladin did not keep tight control over Seljuk lands, however. As a result, Iraq, Egypt, and Syria fell from Turkish control. A group of former Turkish slave soldiers took control in Egypt. For a time, they also held control over Syria and Iraq. These former slave soldiers, now rulers, were known as the **Mamelukes** (MAM-uh-looks). They kept power in Egypt and a few nearby territories until 1517. They were conquered by the Ottoman Turks at that time.

The Mongols. In the 1200s, nomads from Mongolia began a century of conquest that changed the history of the world. For the Middle East this invasion was more harmful than the Seljuk invasions. The Mongol leader Genghis Khan (about 1167–1227) led one of the world's great military machines. The Mongols rode their horses across Central Asia and the Middle East. Behind them, they left death and destruction. The successors of Genghis, called **khans,** conquered much of Russia by 1241. The fierce Mongols then invaded the Middle East and captured Baghdad in 1258. Hulagu Khan, the grandson of Genghis, let his soldiers destroy one of the world's great centers of learning. The last Abbasid caliph, al-Musta'sim, along with hundreds of his officials, was killed. Baghdad was sacked and left in flames. The great irrigation projects in the Tigris-Euphrates valley, upon which much of the agriculture of the land depended, were destroyed by the Mongols. Mongol armies continued to sweep westward into Syria. Alarmed, the Mamelukes in Egypt put together an army to battle the Mongols. The two armies met in battle in Palestine. It was there, in 1260, that the Mongols were finally stopped before they could reach North Africa.

Many Mongol leaders, for example, the khan of Persia and various khans in the Volga River region of Russia, became Muslims. In this way, the Islamic religion spread north into Central Asia. When the

Crusaders surrounding Damascus, Syria. This scene was painted by a European to illustrate a Latin manuscript. It was probably painted many years after the actual event.

Mongol dynasty of Persia was overthrown in 1359, the Turks once more took control. But the Middle East suffered again when another Mongol conqueror, Tamerlane, or Timur, put together an army of Turks and descendants of the old Mongol tribes. Tamerlane tried to build an empire like Genghis Khan's. To do this, he led his troops through parts of southern Russia, Iraq, and Syria. Wherever he went, Tamerlane ordered the slaughter of men, women, and children.

The Mongols and their successors put an end to the unity of the Middle East. In time, most of the Mongols became Muslims. But they created separate dynasties of rulers who governed sections of the region. The Mamelukes still ruled Egypt, Palestine, and Syria. But North Africa and Spain were ruled by several separate Muslim dynasties. And the territory east of Syria often changed hands.

Yet slowly the Middle East began to recover from the Mongol invasions. A new people, the Ottoman Turks, arrived on the scene in the 1300s. By the middle of the 1500s they had taken over most of the Middle East. In the next chapter you will see how the Ottomans reunited the Middle East and took on the role of Islam's chief power.

129

REVIEWING THE CHAPTER

I. Building Your Vocabulary

Match the word in Column A with the phrase in Column B that best defines it.

Column A	*Column B*
1. caravanserai	a. "People of the Book" protected by Muslims
2. *jizya*	b. a mystical religious movement within Islam
3. *dhimmis*	c. desert inns
4. patriarchal	d. poll tax
5. Abbasids	e. ruled by men as opposed to women
6. Sufism	f. successors to the Umayyads
7. sheikh	g. a combined hospital and medical school
8. Maghrib	h. the western part of North Africa
9. astrolabe	i. a tribal chief
10. *bimarastan*	j. an instrument for measuring the position of the stars in the heavens

II. Understanding the Facts

Write the letter of the term that best completes each of the following sentences or answers the following questions.

1. The capital of the Abassid empire was
   a. Baghdad. b. Cairo. c. Damascus.

2. A Muslim city known for its linen and steel was
   a. Baghdad. b. Cairo. c. Damascus.

3. Spain in 756 came under the control of
   a. the Berbers. b. the Umayyads. c. the Abbasids.

4. Moses Maimonides was a
   a. rabbi, physician, and philosopher. b. diplomat in Spain.
   c. Jewish poet and thinker.

5. The famous "House of Wisdom" at Baghdad was a
   a. center for religious training.   b. museum.
   c. scientific academy, observatory, and library.

6. For the Arab study of higher mathematics the concept of zero
   was important. That concept came from
   a. ancient Greece. b. India.   c. Egypt.

7. The Arabs made important contributions to the field of
   a. medicine.   b. archaeology.   c. Asian languages.

8. Which of the following did Omar Khayyam write?
   a. *The Thousand and One Nights*
   b. *Guide to the Perplexed*   c. *The Rubaiyat*

9. Avicenna is famous for his work in the history of
   a. medicine and philosophy.   b. art.
   c. military conquest.

10. When and where were the Mongols stopped in their invasion of
    the Middle East?
    a. Kiev in 1241   b. Baghdad in 1258   c. Palestine in 1260

III. Thinking It Through

1. How did the Arabs affect the growth of both seaborne and overland trade?

2. What was Baghdad's position in the world in the ninth century?

3. What factors helped Spain prosper during the years of Muslim
   rule?

4. Why were the Crusades of greater importance to Europe than
   to the Middle East?

5. What effect did the Mongol invasions have on the Middle East?

DEVELOPING CRITICAL THINKING SKILLS

I. Relating Cause and Effect

Which of the following is the cause and which the effect? Explain
the relationship between the two statements.

1. a. The Abbasid revolution was successful.

   b. A new capital was built at Baghdad.

2. **a.** Wealth captured in battle, taxes, and trade poured into the capital.
   b. Baghdad became a center of culture.
3. **a.** Abd-al-Rahman fled to Spain.
   b. An independent Umayyad emirate was set up.
4. **a.** The Arabs adopted Byzantine, Egyptian, Syrian, Mesopotamian, and Indian art forms.
   b. Islamic art expressed new techniques and achieved a unique style.
5. **a.** The Abbasid caliphate was weakened.
   b. In Syria, Arabia, and even in Iraq itself, independent dynasties came into being.

II. Writing an Essay

Write a three-paragraph essay supporting the following generalization: From about 750 to 1500, Islam was the main civilization in the Eastern Hemisphere outside East Asia.

INTERPRETING A SECONDARY SOURCE

As you have read, the destruction of Baghdad in the middle of the thirteenth century was a terrible blow to the Islamic Empire. Read the description below and answer the questions that follow it.

> Twenty-five years after Ghenghiz's death, Hulagu, the younger brother of the legendary Kublai Khan, was [sent] to Persia with orders to crush . . . the Caliphate, which was still centered in Baghdad. . . . In 1257 he marched against the caliph, the last of the . . . Abbasids, and a weak and pleasure-loving character. Besieged and assaulted in Baghdad, the caliph was [tricked] into surrendering. . . . But Hulagu was no respecter of promises, and had him beaten to death in a sack. The city was taken and was given over to massacre and looting for a week. According to one account, nearly a million people were [killed], often to the accompaniment of . . . torture and mutilation. This must be an exaggeration, but certainly a very small [number] of the inhabitants escaped with their lives. After being . . . looted, the palaces and mosques were burnt. And in the flames many other buildings were destroyed.
>
> Muslim civilization and culture was at a high level in the thirteenth century. With the sack of Baghdad it received a setback from which it never fully recovered. Only the fact that Hulagu's army was later

defeated by the Mamelukes saved Egypt, the last independent stronghold of Muslim culture, from being blasted and overrun.

Adapted from Julian Huxley, *From an Antique Land: Ancient and Modern in the Middle East.* Boston: Beacon Press, Boston, 1966.

1. According to this passage, how important was the Mongol attack on Baghdad?
2. What saved Muslim culture from total ruin?

ENRICHMENT AND EXPLORATION

1. Prepare questions for an interview with one the following noted Muslims: the great caliph Harun al-Rashid; Abd-al-Rahman, founder of the Spanish emirate; al-Razi, the author of studies on smallpox and measles; Avicenna, the philosopher; the Crusader Richard the Lion-Hearted; the Turkish leader Saladin; Moses Maimonides, the philosopher; and the Mongol Hulagu. Then research the individual's life to see if you can find answers to your questions. Present them to the class in the form of an interview.

2. If you have studied algebra or are studying it now, research examples of Arab contributions to algebra.

3. Prepare a list of English words that are derived from the Arabic. What do they suggest about Arab influence on European civilization?

4. Find out how important the astrolabe was to Christopher Columbus and other European explorers. Would their voyages have been possible without the invention? Give reasons for your answer.

THE OTTOMAN EMPIRE
1280–1914

1280–1326	The rule of Osman I
1450–1600	*African empire of Songhai*
1451–1481	The rule of Muhammad II
1453	Ottomans capture Constantinople.
1481	Ottomans control Anatolia and the Balkans.
1492	*Columbus reaches North America.*
1520–1566	The rule of Suleiman I
1529	Ottomans' first siege of Vienna fails.
1570s	Ottomans control most of North Africa.
1683	Ottomans' second siege of Vienna fails.
1700s	Europeans take advantage of Ottoman debts to win privileges.
c. 1760	*Industrial Revolution begins in Great Britain.*
1774	Russia gains north coast of Black Sea.
1776	*American colonies declare independence from Great Britain.*
1789	*French Revolution begins.*
1798	Napoleon Bonaparte invades Egypt.
1818–1824	*Spanish colonies in the Americas become independent.*
1821–1830	Greek War of Independence
1822	Egypt captures Sudan.
1827	European powers destroy Egyptian fleet at battle of Navarino.
1830	French invade Algeria.
1854–1856	Crimean War
1869	Suez Canal opens.
1881	French occupy Tunisia.
1882	British occupy Egypt.
1911	Italy takes control of Libya.
1912–1913	Balkan Wars
1913	Young Turks gain power.
1914	World War I begins.

The Rise and Decline of the Ottoman Empire (1280–1914)

6

Many tribes and peoples moved from Central Asia to the West. But only the Ottomans were able to unify the huge territories that came under their control. So great was their military power that, in the 1500s and 1600s, they seemed about to extend their power deep into Europe itself. In this chapter, you will learn how the Ottomans gained power and what caused their eventual decline.

THE OTTOMAN EMPIRE, FROM ITS ORIGINS TO THE END OF THE EIGHTEENTH CENTURY

Origins and Early Success of the Ottoman Empire. The Ottoman Turks were already Muslims when they reached Anatolia, the Asiatic part of modern Turkey. For them the struggle against the Byzantine Christians was a continuation of the holy war to spread Islam. Ottoman warriors known as *ghazis* (GAH-zeez), a kind of brotherhood of frontier fighters, settled the border areas. Gradually they chipped away at non-Muslim lands. In this way more and more territory came under Islamic control.

Like the ancient Romans, the Ottoman Turks were a military people. They conquered new lands. But they also learned from their more civilized neighbors. As *ghazis*, they proved that they—and not the Arabs—had become the chief defenders of Islam in the Middle East.

The Ottoman Turks took the name "Ottoman" from one of their early leaders, Osman I. It took only a short period of time in the 1300s for these Turkish tribesmen to control large areas of the Anatolian plateau. Through conquest or diplomacy new lands fell to them with great speed. By 1301 they had moved into the northwestern part of Byzantine Asia Minor. By 1402 all that was left of the once powerful Byzantine Empire was a small area on the European side of the Bosporus, the water separating Europe and Asia. When the Ottoman Turks took Constantinople in 1453 they brought to an end one of the world's longest-lived empires.

The Ottoman Conquest of Constantinople.　Constantinople was one of the great centers of the medieval Christian world. It was also the last unbroken link to the empire of ancient Rome. Its conquest was a goal of Muhammad II, "the Conqueror," who ruled as sultan from 1451 to 1481. Muhammad's first step was to build a fort on the European side of the Bosporus. His aim was to cut off the entrance to the city from the Black Sea region. After careful planning he began the attack in April of 1453. A huge army of more than 150,000 men faced 5,000 Byzantines. The Ottomans bombarded the city for over 50 days. At last their navy prepared to sail into the harbor, the Golden Horn. There they found a huge iron chain built by the Byzantines to prevent an invasion.

In late May, after the sultan had some 70 small ships dragged overland from the Bosporus to the Golden Horn, the Ottoman attack succeeded. For three days the Turks looted the city. Muhammad himself rode horseback into the great cathedral of Saint Sophia. In Greek it is called Hagia Sophia, meaning "Holy Wisdom." He ordered its mosaics whitewashed and the building made into a mosque. The city that had been the seat of the Eastern Orthodox Church was now capital of a powerful Islamic empire.

Muhammad set out at once to build Ottoman power. He next annexed southern Serbia in the Balkans (see map, pages 140–141). When the pope called for a crusade to push the Turks back into Asia, Muhammad defeated a combined Hungarian and Venetian force. By the time of his death in 1481, the Ottomans were in control of Anatolia and the Balkans and were threatening southern Italy.

Ottomans Become a World Power.　For some two hundred years, the Ottomans continued to conquer new lands. They seized major land routes to the east and made Ottoman ports important points of world trade. At Turkish markets the cotton goods and spices of India were traded for the woolens of Italy and northern Europe. Turkish fleets of oar-driven ships sailed the eastern Mediterranean and the Red Sea. In

The Hagia Sophia. This Byzantine cathedral was completed in A.D. 537. It was converted to a mosque after the conquest of Constantinople in 1453 by the Ottomans. Today it is a museum.

the 1500s the Ottoman Empire became a major Mediterranean force. It was equal to any power in Europe.

It was the sultans Selim I (1512–1520) and his son Suleiman (soo-lay-MAHN) the Magnificent (1520–1566) who transformed the Ottoman state into a leading world power. Once in control of Anatolia and southeastern Europe, Selim turned his attention to the Islamic heartland. In 1517 he crushed the Mamelukes and sacked Cairo. With Cairo secure, grain-rich Egypt and all of the lands once under Mameluke control soon fell to the Ottomans. The same year, Mecca, Medina, and Jerusalem came under Ottoman control. Thus, the Ottomans ruled Islam's holy cities as well as the city holy to Jews and Christians.

Suleiman the Magnificent, a man of great intelligence, continued the conquests started by his father. In 1521 he captured Belgrade. In 1522 he seized the island of Rhodes. In the West, he used Spain's rivalry with France to extend Turkish control in the Mediterranean. Helped by pirates, he set up bases in Algeria and defeated a Venetian fleet in 1548. From the Hapsburg rulers he gained control of Hungary and the payment of a yearly tribute. Only the problem of supplying his army over a long distance kept Suleiman from taking Vienna in 1529.

137

Suleiman built an alliance with France against Spain in the 1530s. Through this alliance, France became the first major European power to recognize the Ottoman Empire's equal status. One Ottoman writer referred to the king of France as a "bey" in his relation to the sultan. The bey was only head of a province; the sultan was head of an empire.

Under Suleiman's rule Ottoman civilization reached its peak. The mid-1500s saw a flowering in the arts. The empire's vast wealth was spent on numerous building projects. Foreign workers and artisans were brought to work on Constantinople's mosques under the direction of a great architect—Mimar Sinan. In literature, this was the age of the classical poet Baki. He was perhaps the greatest lyric poet in the Turkish language. Baki's poems, mainly his writing on the death of Suleiman, combine a majestic style with great depth of feeling. The period also saw an unfolding of all that was characteristic of Ottoman civilization.

Those who ruled after Suleiman continued the struggle with Spain into the late 1500s. They attacked lands along the western Mediterranean coast and fought over Tunis. Though defeated by a Spanish-led force in a sea battle at Lepanto in 1571, the Ottomans were, in the 1570s, in control of most of North Africa.

The Ottomans Fight with Safavid Persia.   On their eastern front the Ottomans came into conflict with Safavid Persia. The Safavids were one of the area's other chief Islamic powers. In 1511 Ismail, a new **shah,** or ruler, had taken power in Persia. He ruled that Shiite Islam would be the country's religion. In an effort to spread this brand of Islam he asked many Turkish tribes for help. Thus, began a struggle with the Sunni Ottomans. In 1514, near the Caspian Sea, Selim I defeated the Safavids in battle. Twenty years later Suleiman drove them out of Mesopotamia and took Baghdad. For over two hundred years the two empires fought almost constantly and at great cost to each other.

The peak of Safavid power came during the rule of Shah Abbas the Great (1587–1629). Abbas rebuilt the Persian Empire by gaining new lands in the east and by setting up a well-trained bureaucracy. As a symbol of his success he built a new capital, Isfahan. In the 1600s Isfahan became one of the great centers of Muslim art and architecture.

The Ottoman State and Society.   Having conquered vast territories, the Ottomans ruled over different areas and peoples. They set up their government around three major units, known as the Ruling Institution. The first of these units was administrative, the second was military, and the third was religious. The sultan stood at the top of the whole structure.

He was the absolute ruler and also commander-in-chief of the Ottoman army.

Government officials were known as the "People of the Pen." These included ambassadors, provincial governors, and secretaries. They also included the scholars or clerks who kept tax records and wrote official letters. The empire was divided into provinces and sub-provinces. Leading people in each unit were appointed to govern. These governors, or **pashas,** had several responsibilities. They had to raise an army in time of war. They also had to police the countryside and maintain order. Finally, they had to collect taxes. To raise money a system of **tax-farming** was used. Under tax-farming, the sultan awarded a pasha with a province and told him how much money the territory had to bring in to the sultan's treasury. It was then the pasha's job to raise the needed sum. Any extra amount was his to keep. The pasha in turn subdivided his province and had his officials send him a required sum. The rest was theirs to keep, and so on down the line.

The second unit, the military, was made up of the so-called "People of the Sword." This group included all soldiers. Non-Muslims were kept out of the Ottoman army. But because the sultans could not always depend on the army to keep the peace in the territories, a new unit of crack soldiers was set up. This elite corps was the famous **janissaries.** They were expertly trained soldiers who were loyal to the sultan alone. The first janissaries were Christian boys who were brought to the capital to serve in the Turkish army. There, they were educated as Muslims and rigorously trained.

The janissaries lived in special barracks, received certain privileges, and followed the Ottoman way of life. However, they were not allowed to marry. The janissaries were, in fact, part of an institution upon which the power of the empire rested—the Slave Institution. All members of this group were legally the sultan's slaves. All owed their status to the sultan. When they died, all their property returned to the sultan. Dependent on the state for their lives and careers, they were fiercely loyal to their commander-in-chief. Government workers or army officers could all legally be members of the Slave Institution.

The third unit in the Ottoman Empire was made up of the religious leaders. These were the Islamic scholars and great officers of Islam, the ulema. It was the ulema who helped define Ottoman law and practice. They supervised charities, orphanages, and schools. It was their rule to judge matters of criminal, commercial, and civil law.

Christians and Jews did not take part in running the empire. And they were not permitted to join the army. But the Ottomans recognized

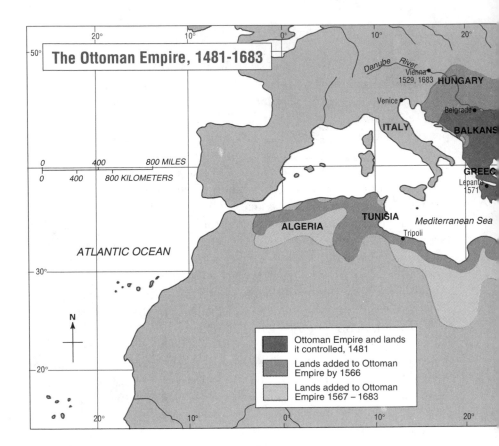

The Ottoman Empire, 1481-1683

Ottoman Empire and lands it controlled, 1481

Lands added to Ottoman Empire by 1566

Lands added to Ottoman Empire 1567 – 1683

the importance of the minorities. These groups helped to keep up the active trade of the empire. They also brought important knowledge and skills to the professions.

Religious minorities lived in their own communities within the empire. Each community, or *millet*, was headed by state-appointed religious leaders. In this way, the Armenian Patriarch headed the Armenian community, the Greek Orthodox Patriarch led the Greek Orthodox, the Chief Rabbi was chief of the Jewish community, and so on. Each of these leaders was held responsible for his **millet**. The *millets* were self-contained. Contact between Muslims and non-Muslims was kept to a minimum. As in Islam, matters of personal law such as marriage, divorce, and religious practice were handled by the *millet*. Serious matters, however, had to be judged by the Muslim courts.

The Ottomans actively welcomed those who sought freedom from persecution. In the case of the Jews, this was a time of great persecution.

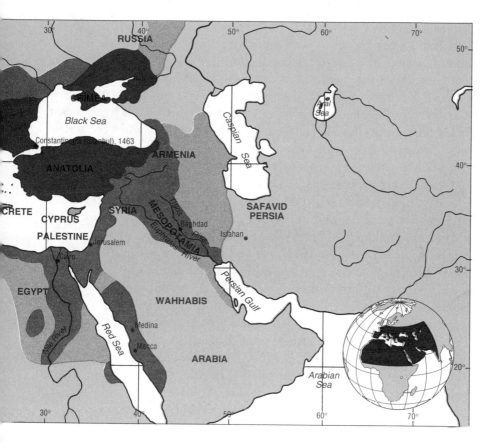

When the Muslims were driven out of Spain in 1492 the Spanish rulers tried to make the country totally Christian. Thousands of Jews were forced to convert to Christianity or to practice their faith in secret. Those who refused had to flee. Some went to Holland. Others went to the Americas. Still others went to the Ottoman Empire, which welcomed them openly. Large Jewish communities sprang up in the Balkans and in Constantinople. These newcomers were the original **Sephardim,** or Spanish Jews. Their language was Ladino, a mixture of Spanish and Hebrew. The Sephardim joined the Jews who had lived under Byzantine rule for centuries.

Christian soldiers of fortune came to the Ottoman Empire to advise the sultans on military matters. Hungarians, with their knowledge of firearms, made the guns that helped the Ottomans win their wars of conquest. Greeks served in the empire's navy and led in the field of commerce. Other Europeans acted as interpreters.

Internal Factors Contributing to the Decline of the Empire. In the late 1600s a few pieces of territory were added to the empire. But the great victories of earlier years were over. The Ottomans simply could not break down the opposition of the Safavids in Iran, the Hapsburgs in eastern Europe, or a newly emerging power—the Russians in the Ukraine. The Ottomans tried once again to capture Vienna in 1683, but failed to take the city. The 1690s saw much of Hungary and what is now Yugoslavia slip away from Ottoman rule. And the Russian presence in the Black Sea was a bitter fact that the sultans had to accept. The peak of Ottoman power was over.

What had gone wrong? Part of the explanation is to be found in the internal affairs of the empire. Part is in developments that took place outside the Middle East. Internally, the efficiency of the Ottoman state began to break down. Nowhere was this more clearly seen than at the top of the Ottoman power pyramid—in the sultanate itself.

The early sultans carried out their duties with great distinction. Some of them were brilliant rulers. But in the 1600s dedication gave way to inefficiency. There was no fixed way to choose a sultan. Often brothers fought over the succession. (To secure his throne against his rivals, one sultan around the year 1600 had his 19 brothers put to death!) Frequently a sultan's wives conspired with palace officials over which son should rule. If a young sultan was weak, his mother could play an important role behind the throne. Palace intrigues often brought weak sultans to the throne.

As the power of the sultans declined, the state became more dependent on the janissaries. The key role they played in the military made them open to violence and blackmail. They began to expect and demand greater privileges. For example, the janissaries gained the legal right to marry. Once they had families, they passed on their status to their sons. Thus, the janissaries ended the basic nature of the Slave Institution. They took advantage of the weakness of the later sultans and tried to destroy those who opposed them.

Never sure of how long they might remain in power, the provincial governors taxed the people at high rates. Their plan was to get rich while they could. The Ottoman system of tax farming had been tied to military conquest. Now that the empire had stopped growing, the system began to break down. The state was forced to raise taxes. And this only added to the poverty and discontent of the people. As the economy declined, the tax-farming system proved inefficient. The underpaid bureaucracy grew weak and corrupt.

Also important in the decline of the Ottomans was their belief in

CASE STUDY:
The Ottoman Siege of Vienna

A major defeat for the Ottoman Empire came during its siege of Vienna in 1683. The following reading is an account by an Ottoman.

> A prisoner was captured and questioned. He said that the Austrian emperor had sent letters to every side appealing for help to all the kings of Christendom. Only the king of Poland . . . had come to his aid in person and with troops and with the soldiers and hetmans [chiefs] of Lithuania and with 35,000 cavalry and infantry of the Polish infidels. The Austrian emperor had also sent his own men together with such reinforcements as he had been able to get from the rest of Christendom . . . altogether 120,000 infidels. All these gathered together in this place . . . to attack the soldiers of Islam who were in the trenches around Vienna . . . .
>
> Everything that was in the imperial [Ottoman] camp, money and equipment and precious things, was left behind and fell into the hands of the people of hell. The accursed infidels in their battalion (may it be crushed) came in two columns . . . . entered the fortress . . . stormed the trenches . . . captured the imperial army camp. Of the disabled men whom they found in the trenches they killed some and took others prisoner. The men remaining in the trenches, some 10,000 of them, were incapable of fighting, having been wounded by guns, muskets, cannon, mines, stones, and other weapons, some of them lacking an arm or a leg. These they at once put to the sword and, finding some thousands of their own prisoners, freed them from their bonds and released them. They succeeded in capturing such quantities of money and supplies as cannot be described.

(Adapted from Silihdar Tarihi, reprinted in Bernard Lewis, *The Muslim Discovery of Europe*. New York: Norton, 1982.)

1. How did the chronicler describe the forces assembled against the empire?
2. What did the Europeans do with the prisoners?
3. Was the Ottoman Turk who wrote this description correct, according to Islamic tradition, in calling his European enemies "infidels," that is, unbelievers?

Muslim superiority. The empire's early successes had helped strengthen this belief. But the early sultans were open-minded. They looked to the West for modern technology, especially in military matters. They encouraged the study of Greek thought and philosophy. In sharp contrast, the later sultans grew more rigid in their thinking. They came to believe that nothing of value could be learned from non-Muslims. They assumed that little of the cultural or economic life of non-Muslims could have any effect on the Ottoman state. At a time when Western Europe was undergoing a rebirth in thought and technology—the Renaissance— the Ottoman Empire remained isolated and stagnant.

Outside Factors Contributing to Ottoman Decline.   In time, the impact of European technology began to overtake the Ottomans. European weapons were superior to those of the Ottomans and inflicted heavy losses. Furthermore, the Middle East began to lose its place at the center of world trade. In 1488 Bartholomew Diaz rounded the southern tip of Africa. Along with other Portuguese explorations, this voyage led to others. Vasco da Gama's journey up the East African coast to India and back came in 1497–1499. In 1503, a Portuguese military expedition, again led by da Gama, won its first sea battle against Arab naval forces. In one quick stroke the Europeans cut their way into the Indian spice trade.

In the centuries that followed, the role of the Islamic middlemen in world trade declined. Gradually the money from trade—once the support of the Ottoman state—began to dry up. Also, the European traders began to shift their focus away from the Mediterranean Sea to the Atlantic Ocean. Europeans could now reach East Asia directly. At the same time they opened up the vast riches of the newly discovered Americas.

Spain's great South American empire flooded the Mediterranean—and the world—with cheap silver. This caused severe inflation everywhere. The cheap silver also cut the value of the standard Ottoman coin. As a result the Ottomans could not afford to buy many trade items from other lands. Widespread poverty followed. For their part, European merchants took advantage of the Ottoman Empire's bad situation. They did this by trading more actively in the Middle East. In the 1700s, as many Ottoman merchants fell into financial ruin, Europeans demanded further **capitulations.** Capitulations are the conditions of a surrender. In this case, the Ottomans were surrendering to Western bankers who demanded trading privileges and control over Ottoman trade. With that control came a special status in the empire.

144

Thus, Westerners gained great control over Ottoman trade. With that control came a special status within the empire. At the end of the 1700s the Ottoman Empire suffered several setbacks at the hands of the Russians. In the Treaty of Kuchuk Kainarji in 1774 the Ottomans gave Russia control of the northern coast of the Black Sea (see map, pages 140–141). The treaty also gave Russia a valuable share of capitulations. And it recognized the tsar's authority over the sultan's Christian Orthodox subjects. In 1783 Tsarina Catherine the Great took control of the Crimea. This was the Ottomans' first major loss of basically Muslim territory. Before long, the English and French were fighting in Egypt as the wars of the French Revolution spread into the Middle East.

THE IMPACT OF THE WEST

From the end of the 1700s the Ottoman Empire found itself more and more on the defensive. Dramatic changes within Europe changed the social, economic, political, and diplomatic relations of the entire Middle East.

Impact of the Age of Revolution.   The end of the 1700s saw a double revolution whose impact can still be felt today. These revolutions took place in two countries—England and France. In England the revolution was economic. In France it was political.

The great changes which began in England at the end of the 1700s became known later as the "Industrial Revolution." Using nonhuman sources of power and machines, the English and then the Europeans built up their levels of production. Within a short time they were far ahead of their non-European competitors. Thus, they were able to flood the Middle East with cheap manufactured products.

While this was happening, Middle Easterners continued to rely on costly handcrafted goods. Unable to compete with other countries, the Middle East turned into a backward consumer market. Like India, the region found itself supplying cheap raw materials to Europe as it imported finished goods. For example, British factories made cloth from Egyptian cotton. The finished cloth was shipped back to Egypt. Then it became a less expensive item within Egypt than locally produced textiles. The whole Middle East was gradually drained of both currency and raw materials. A huge debt with the West resulted.

The French Revolution of the 1790s let loose new ideas of freedom, citizenship, and the role of the state. Peoples of Europe began to think of themselves as belonging to nations. The idea took hold that every people ought to have its own country with clearly defined borders and its own government. This is known as **nationalism.** The French Revolution brought about a huge change in the role of the state. Male citizens were now expected to serve in a national army. (Before, rulers had used mercenaries, or professional soldiers, to fight their wars.) The bringing together of an entire nation's resources was one of the major influences of the French Revolution.

With the idea of loyalty to the state came the principle that rulers needed to recognize their subjects' wishes. This was a "liberal" idea. The belief that the citizen had basic rights and that his or her welfare could be improved through education and higher standards of living were other "liberal" ideas. These ideas and many others were spread throughout Europe by the armies of the French Revolution and their leader, Napoleon Bonaparte.

The powerful ideas of the French Revolution did not go unnoticed in Constantinople. In 1792 and 1793 Sultan Selim III (1789–1807) proclaimed a series of new rules. These came to be known together as the "New Order." These rules reorganized the army and ended many abuses. They reformed the tax structure, adding taxes on tobacco, spirits, and coffee. They set up permanent embassies in the European capitals. A new body of young army and naval officers was created. They were chosen because they were familiar with some aspects of Western civilization. But from the first, the reforms caused trouble. Some within the empire were against the whole idea of reform. Selim was overthrown and murdered, and most of the leaders of the reform party were killed. It took 20 years for Selim's successor, Mahmud II (1808–1839), to win over the religious leaders to the idea of reform. He challenged the janissaries and did away with them in 1826.

Thus, the Middle East was pulled out of its isolation by political and economic events in Europe. The rivalries of the Great Powers also had an effect on breaking down the isolation of the region. At first, the major struggle was between Britain and France. Their struggle took place mainly in the period up until 1815. Then the struggle for influence in the region was between Britain and Russia. In the 1800s Britain was the world's industrial giant and the major force in the Middle East. Finally, toward the end of the 1800s, the struggle was between Britain and its new rival, imperial Germany. The Ottoman Empire managed to survive Napoleon's wars of conquest in one piece. It continued on as "the sick man of Europe" until World War I. But this was only because the British, Russians, and French balanced out each other's designs upon it.

146

Napoleon and the Middle East.   Napoleon Bonaparte's conquest of Egypt in 1798 did several things. It drew attention to the Middle East's strategic importance. And it also made the region the center of a major power struggle. In May 1798, as the "star" of the French army, Napoleon sailed with 35,000 men for Egypt. His aim was to strike at the British Empire by starting an invasion of India. He landed near Alexandria in July 1798, defeated the Mamelukes, and took Cairo. But the young general failed in his goal. Under the command of Admiral Horatio Nelson, the British destroyed or captured most of the French fleet at the Battle of the Nile in August 1798. Cut off from France, Napoleon still managed to invade Syria early in 1799. But he had to leave his army just a few months later. He returned home, where he seized control of the shaky French government.

To the world at large, Egypt and Syria had long been forgotten. Little value was attached to them. Napoleon, however, saw the importance of their geographical position. Both are at the crossroads of three continents—Asia, Africa, and Europe. Throughout the 1800s the entire region was the scene of continued military conflicts.

Strains within the Empire.   New ideas from revolutions in Europe, such as nationalism, had widespread impact throughout the Ottoman Empire. Three examples—Arabia, Egypt, and Greece—show different responses to Western influence.

In the Arabian peninsula a new movement against Turkish rule developed. This movement started in the middle of the 1700s and was the work of the **Wahhabis.** An entirely Muslim movement, the Wahhabis were religious in nature, anti-Turkish and anti-Western. Their anger was aimed against what they considered to be the religious looseness and corruption of the Ottoman government. Specifically, they saw the sultan himself as corrupt. The Wahhabis denounced the introduction of Western reforms. They called the reforms the "ungodly inclinations towards the filthy devices of the Frankish infidels." They urged a stricter, more puritanical devotion to Islam. Wahhabism helped the Saud dynasty to establish in the late 1800s what is today modern Saudi Arabia.

For political reasons government schools in the Ottoman Empire taught in Turkish. Arabic was neglected on purpose. However, Western—especially American—missionaries taught in Arabic. In the 1860s schools like the Syrian Protestant College, which later became the American University of Beirut, taught in Arabic. The teaching of Arabic led to a revival of interest in Arabic literature. And the past glories of Arabic civilization were re-examined. These developments in turn increased feelings of Arab nationalism. These influences, however, were limited to a small group of intellectuals, in Beirut and to a lesser extent in Damascus.

In Egypt, even during the great days of the 1500s, Ottoman power never uprooted the old Mameluke landed establishment. By the 1600s governors sent by the sultan were often resisted or assassinated. By 1700 power in Egypt was once again in Mameluke hands. The Ottoman pasha was little more than the ambassador of a foreign government. In the early 1800s a tobacco merchant of Turkish origin, Muhammad Ali, directed the country's break with Constantinople in everything but name. He created a dynasty that endured until 1952.

Born in Albania, the gifted Muhammad Ali became a soldier in the Ottoman army. Soon he was Egypt's governor. With France's financial help, he gained almost complete independence for Egypt. In time, the country was on the road to economic and social development. Muhammad Ali reorganized the local administration. He also built up the economy by industrializing Egypt's textile production. With French advisers he remade his army along European lines and helped the sultan put down a Wahhabi invasion of Syria in 1818. By 1822 Muhammad Ali captured the Sudan. He gave Egypt the most powerful Muslim fleet in the Mediterranean.

The Greek independence movement succeeded in the 1820s. Its success was the result of revolutionary developments in Europe and the action taken by the great powers. Alexander Ypsilanti (ip-suh-LAN-tee), a Greek who had served in the Russian army, led a revolt against the Ottoman state in 1821. His aims were nationalistic and he asked the Russian tsar for help. As leader of Orthodox Christian Europe, the tsar saw it as his duty to protect the Orthodox Christians in Ottoman lands.

For diplomatic reasons of their own the Great Powers all supported the Greek revolt. In 1827, the sultan asked for Egyptian help in putting down the rebellion. But a combined British, French, and Russian fleet came to Greece's aid. At the Bay of Navarino, in southwestern Greece, the Egyptian fleet was destroyed. Soon after, the Greeks won their independence. Thus, a way was set for other ethnic groups to seek national liberation from the Ottoman Empire.

Russia, Britain, and the Middle East.   As you have read, since the 1770s the tsar had claimed the right to protect Orthodox Christians within the Ottoman Empire. He also saw himself as the patron of the Slavs and their hopes for independence. These movements, however, could only achieve success at the sultan's expense. Within the Balkan peninsula a number of Slavic peoples lived under Islamic rule. There were Bulgarians, Albanians, Serbs, Croatians, Bosnians, Montenegrins, Herzegovinians, and others. Many looked to Russia for support and independence. This factor, along with Russia's age-old search for a warm-water port, shaped Russian policy in the 1800s.

As the world's great naval and industrial power of the 1800s, Britain saw itself in a special role. Britain became the guardian of the decaying Ottoman state. It also believed that the Russian expansion had to be contained. But neither Britain nor France could accept Russian control of the eastern Mediterranean trading centers. More and more in the 1800s, the two nations acted together to stop Russia.

The Crimean War, 1854–1856. The short-term cause of the Crimean War was a dispute in the province of Palestine. The conflict was over the question of control of the "Holy Places." In recent years monks of the Greek Orthodox church had looked after these holy sites. Now Roman Catholics, supported by the French emperor, sought to regain a role in their upkeep. War broke out, and Britain, France, and the Ottoman Empire were pitted against Russia. The war revealed how truly weak the Ottomans were. Even though it was fought over territory under Ottoman rule, the Ottomans were almost incidental to the war itself.

Turkish and British troops during the Crimean War. Along with the French, they fought the Russians. The war was badly managed and commanded. Over 250,000 soldiers died on each side, mostly from disease.

The British blockaded Russia's ships. French and British armies invaded the Crimea (Russia's peninsula on the Black Sea). Both sides suffered heavy losses because of battles and, more than that, disease. Russia finally asked for peace. What the peace settlement showed the Ottomans was that their survival depended on European rivalries, especially on British and French support against the Russians.

FROM THE ERA OF REFORM TO WORLD WAR I

The 1800s saw the continuing decline of the Ottomans, despite serious efforts to reform the structure of the Ottoman state. The changes came too late. The rapid decline of the Ottomans in the years before World War I led to great internal conflicts. And once the Europeans could agree on how to carve up the Ottoman Empire, things began to fall apart rapidly.

Ottoman Attempts at Reform. The end of the janissaries in the 1820s opened up a period in Turkish history known as the **Tanzimat,** or the Reorganization. In 1839, the sultan proclaimed sweeping changes. He guaranteed the basic rights of life, liberty, and property. And he promised financial and military reforms. In 1856, as a direct response to the Crimean War, the Ottoman government issued the *Hatt-i Humayun* (HAHT-ee hoo-mah-YOON). This was the major Turkish reform edict of the 1800s. Its aim was to create a national citizenship on European lines. It did away with the system of *millets*, ended the civil authority of the religious leaders, and guaranteed equality before the law. Christians and Jews could now gain public office and entrance into the army. The *Hatt-i Humayun* changed the tax structure, did away with torture, and brought about prison reform. War was declared on graft and bribery in the Ottoman bureaucracy.

In the 20 years following the Crimean War, the Ottoman state made a real effort to carry out the principles of the *Hatt-i Humayun*. Western ideas were welcomed into the empire. Newspapers were set up. Turkish translations of European (especially French) authors were promoted. A railroad linking the Black Sea and the Danube was built. In the late 1860s, Abdul Aziz (1861–1876) became the first sultan to visit Europe.

Reaction within the Ottoman Empire. The reform spirit was not approved by everyone. Both Christian and Muslim religious leaders opposed much of it. They feared that the empire was becoming a secular state. The end of their influence and incomes seemed in sight. What future could they have in a Westernized Ottoman state? For this reason, in the 1870s, they blocked efforts to reorganize the empire.

What is more, the bulk of the peasantry cared little about the whole matter. Moreover, the Turkish reformers were not that well-equipped to do the job. There were simply too few Turks with the education, skills, training, and experience to do the work their government asked of them. The corruption of the sultans was another problem. Abdul Aziz borrowed money freely and spent it lavishly. In 1875 Bulgarian and Serbian uprisings added to the government's unsteadiness. Such movements for autonomy were a threat to the empire. The Ottomans put them down brutally.

In 1876, with the backing of the reform party, a brilliant administrator, Midhat Pasha, overthrew Abdul Aziz. He placed Abdul-Hamid II on the throne. During the early months of his reign the new sultan took up the cause of reform. He proclaimed a new constitution providing for an elected parliament and a variety of rights. Elections were held and parliament met. But in 1877 Abdul-Hamid's real motives became clear.

Gaining control of the army, the sultan banished Midhat Pasha. He then called an end to sessions of the parliament. The constitution was allowed to lapse. For over the next 30 years Abdul-Hamid kept a strong hand on the government. He drove thousands of his reform-minded subjects out of the empire. These reformers, called the **Young Turks**, numbered in the tens of thousands. In exile in Paris and Geneva, they plotted the creation of a liberal Turkish state.

In 1881 the Ottoman government went bankrupt for a second time. Now it was forced to hand over almost the entire tax system of the empire to foreign bankers. When payments on the loans resumed, Western bankers became active supporters of the sultan. A thoroughly reformed and modernized Ottoman Empire was really not something the European governments wanted. After all, if a new government were set up in the empire, it might refuse to pay the sultan's debt. Liberals in England and France might call for human rights and an open parliamentary system. But it seemed that none of the Europeans wanted what the Young Turks wanted. This was an Ottoman Empire strong enough to challenge the Great Powers as a political equal.

The New Imperialism. The second half of the 1800s saw a surge of empire building on the part of the major European powers. This movement came to be known as the new **imperialism**. In their search for markets and national honor, the wealthy nations tried to impose a new order on the less developed parts of the world. They did this in a number of ways. They took control by seizing colonies. Or they set up spheres of influence. Another method was to rule through a local, weak "puppet" ruler. Decaying as it was, the Ottoman Empire proved an obvious victim at the hands of the West.

Many European imperialists had aims other than the search for markets and glory. They believed they were civilizing undeveloped corners of the world. It was, they argued, their duty to bring modern technology, education, and Christianity to those peoples who had no opportunities for improvement. But the presence of European armies and European fleets could easily inflame the national sentiments of local populations.

The British and French in North Africa. Under the rule of Muhammad Ali's grandson, Ismail Pasha, Egypt seemed on its way to modernization. In the 1860s the country's wealth grew at a rapid rate. This was a result of the cotton shortage created by the American Civil War. With cotton prices soaring, Egypt jumped in to meet world demand. In the period 1861–1865 the country's cotton production increased more than four times. In the hope that the cotton boom would continue, Ismail Pasha borrowed from European bankers in a rush to modernize the country. He financed the building of railways, telegraphs, harbor works, and finally the Suez Canal.

Using advanced techniques, a French engineer, Ferdinand de Lesseps, built a canal linking the Mediterranean to the Red Sea. The French public bought shares in the Suez Canal Company, and the Egyptian government backed the project. Upon completion in 1869, the Suez Canal cut the sea route from Europe to India in half. Ships no longer needed to sail around Africa. The British, having failed to invest in its construction, were now anxious to win control of the canal.

By the 1870s Ismail's finances were in terrible shape. When he tried to mortgage his share of the Suez Canal Company, British Prime Minister Benjamin Disraeli seized the moment. He raised 4 million pounds and bought Ismail's stock. In one quick stroke the British took over control of the Suez Canal. Egypt now had no control over or direct benefit from a canal that crossed its own country.

By 1876 bankruptcy forced Ismail Pasha off the throne. Egypt was forced to accept the dual financial control of Britain and France. The Egyptians rebelled under the leadership of Colonel Arabi Pasha. This revolt was one of the first truly nationalist uprisings against European

Suez Canal construction workers removing earth. Men with shovels, camels, and mules were replaced by workers with dredges, barges, and a railroad in 1864. In what year was the canal completed?

domination. But British interests were at stake, and in 1882 the British put down the rebellion, and Egypt came into the British sphere of influence.

Like Egypt, other Ottoman provinces in North Africa found themselves subject to imperial control. In Algeria the French had launched an invasion as early as 1830. It took a bloody 18-year war against stiff Arab resistance before French forces won out. Once the fighting ended, the French began to settle in Algeria. After 1871 the country received a civil administration with the status of a department of France.

In Tunisia, where the French had loaned the bey of Tunis money, France gained a sphere of influence. In 1881, the bey's government declared bankruptcy. France moved in at once and declared the country a **protectorate.** A protectorate is a country that is controlled by a stronger nation, in this case France. In 1911, after a failed attempt to take over Ethiopia, Italy seized Tripoli from the Ottoman Empire. It renamed the country Libya.

An English magazine illustration showing the British in Egypt in the late nineteenth century.

The Young Turks, 1908–1914. From the 1870s the Ottoman Empire faced a series of setbacks. The Russo-Turkish War of 1877–1878 forced the Ottomans to let go of several territories. The empire's holdings in the Balkans were reduced to no more than Albania and Macedonia. In 1912 and 1913 two Balkan wars led to independence for Albania and to Macedonia's becoming part of Greece. Within the empire these losses set off a series of constitutional crises.

In 1908 Young Turk army officers rebelled. They forced Abdul-Hamid to restore the constitution and call together a parliament. For a time it appeared as if Turkey would finally have a liberal government. But the Young Turks succeeded no more than Abdul-Hamid in holding back the tide of collapse.

In 1909 Abdul-Hamid encouraged Muslim conservatives to rise up against parliament. This rebellion was put down by the army. Abdul-Hamid was then overthrown and sent into exile. The constitution of 1876 was restored with a free legislature and a new sultan, Muhammad V. This sultan was a figurehead, however. He had no real power. The Young Turks struggled for basic democratic rights such as freedom of speech, assembly, and the press. Nevertheless, they were faced with the old problem of nationalism within the empire. The Balkan wars of 1912–1913 had resulted in crushing losses. Arabs, Armenians, Lebanese,

154

and Syrians were all calling for independence. As their demands increased, the Young Turks adopted harsher measures. In 1913 a group of politically minded army officers within the Young Turk movement seized power. They aimed to prevent the empire's collapse. Through ruthless means they sought to put down opposition in the center and borderlands.

An 1897 German cartoon showing the Ottoman Empire as a sick man. The European powers are shown as doctors ready to operate. In the original caption, John Bull (England) says to the others: "The sickness cannot be allowed to progress any further. I am for amputation." By 1897 which European countries had carved up and taken over the parts of the Ottoman Empire?

The Origins of World War I. In the years before World War I, the Ottoman Empire was gradually drawn into Germany's camp. Germany had been a major world power since its unification in 1870. German leaders dreamed of a Berlin-to-Baghdad railway. The German kaiser (emperor) sought to extend German influence throughout the Middle East—and to challenge Britain wherever possible. After 1905 tensions in Europe reached a fever pitch. The race to build larger armies with the latest weapons increased. And Germany's aggressive claims for world power status nearly resulted in war on more than one occasion before 1914.

With France and Russia allied against a growing German military threat, Turkey shifted toward the German camp. After all, Russia had been the chief Ottoman enemy for centuries. For their part, the Russians were happy to see the straits connecting the Black Sea to the Mediterranean in the hands of a weak sultan. Control of the straits by Germany was another matter, however.

The instability in the Balkans remained a source of serious international concern. It would be the direct cause of World War I because it made Russia and Austria want to seek influence there. When war finally broke out in the summer of 1914, it was the first conflict since the time of Napoleon to involve all the major European powers. World War I signaled disaster and the end of the Ottoman Empire.

REVIEWING THE CHAPTER

I. Building Your Vocabulary

On a separate sheet of paper write the word or phrase from the list below that correctly completes each sentence.

ghazis	pasha	*Hatt-i Humayun*
Tanzimat	janissaries	shah
Libya	Wahhabis	tax-farming
imperialism	protectorate	pasha

1. The major Turkish reform edict of the nineteenth century was known as _____.

2. The _____were a kind of brotherhood of Turkish frontier fighters.

3. In the Ottoman Empire, a provincial governor was known as a _____.

4. To raise money the Ottomans introduced a system known as _____.

5. The Ottomans called the era of reform, or reorganization, that began in 1839_____.

6. In the late 1800s, a group known as the _____ assumed power in what is today Saudi Arabia.

7. Formerly known as Tripoli, _____ became an Italian colony in 1911.

8. Expertly trained soldiers loyal to the sultan alone were known as the _____.

9. The ruler of Persia was known as a _____.

10. A country partly controlled by another and dependent upon the other country is known as a _____.

II. Understanding the Facts

Write the letter of the word or phrase that best completes the following sentences or answers the following questions.

1. By the 1400s, the last unbroken link to the Roman Empire was located at
   a. Rome.   b. Jerusalem.   c. Constantinople.

2. The peak of Ottoman power was during the reign of
   a. Suleiman the Magnificent.   b. Selim I.
   c. Selim III.

3. Baki is famous in the history of Turkish
   a. architecture.   b. poetry.   c. medicine.

4. Which of the following statements about the Ottoman system of tax-farming is true?
   a. It resembled the tax system of most modern European countries.
   b. It was ineffective because it enacted a direct federal tax.
   c. Through its very nature it promoted corruption.

5. Which of the following comparisons between Spain and the Ottoman Empire in the 1500s is false?
   a. In the 1500s both Spain and the Ottoman Empire were major forces in Mediterranean trade.
   b. In the 1500s both Spain and the Ottoman Empire practiced religious toleration.
   c. In the 1500s both Spain and the Ottoman Empire were great military powers.

6. The importation of silver from Spanish America affected the Ottoman Empire in the following way:
   a. It had no impact.
   b. It caused severe inflation and a crisis in trade.
   c. It helped to support the movement for reform.

7. The Treaty of Kuchuk Kainarji in 1774 acknowledged all of the following except
   a. Russian control of the northern coast of the Black Sea.
   b. the tsar's authority over the sultan's Christian Orthodox subjects.
   c. Russian control of the Dardanelles.

8. The chief power in the Middle East in the late 1800s was
   a. Great Britain.   b. Germany.   c. France.

158

9. The territory of the Ottoman Empire first affected by the idea of nationalism was
a. the Fertile Crescent.   b. the Balkan peninsula.
c. the Tigris-Euphrates valley.

10. When France and Russia allied in the period before World War I, the Ottoman Empire formed an alliance with
a. Britain.   b. Germany.   c. Italy.

III. Thinking It Through

1. How did the changing nature of the janissaries influence the decline of the Ottoman Empire?

2. What impact did the voyages of Vasco da Gama have on Turkish trade?

3. How did the French Revolution affect the Middle East?

4. How did the Industrial Revolution affect the Middle East?

5. Why was Napoleon Bonaparte important to the history of the Middle East?

6. Why did Britain and France unite against Russia in support of the Ottomans during the Crimean War?

7. How did the new imperialism affect the Middle East?

8. How did the sultan Abdul-Hamid affect events between 1877 and 1908?

9. Why did government schools in the Ottoman Empire teach in Turkish rather than Arabic?

10. Why did reform efforts within the Ottoman Empire fail?

DEVELOPING CRITICAL THINKING SKILLS

I. Relating Cause and Effect

Name one effect of each of the following events.

1. In 1511, a new shah established Shiite Islam as Persia's religion.

2. Many Jews fled from Spain to the Ottoman Empire.

3. The janissaries sought to end the Slave Institution.

4. Great Britain took control of the Suez Canal.

5. The Ottoman Empire suffered crushing losses in the Balkan wars of 1912–1913.

II. Supporting a Generalization

1. Write an essay using the facts in this chapter to support the following generalization: Neither Britain nor France could accept a major power like Russia in control of the eastern Mediterranean trading centers. More and more they found themselves acting together to keep this from happening.

2. What facts support the following generalization: The Ottoman Empire was the sick man of Europe.

ANALYZING A MAP

Study the map on pages 140–141 and answer the following questions.

1. When did the Ottoman Turks conquer Constantinople?
2. Which did the Ottoman Turks conquer first, Mecca or Cyprus?
3. What was the westernmost land that came under the control of the Ottoman Turks?
4. What empire was on the easternmost border of the Ottoman Empire?
5. The first siege of Vienna by the Ottoman Turks, which failed, took place in 1529. The failure of their second siege marked the end of Turkish pressure on Europe. When did the second siege of Vienna take place?
6. Who controlled Armenia?
7. What were the major bodies of water whose shorelines were at least partly controlled by the Ottoman Turks?
8. What Muslim movement gained power in central Arabia in the 1700s?
9. Approximately how far was Constantinople from Baghdad?
10. Why was Constantinople important to the Ottoman Empire?

ENRICHMENT AND EXPLORATION

1. Research the golden age of the Ottoman Empire under Suleiman the Magnificent. Investigate the architecture, poetry, and other aspects of the culture. Prepare a report explaining why it was considered a golden age.

2. Imagine you are a Turkish aristocrat living in Britain in the years between 1789 and 1815. Write a series of short letters home. In them discuss the revolutionary developments taking place around you. You can be for or against what is happening, but give reasons to support your point of view.

3. Draw a map of the Middle East that shows important trade routes for the period between 1500 and 1900. Explain your map to the class.

4. Write an essay on one of the following:

   a. Muhammed I after the fall of Constantinople

   b. Suleiman the Magnificient after the alliance with France

   c. Selim III during the French Revolution

   d. Muhammad Ali after he became pasha of Egypt

   e. Benjamin Disraeli, the British prime minister, after the British acquisition of the Suez Canal

   f. Abdul-Hamid following the end of the reforms of the late 1870s

   g. the Young Turks just after they seized power

TWO WORLD WARS AND THEIR IMPACT

1914–1967

1914–1918	World War I
1917	Balfour Declaration
1917	*Communist Revolution in Russia*
1920	Syria and Lebanon become mandates of France, Palestine becomes mandate of Britain.
1922	Britain grants Egypt independence.
1923	Turkey becomes a republic.
1929	*Great Depression begins.*
1932	Iraq gains independence from Britain.
1939–1945	World War II
1943	Lebanon becomes independent.
1945	The Arab League is formed.
1946	The French leave Syria and Lebanon; Jordan gains independence.
1947	The United Nations partitions Palestine.
1947	*India becomes independent.*
1948	State of Israel declared
1948–1949	Arab-Israeli war
1949	*Communists triumph in China.*
1951	Libya becomes independent.
1952	Egypt becomes a republic.
1956	Egypt nationalizes the Suez Canal; Israel, France, and Britain invade Egypt; Tunisia and Morocco gain independence.
1957–1965	*Most West African countries achieve independence.*
1958	Iraq becomes a republic.
1958–1961	United Arab Republic is formed and dissolved.
1962	Algeria becomes independent.
1967	Six-Day War between the Arab states and Israel

7 Two World Wars and Their Impact: 1914–1967

World War I and World War II shaped the modern Middle East. Before World War I almost all of the region was ruled by the Ottoman Empire. After World War I the victorious powers, especially Great Britain and France, carved up Turkey's former Arab lands. Thus, most of the present-day Arab states began as British and French creations. They were born in the era of imperialism. Many were the direct result of arrangements made between British officials and the Arab leaders who were their clients and whom they later set up as rulers.

Between the wars there were only five truly independent Muslim states in the Middle East: Turkey, Iran, Afghanistan, Yemen, and Saudi Arabia. Although Egypt gained independence between the wars, it remained under British influence until 1952. Iraq, too, gained formal independence from Britain in the early 1930s. But its foreign policy remained linked to that of Britain.

After World War II, most Middle Eastern states became independent. Nationalism, imperialism, modernization, and superpower politics all contributed to the development of the region. This chapter looks at the major changes that shaped the Middle East from World War I to 1967.

THE MIDDLE EAST AFTER 1914

The years from 1914 to 1918 were a turning point for the Middle East. This period saw the fall of several empires: the German Empire, tsarist Russia, the Hapsburg Empire of Austria-Hungary, and the Ottoman Empire.

World War I and Its Aftermath. As you read in Chapter 6, in the years before World War I the Ottoman Empire was drawn into an alliance with Germany. At the end of 1914 it entered the war on the side of the Central Powers, Germany and Austria-Hungary. They were fighting against the alliance of France, Russia, and Great Britain. Most of the fighting took place in Europe. But the Middle East also saw action.

The British sent an army to the Dardanelles in 1915 in an effort to seize the strait, a strategic waterway between the Black Sea and the Mediterranean Sea. The effort failed miserably. The Turks frustrated the attack of the mostly Australian and New Zealand troops at the Gallipoli Peninsula. Then, from Egypt the British moved across the Sinai and Palestine. Meanwhile, in the Persian Gulf region, the Arabs had revolted against the Turks. One leader of this revolt was Faisal (FEYE-suhl), a son of Sharif Husayn of the Hejaz (hej-AZ) in the western part of the Arabian Peninsula. Husayn was the head of the Hashemite family of Mecca. The family traced its descent from the great-grandfather of Muhammad.

During the war, the British made a number of secret agreements with two goals in mind. One was to win the war. The second was to increase their influence in the region after the war. Sometimes, in pursuing both these goals, Britain made promises it did not intend to keep or that contradicted one another. For example, the British government felt it needed the support of Sharif Husayn. Husayn wanted to rule an "independent Arab state" that stretched beyond the Arab Peninsula to include Palestine, Iraq, and Syria. In its correspondence with him, the British government seemed to encourage his ambition. Yet on November 2, 1917, it issued the Balfour Declaration, which stated that it favored "the establishment in Palestine of a national home for the Jewish people." The Balfour Declaration helped win Jewish support for the war in Europe and the United States. Agreements like these that the British made during World War I continue to be important in the Middle East to this very day.

The British negotiated another secret arrangement—this time with France. In 1916 the two nations signed the Sykes-Picot Agreement, which divided up much of the old Ottoman Empire. The two countries agreed that after the war Britain would take control of Iraq, Palestine, and Transjordan and that France would rule Syria and Lebanon.

When the war ended in 1918, the Ottoman Empire collapsed, much as everyone had expected. The sultan agreed to give up all of his non-Turkish territory. Arab lands that had been part of the Ottoman Empire for nearly four hundred years were now occupied by Allied troops.

Nationalists throughout the region quickly discovered that they had no reason to rejoice. No sooner were they free of Turkish rule than the newly formed League of Nations divided the region into political units called **mandates.** A mandate was an order giving a country the right to rule a territory until it was ready for independence. Britain and France were immediately issued mandates to govern the region. Those mandates were based on the terms of the Sykes-Picot Agreement. The mandates created nations that had never existed before. For example, the British received a mandate over Iraq. But there had never been a nation called Iraq, and people in the region did not think of themselves as Iraqis. Under the Ottomans, what was now Iraq had been three separate provinces. Similarly, Syria and Lebanon had never been countries in their own right.

Many Arabs felt betrayed. In Syria, a group led by Faisal tried to set up an independent country. Although the rebels had some support from Britain, France put down a revolt in 1920. In Iraq, a number of groups rebelled. The British restored order and, in 1921, they made Faisal king of the new country. At about the same time, they made yet another of Husayn's sons, Abdullah, ruler of Transjordan. The British ruled both countries indirectly. Although Iraq, for example, became independent in 1932, it was no secret that it was the British who ran the country. One British official boasted that the country's effectiveness was "entirely due to British airplanes. If the airplanes were removed tomorrow, the whole structure would inevitably fall to pieces."

The British governed Transjordan in a similar way. Only in Palestine did they rule directly. There they could not install a king because of the obligations they had undertaken in the Balfour Declaration and repeated in the mandate. They had to keep the peace between the Arabs and the Jews, an increasingly difficult task.

The Arabs were able to establish independent kingdoms in only one part of the old Ottoman Empire—the Arabian Peninsula. Ibn Saud (sah-OOD), the founder of Saudi Arabia, had been fighting for control over the peninsula since long before World War I. After the war, he was able to enlarge the area under his control. Sharif Husayn also took advantage of the fall of the Ottoman Empire by creating the Kingdom of Hijaz in the western part of the Arabian Peninsula. In 1925, however, it fell to the Saudis and became part of Saudi Arabia, which now stretched from the Persian Gulf to the Red Sea.

Although the British had no hand in setting up Saudi Arabia, they had considerable influence over it. They had subsidized Ibn Saud throughout World War I to keep him from helping the Ottomans. Also, with no known resources and few links to the outside world, an independent Saudi Arabia posed no threat to Britain. The same was true of part of the neighboring country of Yemen.

Britain and the New Role of Oil.   The Middle East had been important to the British since the early 1800s. It was the gateway to India, which was the jewel in the British imperial crown. After World War I, the Middle East took on new importance. It was a major source of oil, the fuel that now provided most of the energy of the industrial world.

British companies had begun drilling in the region before World War I. Their first explorations for oil were in Egypt and Iran. By World War II, the region's estimated reserves were a fifth of the world's total. Oil became the most important cargo shipped through the Suez Canal. Protection of the canal and the oil lifeline was a major reason for the continued British presence in Egypt.

After a major oil discovery in Iraq in 1927, a pipeline to the Mediterranean was opened. In 1928 private British, French, and American oil firms formed the Iraq Petroleum Company. By the mid-1930s, Iraq was the second largest oil producer in the Middle East.

In the Persian Gulf state of Kuwait, disputes broke out in the early 1930s between British and American oil companies. They were competing for **concessions.** By granting a concession to a company, a government allowed that company to tap the country's oil resources. In the end, the companies applied jointly for a concession. Kuwait later became Britain's chief supplier of oil. In 1933 Ibn Saud granted a concession to Standard Oil of California. In 1944 the Texas Oil Company, Standard Oil of New Jersey, and Socony-Vacuum joined Standard Oil of California to form the Arabian-American Oil Company (Aramco).

Except for Saudi Arabia and Yemen, the Arabian Peninsula and the Persian Gulf were under direct or indirect British control. Thus, Britain remained the main power in the Middle East until 1945.

TURKEY AND IRAN: TWO ATTEMPTS AT MODERNIZATION

Turkey and Iran are two nations with unique historical traditions. Both once ruled great empires. Both are Islamic states, but neither country's language is Arabic. In the years after World War I, Turkey and Iran tried to remake themselves as modern states. While doing this, both nations tried to throw off direct Western influence.

The Birth of Modern Turkey. Faced with occupation by the Allies in 1918, the Turks resisted strongly. They drove the Greeks and the Allies out of Turkey. The Turks were helped in this by the Soviet Union. Under the leadership of Mustafa Kemal (kuh-MAHL), the Turks kept their hold on Asia Minor and both sides of the Dardanelles. For over two years the Turks waged war against Greece, their traditional enemy. Peace did not return until 1922.

Mustafa Kemal launched a revolutionary plan for Turkey. In 1923 the sultanate was done away with. This event marked the birth of the Turkish Republic. The new republic was founded as a national state with the Turkish people sovereign, a change from the old Turkey, which had been organized as a group of religious communities. The people were given the right to vote, and a parliament was set up. The president of the republic was granted strong powers.

The creation of the Turkish Republic created difficulties for many Turkish residents. Certain minority groups in Turkey had been persecuted during Ottoman times. One of these groups, the Armenians, had suffered greatly at the hands of the Turks. The persecution had begun in the late 1800s and climaxed with the forced deportation of the Armenians in 1915. The Turkish government, fearing that the Armenians would aid the Russians, ordered the whole Armenian population out of the country. Hundreds of thousands of Armenians were killed or died of starvation as a result of the expulsion. Once in power, the leaders of the new Turkish Republic tried to make the nation mainly Turkish. As a result, about 1.4 million Greeks were forced to move from Turkey to Greece. In exchange, about 400,000 Turks living in Greece were forced to move to Turkey. This exchange caused great hardship for both peoples. It burdened the Greek and Turkish governments with a crippling refugee problem. Greeks who had lived in Asia Minor since the time of the Byzantines were uprooted from their homes. But the forced exchange of peoples did enable the Turkish Republic to achieve its goal of transforming the country into one consisting mainly of Turks.

Separation of Church and State in the Turkish Republic. In the new Turkey, for the first time in any Muslim country, church and state were separated. The Turkish Republic declared religion a matter of private belief. All religions were to be tolerated. The government was reorganized on secular lines. New laws were written, based on a European model rather than on the Koran. For the Islamic world, this alone was a revolutionary change.

Mustafa Kemal outlawed polygamy, the right of a man to have more than one wife at a time. He urged women to stop wearing veils and called for them to seek public office. He called for his people to wear Western clothes, and he made the use of the Western alphabet a legal requirement. Turks who could read and write with the Arabic alphabet now had to learn to do so with the new alphabet. At the same time, illiteracy was greatly reduced. Turkey adopted the Western calendar and the metric system. People were required to select a family name for themselves. Kemal himself took the name Atatürk (AT-uh-turk), meaning Father of the Turks. He moved the capital from Constantinople to Ankara in Asia Minor. Constantinople was renamed Istanbul.

Kemal Atatürk giving instructions in the newly introduced Latin alphabet, 1928. As leader of the Turkish Republic, he favored secularism, nationalism, and the increased power of the central government. He looked to Western nations for ideas and support.

Atatürk had mines, railroads, and factories developed for the new republic. Most of these industries were owned by the government. Lands once owned by Greeks were given to landless peasants. Certain businesses were taken over by the government. Railroads and telegraph lines linked the nation. And, while Atatürk accepted aid from what was then the Soviet Union as a means of limiting Western influence, he put down communism. For Atatürk, the Turkish revolution was a purely Turkish achievement. And he often used severe methods to achieve his ends.

After Atatürk's death in 1938, Turkey shifted several times between democratic and military rule. But the state's planning and the modernization Atatürk had started continued. With United States help after World War II, Turkey successfully fought a communist takeover. In 1952 Turkey became a member of the North Atlantic Treaty Organization (NATO). This military alliance includes the United States, Canada, and most of the democratic countries of Western and Southern Europe. Turkey allowed U.S. military bases within its borders. With its 700,000 soldiers, Turkey's armed forces are the second largest in NATO.

Present-day Turkey faces many problems. One is Turkey's continuing dispute with Greece, its neighbor and fellow member of NATO. The dispute is about control of the island nation of Cyprus. Greece and Turkey each supports its own ethnic group in the conflicts between the Greek majority and the Turkish minority on the island. Turkey also

Street scene in modern Ankara, Turkey's capital.

faces serious domestic problems. There have been industrial strikes, student protests, and economic problems. In 1983 the Motherland party came into power in free elections. It put an end to military rule, although the military still has considerable influence.

The Emergence of Modern Iran. By 1907 Britain and Russia both had spheres of influence in Persia (Iran). This country was rich in oil reserves, but its government was very corrupt. The ruling Qajar (KAH-jahr) dynasty granted foreigners the right to do business in Iran. Though these concessions helped the upper class, they did little to improve life for most of the people. During World War I, Persia became a battlefield for Russian, Turkish, and British troops. After the war, Persia was in a state of chaos. Famine had left the nation exhausted. Its treasury was empty, and the central government had completely broken down.

The Anglo-Persian Treaty of 1919 was designed to restore some order to Persia. But the Persians viewed it in a different light. To them, the treaty was only a disguised effort to make the country into a British **protectorate.** A protectorate is a country that is partly controlled by another nation. The Persians turned down the British offer of aid. British financial and military experts left the country.

Between 1921 and 1925 a young army officer, Reza Khan, moved steadily on the road to supreme power. He achieved absolute control through the military. In October 1923 Reza Khan became the prime minister of Iran. Two years later, a Constitutional Assembly voted to end the Qajar dynasty. In 1925 Reza Khan was declared **shah,** or king. He became the first ruler of the new Pahlavi (PAH-lah-vee) dynasty. The ancient empire of Persia had become the modern nation of Iran.

Modernization in Iran during the 1920s and 1930s. Reza Shah's chief goal was to free the country of foreign control. The most hated symbol of Western influence had been the system of granting privileges to foreigners living in Iran. For example, foreigners did not have to abide by the decisions of Iranian courts. By 1928 Reza Shah brought forth a new legal code. This ended all privileges to foreigners. It was a major victory in his attempt to build national self-respect.

Reza Shah made sweeping changes in other areas, too. In education, a Western-style curriculum was introduced, and girls' schools were set up for the first time. Women were urged to put aside the veil. Divorce laws were changed in their favor. In 1935 the University of Tehran was founded. The following year a program for adult education was started to end illiteracy and to give training in citizenship.

The shah's legal and educational reforms had a major impact on Iran. The reforms broke with Islamic tradition. They thus caused a serious break in the social order. The reforms reduced the role of the religious orders and laid the basis for a secular state. No other ruler had ever challenged the authority of the Islamic judges. The process of change started by Reza Shah in the 1920s and 1930s would have violent results in the late 1970s.

To modernize his country, the shah supported commerce, transportation, and industry. His major achievement was the Trans-Iranian Railway. Built between 1927 and 1938, it linked the Persian Gulf and the Caspian Sea. The railway was paid for by means of a tax on sugar and tea, without a single foreign loan. The shah also tried to reduce the country's dependence on the Soviet Union. Between 1938 and 1941, the Soviet Union's share of Iran's exports fell from over 34 percent to less than 2 percent. In contrast, Nazi Germany's share of Iranian exports rose to 47 percent. Iran's reliance on Soviet-made textiles was reduced when textile factories were built in Isfahan and Tehran.

Iran from 1941 to the Early 1970s.   The shah's search for independence from the Soviet Union and Britain drove him closer to Nazi Germany. By 1941 Germany was operating an effective spy system in Iran. The German invasion of the Soviet Union that same year made this system a real threat to the Allies. The shah would not allow the Allies to use the Trans-Iranian Railway to send war supplies to the Soviet Union. When the shah turned down Allied demands for the eviction of a large number of Germans, the Soviets and the British invaded the country. In 1941 Reza Shah was forced to step down by the Soviets and British in favor of his son, Muhammad Reza Shah Pahlavi.

The British thought of the Allied troops in Iran as a temporary necessity. The Soviets, on the other hand, used the chance to foster a separatist movement in the areas held by Soviet troops. Only after heavy diplomatic pressure was applied were Soviet troops removed from Iran's northwestern province.

By 1951, under Prime Minister Muhammad Mossaddegh, the Iranian oil industry was **nationalized,** that is, taken over by the government. The British responded with a blockade of the country. In 1953 the British and Americans backed the young shah in a **coup d'état** (koo day-TAH), or a sudden seizure of power by a group of persons in authority. This coup toppled the elected government of Mossaddegh. The shah, a figurehead since 1941, became the ruler of Iran. Many people saw the coup as a return of foreign privilege in Iran.

Reza Khan became shah of Iran in 1925 and ruled as Reza Shah Pahlavi for 16 years. He is shown here with his three children, the future shah Muhammad Reza Pahlavi, Princess Ashraf, and Princess Shams.

In the early 1960s the shah started a series of economic and social reforms known as the White Revolution. One change was launched through the Land Reform Act of 1962. This law forced the landed majority, including the religious leaders and many of the shah's opponents, to give up lands for redistribution to farmers who worked the land. In the years from 1960 to 1972 the percentage of owner-occupied farms climbed from about 25 percent to over 75 percent. Per capita income rose from about $175 in 1960 to $2,500 in 1978, mainly because of increased oil revenues. The country's power structure was greatly changed by the White Revolution. It broke the power of the landlords and cleared away the last remnants of feudalism. The White Revolution also gave the shah a new base of support in the middle and lower classes.

DEVELOPMENTS IN THE FRENCH MIDDLE EAST

France was a major power in the Middle East until World War II. It controlled most of North Africa and part of the Middle East. After 1945 Syria, Lebanon, Algeria, Morocco, and Tunisia gained independence from French rule.

Algeria. As you read in Chapter 6, Algeria had come under French rule in the middle of the nineteenth century. The French turned the country into a rich agricultural colony. Until 1900, France administered it as a **département** of mainland France. This meant it was ruled by the central French governing body located in Paris. The French built railways, hospitals, and schools. Although they were primarily for their own benefit, they also benefitted the Algerians. However, these improvements only frustrated the Algerians, for they made them painfully aware of their own lack of political power. Sooner or later France had to face Algeria's growing desire for freedom.

After World War II, the Algerian independence movement grew stronger. Nine million Algerians saw about one million French Algerians holding most of the country's manufacturing and agricultural wealth. But from the French point of view, independence meant the forced exile from the country of the hundreds of thousands of French who lived in Algeria.

In 1954 the Algerian National Liberation Front (N.L.F.) led an open revolt against French rule. But the French refused to accept an independent Algeria. Several years of bloody conflict followed, with over 250,000 people killed. Finally, after a new French government came to power under Charles de Gaulle, France accepted Algerian independence in 1962. Ahmed Ben Bella, a leader of the N.L.F., became Algeria's first prime minister. He was overthrown by Colonel Houari Boumedienne, who ruled until his death in 1979. Chadli Bendjedid was then elected president.

After the French left, the newly independent government set out to make Algeria a socialist state, with government ownership and control of industry. At the same time, the government started a major drive to redirect the cultural life of the country. It hoped to create an Islamic nation. Arabic replaced French as the official language. Teachers were brought in from other countries to instruct young people in Arabic. Islamic scholars were invited to teach in the new nation. As in other Islamic countries, Friday became the day of rest. In the new Islamic nation, women lost much of the independence they had won as freedom fighters. Yet Algeria's leaders did not erase all of the country's French legacy. They kept the schools, hospitals, and railways. They had no intention of eliminating the benefits of French rule.

Tunisia. Tunisia had been a French protectorate since 1881. In the 1930s an independence movement emerged, led by Habib Bourguiba (boor-GEE-buh). Although France had granted Tunisia a degree of self-rule after World War II, the French colonists in Tunisia opposed full independence. Despite these differences, Tunisia was granted independence in 1956. Bourguiba became the country's first president.

Morocco. Morocco was the last country of the Maghreb, northwestern Africa, to be invaded by the French. Spain also took control over part of Morocco. Moroccans put up great resistance to European domination. Protected by the rugged mountainous terrain, Moroccan fighters for independence held out from about 1911 to the mid-1930s. Nevertheless, during this period, the French built factories, mines, schools, and hospitals in their protectorate. After World War II, the nationalist movement grew at a faster pace. In 1956, France and Spain gave up their claims to Moroccan territory and the country became independent. A year later the former sultan became king as Muhammad V. In 1961 his son succeeded him as Hassan II. The following year Morocco adopted a constitution that made the country a constitutional monarchy.

Syria and Lebanon under the French Mandate. In March 1920 Arab nationalists held a congress in Damascus. They called for total independence and proclaimed Faisal king of Syria. Neither Britain nor France recognized this proclamation, however. Instead, as you have read, Allied leaders agreed to give France responsibility for Syria and Lebanon under the League of Nations mandate system. This meant that France would make and enforce laws for Syria and Lebanon, while supervised by the League of Nations. As you read earlier, the French overthrew Faisal and forced him into exile.

Throughout the period of the French mandate in Syria, religious and ethnic differences created instability. In the cities, a few wealthy families enjoyed great luxury while most of the people lived in poverty. Poor peasants lived and worked almost as serfs on the vast estates of the landed families. The leading families — the rich landlords and well-to-do merchants — organized the resistance to French rule. The occupying French proclaimed Syria a republic in 1941 and granted complete independence in 1944.

Algiers, 1962. Algerians celebrating their independence from France.

After independence, the wealthy families became the government leaders of Syria, but once in office, they proved to be poor rulers. Syria's rising lower middle class began to challenge them for power. This class supported the nationalist military, and in March 1949, army officers staged a bloodless coup. Then they in turn were overthrown in August.

By 1951 Syria had had its fourth coup in two years. The country was to be plagued by a series of military takeovers for two decades.

In the 1920s, the French created the new country of Lebanon out of a portion of Greater Syria. It consisted of a region called Mount Lebanon, which was largely Christian, and predominantly Muslim surrounding areas. Differences between Christian groups and Muslims over the independence of Lebanon were a growing problem in the 1930s. The Muslims did not want to be separated from Greater Syria. Private militias and paramilitary organizations formed along religious and communal lines. Conflict was avoided by an unwritten settlement in 1943. This settlement is known as the National Pact. In return for Muslim acceptance of Lebanese independence, the Christians ended their dependence on French protection. The Christians also agreed that Lebanon would become an Arab state. Lebanon became independent in 1943, with Christians and Muslims sharing power in the government.

Following World War II, in 1946, French troops left Lebanon as well as Syria. During a rebellion by Muslims in 1958, the Lebanese president requested American help. Thousands of U.S. Marines intervened to help restore peace. The country was to be torn by internal religious and political conflict for decades.

PALESTINE, A TROUBLED LAND

Conflict between cultures and peoples is no stranger to the Middle East. Nowhere in the region is this truer than in the ancient land of Palestine, which Arabs and Jews have each claimed as their own and whose disputes have meant bloodshed and bitterness for the better part of the twentieth century.

Modern Zionism.   As you read in Chapter 3, Hebrew civilization arose in the ancient Middle East. After the Romans destroyed the second temple in Jerusalem in A.D. 70, many Jews were forced to leave Palestine. Although a few remained on the land, many more were dispersed to other areas of the Middle East and to Europe. By the early Middle Ages, there were Jewish communities in Palestine, Egypt, North Africa, Spain, Italy, and the Byzantine Empire. Some Jews settled in Germany and other parts of Eastern Europe. Others moved into Western Europe and into the Black Sea region of Russia. In some of these places, as the medieval period ended, Jews were able to preserve their religion and traditions. They participated in commerce, trade, banking, and the professions. In other places, however, they were excluded from the lives of the communities in which they lived.

The Jews of the **Diaspora,** as this mass dispersal was called, never gave up their hope of returning to Palestine. The idea of Israel lived on for centuries in the traditional Jewish prayer, "next year in Jerusalem." By the late 1880s, about 25,000 Jews lived in Palestine, many on newly formed agricultural settlements.

Towards the end of the nineteenth century rising **anti-Semitism,** or prejudice against Jews, in Europe prompted some Jews to work harder for the goal of a new life in Palestine. In the late 1880s, thousands of Jews were killed in Russia during massacres known as **pogroms** (poh-GROHMZ). Waves of anti-Semitism spread to Western Europe. In 1896, an Austrian journalist who was Jewish, Theodore Herzl (HERT-suhl), came to believe that Jews could never lead normal lives in countries where they were dominated by non-Jews. Herzl believed they would always be persecuted because of their religion. Herzl wrote a book, *The Jewish State,* in which he urged European Jews to rebuild the Jewish nation. He advocated a homeland in Palestine. Under Herzl's leadership, Zionism (ZEYE-uh-niz-uhm) began to emerge as an organized movement. Zionism is a movement that calls for the reestablishment of a national Jewish state in Palestine.

Under Herzl's leadership, the First Zionist Congress met in Basel, Switzerland, in 1897. It created the World Zionist Organization. It also adopted a national flag, a national anthem, and a resolution calling for a "home in Palestine." The Jewish National Fund was founded to turn that dream into a reality. It purchased land in Palestine from the Ottomans. Zionism was similar to the European nationalist movements of nineteenth-century Europeans. The Italian people of the many Italian states had joined together in a united Italian nation. The many small German states had also joined together in a unified Germany. Zionism was also similar to the twentieth-century national liberation movements of non-European peoples freeing themselves from colonial rule. In the years before World War I, the number of European Jews in Palestine increased; by 1918 there were some 80,000 Jews in Palestine.

The Balfour Declaration. From World War I to the end of the British mandate, Zionists sought the help of Great Britain and, to a lesser degree, the United States. Dr. Chaim Weizmann (VEYETS-muhn), a chemist and Zionist leader, helped the British Ministry of Munitions in the development of improved explosives. In return, Weizmann won the support of, among others, Arthur Balfour, the British foreign secretary, and David Lloyd George, the prime minister. At that time, Great Britain was seeking as much support for its war effort against Germany as possible. Lloyd George believed that a British-sponsored homeland for the Jews in Palestine would win Jewish support, especially from Jews in the United States. The result was the Balfour Declaration of November 1917.

The Balfour Declaration was a published statement from the British foreign secretary to Lord Rothschild, head of the British branch of the prominent Jewish banking family. Merely 67 words in length, the declaration stated: "His Majesty's Government views with favour the establishment in Palestine of a national home for the Jewish people, and will use their best endeavors to facilitate [help] the achievement of this object, it being clearly understood that nothing shall be done which may prejudice the civil and religious rights of existing non-Jewish communities." While offering the Jewish people a national home, the Balfour Declaration made a point of saying that its support for a Jewish homeland would not violate the rights of the non-Jews who lived in Palestine. But, as you have read, other promises had already been made to the Arabs which seemed to contradict the declaration. Thus, the British appeared to promise the Jews more than they may have meant to deliver. At the same time, they ignored earlier commitments to the Arabs. In the years between World War I and World War II this would only serve to intensify friction between the two groups.

Palestine Between the World Wars.   Palestine formally became a mandate of Great Britain in 1920. The Arabs had reacted bitterly to the Balfour Declaration of 1917. Now, in the period between the world wars, the most heated issue of the British administration of Palestine was Jewish immigration into Palestine. The Palestinian Arabs worked actively to limit, or even end, this immigration. There were increasing numbers of violent incidents between the Arab and Jewish communities. By the end of the 1920s, only small numbers of Jews were entering Palestine. In this period, the Arabs of Palestine turned their attention to other issues, believing that the Zionist movement was melting away.

Within a few years, however, drastic changes in the situation of Jews occurred. The 1930s saw the rise of Nazism in Germany and with it, the persecution of Jews. Rabid anti-Semitism intensified in Eastern and Central Europe. As a result, European Jews fled to Palestine in greater numbers. By the outbreak of World War II there were roughly 450,000

Jews in Palestine. This was still a minority—only about 30 percent of the total population.

In 1936 an Arab High Committee was formed. It tried to unite the Palestinian Arabs in opposition to Jewish immigration. Arab attacks on Jews became more frequent and soon amounted to civil war. This situation lasted for three years. For the Arabs, the partition, or division, of Palestine was not acceptable. They were the majority; their birth rate was high. Over the previous 50 years, attracted by the economy in the area, thousands of Arabs had moved into the region. Meanwhile, Great Britain had concluded that Jews obviously were not going to help the Nazis in any coming world conflict. However, something had to be done to gain Arab support for Britain. In 1939, the British government issued a White Paper. That document limited to 75,000 the total number of Jewish immigrants to be allowed into Palestine over the next five years. It also decreed that after those five years there would be no further Jewish immigration. As it turned out, these were the years during which Jews unsuccessfully sought to escape from Nazi-controlled Europe.

The Impact of the Holocaust.   At the end of World War II, a shocked world learned the truth about Adolf Hitler's death camps. Of Europe's 10 million Jews, 6 million had been murdered by the Nazis. As you read in Chapter 2, this attempted **genocide**, or murder of a whole people, became known as the **Holocaust**. During the Holocaust, 1.5 million Jewish children were murdered. More than 2.5 million Jews were put to death at one camp, Auschwitz (OW-shwitz), alone.

Before World War II, many Jews rejected the idea of a Jewish state. However, Zionism gained more supporters after the war. Between 1945 and 1948 the leadership of the United States began to favor the Zionist cause. President Harry S Truman urged that the European Jewish refugees be immediately admitted to Palestine.

At the same time, the British were unable to follow a firm policy. World War II left Britain exhausted. The British now found it impossible to control the Arabs and Jews. One Jewish group blew up British headquarters in a hotel in Jerusalem. Many British soldiers and civilians died in the explosion. British policy tried to weaken the Zionists. The British refused to let Holocaust survivors into Palestine. They also tried to take weapons away from Jewish farming settlements, despite the danger of Arab attack. Criticized by both sides, Britain turned over the issue of Palestine to the United Nations.

The Arabs, for their part, tried to win sympathy for their cause.

179

CASE STUDY:

The Pioneers

Shmuel Dayan was the father of the famous Israeli general and statesman, Moshe Dayan. The elder Dayan came to Palestine in 1908 as a
teenage immigrant. His generation was among the first to clear land,
drain swamps, irrigate the desert, and build settlements in the Jewish
homeland. In this excerpt from his account of these early days, we learn
about the ideals of these early pioneers and of the difficulties they faced.

> Nahalal [the village] was founded with the aim of building a
> society where . . . everyone would be a worker in his own right,
> living by his own work. There would be no exploiters and no
> exploited. We have succeeded in our aim and created a new
> society, a creative, productive society living directly from the land
> and the work of its hands.
> Our economy has been built on the family and its work, and
> we have employed paid labor only in very exceptional
> circumstances. Our children have done most of the work and
> created the village and everything in it. We ourselves worked too
> hard, for we had to start from nothing. There were not enough
> hours in the day for us, and we worked on in darkness after the
> sun had set. We did not do this for material gain, but because we
> wanted to build here a sound farm economy for the generations
> which were to come after us. We hope that the next generation
> will have an easier time. We, however, have a double task to
> fulfill—to build up Nahalal for the future, and to gain our daily
> bread from its soil now. This is too much for ordinary mortals to
> do. And we are constantly anxious for the peace of our society. A
> dozen times a day we ask ourselves: "Have we really created a new
> society, a juster society?"

Source: Shmuel Dayan, *Pioneers in Israel.* Cleveland: World Publishing Co., 1961.

1. What was the principal occupation in the village?

2. Describe some of the problems the pioneers faced.

3. What were some of the motives and goals of the pioneers?

Some Arab leaders in Palestine had supported Germany during the war. In 1945 they opened Arab information offices in Washington and London. The Arabs asked if it would be just for them alone to pay the price for the Nazi atrocities by accepting Jewish immigrants in Palestine. The Arabs thought they were being punished for the anti-Semitic crimes committed by Europeans in Europe.

Before World War II a unified Arab leadership in Palestine did not exist. The Zionists, by contrast, were much more united. In March 1945 Arab leaders from the neighboring countries of Syria, Lebanon, Transjordan, Egypt, Iraq, Saudi Arabia, and Yemen formed the Arab League. They set out to strengthen ties between Arab states and thus to defend the Arab cause in Palestine.

Creation of the State of Israel.   The emergence of Israel as a Jewish state in Palestine was the key political issue of the Middle East after World War II. The energy and skill of the Zionist founders led to their success. The Zionists had great hopes for their new nation. They wanted to bring the science and democracy of the West to the Middle East. This was part of the root of the whole problem. To many Arabs, Zionism seemed only another form of Western imperialism. The result has been an armed conflict that has gone on to this day.

By 1947, Jews in Palestine were pressing Britain to create a Jewish state. In February 1947, unable to resolve the basic dispute between the Jews and the Arabs, Britain decided to turn the question of Palestine over to the United Nations. In November 1947, the UN voted to end the British mandate and **partition,** or divide, Palestine into a Jewish state, an Arab state, and a small internationally run zone that included Jerusalem. The territory of the Jewish state would occupy 56 percent of the land of Palestine. The separate Jewish and Arab states were to be set up within 11 months.

Immediately after the UN vote, fighting broke out between the Palestinian Arabs and Jews. In the fighting, although the Arabs were aided by other Arab countries, the Jews held on to the portion of the mandate assigned them by the UN. On May 14, 1948, the British high commissioner for Palestine departed, and the state of Israel was proclaimed. It was recognized at once by the United States and the Soviet Union.

War between Israel and the Arab states broke out the day after Israeli independence was declared. Egypt, Transjordan, Syria, Lebanon, and Iraq invaded Israel. Fighting continued on and off until February 1949, when separate agreements were signed by Israel and Egypt,

Lebanon, Syria, and Transjordan. Israel now controlled 77 percent of Palestine, having gained territory in the north, center, and southwest. Transjordan occupied most of what had been the Arab portion in the second partition of Palestine. Israel and Transjordan divided Jerusalem between them. Egypt gained control of the Gaza Strip, a piece of land on the Mediterranean coast (see map on page 184).

What had once been known as Palestine had ceased to exist as a separate entity. Hundreds of thousands of Palestinian Arabs left the new state, giving Israel a Jewish majority. The Israelis claimed the Arabs had fled of their own accord. The Arabs insisted that they had been driven out.

A Democratic Republic in Israel.   The new government of Israel was a parliamentary democracy, similar to that of Great Britain. Its legislature, called the **Knesset** (KNES-et), has the highest power in the government. Political parties are represented in the Knesset according to the proportion of votes they receive in each election. The Knesset elects a president, who is the head of the state. But political power rests with the prime minister, who is usually also the leader of the party with the majority of members in the Knesset, and the cabinet. Hebrew and Arabic were made the official languages of the country.

Jewish immigrants to Palestine, 1947. During and immediately after the Nazi murder of millions of Jews, the British rulers of Palestine tried to restrict and prevent Jewish refugees from reaching Palestine. Ships such as this tried to slip through the British naval blockade.

The Launching of the New Nation.   The new nation of Israel was tiny—about the size of the state of New Jersey. The first Israeli census, taken in 1948, reported a population of close to 900,000. As you read in Chapter 2, soon after the founding of the state, the Knesset passed the Law of Return, which, in keeping with the country's Zionist ideals, gave every Jew the right to immigrate to Israel. Within 20 years of Israel's founding, the Jewish population tripled, largely as a result of immigration. About a quarter of the Jewish population was born in the United States or Europe. Many other Jews had come from North Africa and other Middle Eastern and Asian countries. The number of native Israelis likewise grew, but at a slower rate. Native Israelis are known as **sabras,** named after the fruit of the cactus plant. Israelis liken themselves to the sabra, which is hard and prickly on the outside but tender and sweet within.

Israel did not allow most of the Arabs who had left the country in 1948 to return, so the Arab population, which was about 15 percent of the total in 1948, did not grow very fast between 1948 and 1967. Israel gave the Arabs the same social and political rights as Jews. Israel gave the vote to female Arab citizens before any Arab country allowed its women to vote.

A Modern Urban Society.   From the late 1880s on, the Jewish immigrants to Palestine worked hard to renew the land. They drained swamps, developed irrigation systems, and planted forests. They reclaimed the coastal plains and even parts of the barren desert. Farms sprang up, and the growing of citrus fruits and dairy production were encouraged.

By the mid-1900s, while the people continued to improve the land, the emphasis shifted to manufacturing and commerce. Cities increased in population as the Israelis built factories, refineries, chemical plants, and transportation facilities. By the late 1960s, there were several cities with populations of over 100,000. The most important were Tel Aviv, Jerusalem, and Haifa. Tel Aviv, with a population of more than one million, became a major manufacturing center. The food processing industry as well as the clothing and textile industries were also centered there.

A number of factors helped Israel develop into a modern industrial state. One was that the large percentage of the people who had come from Europe were trained in professions and the trades. Their skills were invaluable in building the new nation.

A second factor helping Israel was the flow of capital into the country. Aid from the United States government alone amounted to many

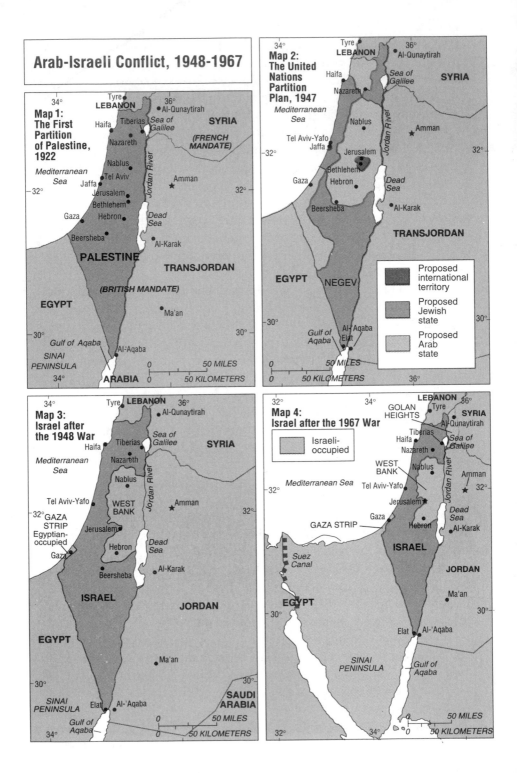

Arab-Israeli Conflict, 1948-1967

**Map 1:
The First
Partition
of Palestine,
1922**

34°

Tyre
LEBANON
Haifa Tiberias *Sea of Galilee*
Nazareth
36°
Al-Qunaytirah
SYRIA
(FRENCH MANDATE)

Mediterranean Sea
Nablus
Tel Aviv
Jaffa
Jerusalem
Bethlehem
Hebron
Gaza
Beersheba
Jordan River
Amman
32°
Dead Sea
Al-Karak

32°

PALESTINE
TRANSJORDAN

(BRITISH MANDATE)

EGYPT

Ma'an

30°
Gulf of Aqaba
SINAI PENINSULA
Al-'Aqaba
34°
ARABIA
30°

0   50 MILES
0   50 KILOMETERS

**Map 2:
The United
Nations
Partition
Plan, 1947**

34°
Tyre
LEBANON
Haifa
Nazareth
Mediterranean Sea
Tel Aviv-Yafo
Jaffa
Gaza
36°
Al-Qunaytirah
Sea of Galilee
SYRIA
Nablus
Jerusalem
Bethlehem
Hebron
Jordan River
Amman
32°
Dead Sea
Beersheba
Al-Karak

TRANSJORDAN

EGYPT NEGEV

Gulf of Aqaba
Al-Aqaba
Elat
30°
30°

Proposed international territory

Proposed Jewish state

Proposed Arab state

0   50 MILES
0   50 KILOMETERS
36°

**Map 3:
Israel after
the 1948 War**

34°
Tyre LEBANON
Haifa
Mediterranean Sea
Tiberias *Sea of Galilee*
Nazareth
Nablus
Tel Aviv-Yafo
32° GAZA STRIP
Egyptian-occupied
Gaza
36°
Al-Qunaytirah
SYRIA
WEST BANK
Jordan River
Amman
Jerusalem
Hebron
Dead Sea
Beersheba
Al-Karak
32°

ISRAEL
JORDAN

EGYPT

Ma'an

30°
SINAI PENINSULA Elat Al-'Aqaba
Gulf of Aqaba
34°
30°
SAUDI ARABIA

0   50 MILES
0   50 KILOMETERS

**Map 4:
Israel after the 1967 War**

32°
34°
GOLAN HEIGHTS
LEBANON
Tyre
36°
SYRIA
Tiberias
Haifa *Sea of Galilee*
Al-Qunaytirah
Nazareth
Israeli-occupied
WEST BANK
Nablus
Mediterranean Sea
Tel Aviv-Yafo
Jerusalem
Gaza
GAZA STRIP
Jordan River
Amman
32°
Dead Sea
Hebron
Al-Karak
ISRAEL
JORDAN
Suez Canal
EGYPT
30°
Ma'an
Elat Al-'Aqaba
30°
SINAI PENINSULA
Gulf of Aqaba
32°
34°

0   50 MILES
0   50 KILOMETERS

184

millions of dollars. In addition, the West German government sent Israel $715 million over a 14-year period. This sum was in repayment for some of the losses suffered by Jews at the hands of the Nazis during World War II. American Jews contributed more than $500 million.

As a result of this influx of money, Israel's gross national product grew in the 1950s and 1960s at a rate of more than 10 percent a year. In terms of per capita income, this represented an increase in this period from less than $100 to more than $5,000 a year. Except for some of the oil-rich Arab lands, this was the highest per capita income in the Middle East. Another indication of Israel's high rate of economic development was the decline in the number of people employed in agriculture as opposed to other occupations. By the end of the 1960s, less than 7 percent worked at farming. More than 36 percent were in industry, and 57 percent were in service work.

Israeli Leadership.   From the founding of the nation until 1977, the dominant party in Israeli politics was the Labor party. By itself or in **coalitions** (temporary alliances) with other parties, it ruled the government. Chaim Weizman was the first Israeli president. His prime minister, David Ben-Gurion, a native of Poland and an ardent fighter for Zionism, led the new Jewish state through its first 15 years. He was followed over the next decades by a number of other effective members of the Labor party. One such leader was Golda Meir (may-EER), who served as prime minister from 1969 to 1974. Golda Meir was born in Russia but grew up in Milwaukee, Wisconsin. In 1921 she and her husband emigrated to Palestine to join the Zionist effort there. She spent a lifetime in Israeli politics. As prime minister, she led Israel through several armed conflicts with Arab states.

Palestine and Jordan.   In 1921, a year after Palestine became a British mandate, the British recognized Abdullah Hussein as the emir (prince or governor) over land east of the Jordan River in Palestine. Abdullah was a son of Sharif Husayn of the Hejaz in Saudi Arabia. The British named the territory Transjordan and allowed the emir limited self-government. In 1922 the first official partition of the mandate of Palestine took place. The mandate was divided at the Jordan River. About 80 percent of the land became the British mandate of Transjordan. The land west of the Jordan River—about 20 percent of the original mandate—became the new mandate of Palestine. As you have read, part of this land west of the Jordan River eventually became Israel, the West Bank, and the Gaza Strip.

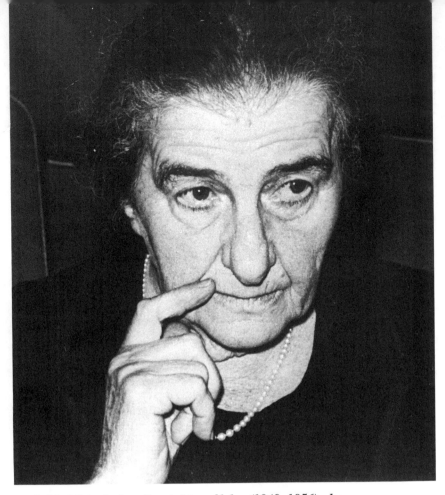

Golda Meir. As Israel's minister of labor (1949–1956), she carried out major housing and road-building programs. As foreign minister (1956–1966), she promoted Israeli aid to new African nations. Meir was Israeli prime minister from 1969 to 1974.

In 1928, Britain formally recognized Transjordan as an independent state under the rule of Abdullah. But the country was still officially under British protection and was supported by a subsidy from the British government. In 1928, Britain signed a treaty giving the new country more independence, although British officials continued to handle not only the nation's foreign affairs but also its finances. It was not until 1946 that Transjordan became fully independent. On May 25, 1945, Abdullah was proclaimed king, and the country's name was officially changed to the Hashemite Kingdom of Jordan.

During the 1948 war with Israel, Jordan gained control of the West Bank and the eastern part of Jerusalem. In 1950, it officially annexed the West Bank. According to the UN's 1947 plan, that area was to have been part of a new Arab state. In 1952, Abdullah's grandson, Hussein, became king of Jordan.

Many Arabs, refugees from the 1948 war with Israel, moved into the West Bank and Jordan. When Jordan lost the West Bank to Israel during the 1967 war, many more Arabs moved eastward across the river into Jordan. One of the country's major problems in the 1960s was how to deal with these refugees, who numbered about one million out of Jordan's three million people. Many of these Arabs consider themselves Palestinians whose land is now held by Israel and Jordan.

EGYPT IN THE TWENTIETH CENTURY

As you have read, Britain gave Egypt independence in 1922 in name only. In reality, because of the Suez Canal, Britain kept up its political control of the country.

Egypt from 1922 to 1952.   Upon independence, Egypt's sultan became king. A parliamentary constitution was adopted, with the king keeping broad powers. Egyptian politics was dominated by landowners and members of the upper middle class. Leading politicians came from the landowning classes. In time, they confronted the country's main authority—the king, and behind him, the authority of the British.

Egypt's Aswan Dam was completed in 1970. It controls the flood waters of the Nile and provides water to irrigate thousands of acres. It also improves river navigation and generates electricity.

With the outbreak of World War II, Egypt's strategic role in Britain's survival again became critical. As the war spread to North Africa, Britain met Germany and Italy in fierce desert fighting. In October 1942, one of the key battles of World War II was fought at El Alamein, within 60 miles (96 kilometers) of Alexandria. The British defeated Germany's "Desert Fox," General Erwin Rommel. Rommel's troops were driven into Libya, and Germany's efforts to seize the Suez Canal ended.

Following the 1948 Arab-Israeli war and the founding of Israel, a series of political crises shook Egypt. Those opposed to Britain's role in Palestine demonstrated against the British. Guerrilla attacks against British troops in the Suez Canal area became more frequent. In January 1952 demonstrators in Cairo took to the streets and burned parts of the city. The months that followed saw the rise and fall of four prime ministers. Rival groups struggled for power. The scandalous lifestyle of the king, Farouk, reduced the prestige of the monarchy. Egypt was more than ready for revolution.

In July 1952 a group of Egyptian officers led by General Muhammad Neguib and Colonel Gamal Abdel Nasser staged a coup in which King Farouk was overthrown. Of lower-middle-class origin, Nasser had fought in the Israeli campaign of 1948–1949. His experiences led him to form the secret Free Officers' Movement. Like Nasser, many others in this group came from the lower middle class. The Free Officers' Movement was a military conspiracy. It had no formal ideology. The conspiracy was basically a response to two factors: the failure of the 1948–1949 war with Israel and the continued British presence in Egypt. The movement appealed to many, particularly the army and the working class.

A number of leaders of the Free Officers' Movement had ties to a group known as the Muslim Brotherhood. It was founded in 1928 by an elementary school teacher in Egypt named Hasan al-Banna. Its goal was to purify Islam. Education and health care were central concerns of the Brotherhood. So were economic improvement and political reform. The Brothers wanted Egypt to become not only a modern nation but also one that acted in accordance with Muslim teachings.

The Brotherhood was a tightly organized and controlled secret society. In the 1940s it increasingly took to terrorism to achieve its goals. It drew its support from the middle class—artisans, traders, teachers, and professionals in cities like Cairo and Alexandria. No one knows for sure how many people belonged to the Brotherhood. There is no question, however, that it was a major political force, not only in Egypt but also in Syria and several other countries.

188

At first, Nasser gave the group considerable freedom. But increasingly the Brotherhood's dream of a unified Islamic state conflicted with his own dream of a unified secular Arab state. After a member of the group made an attempt on Nasser's life in 1954, he tried to wipe out the organization. Some of the leaders were executed by the government, while others were exiled or forced underground.

Pan-Arabism. Nasser's dream of a unified Arab state is known as **Pan-Arabism.** It was a form of nationalism that cut across political boundaries. It rested on the belief that all speakers of Arabic are really part of one nation. The goal of Pan-Arabism was to provide Arabs with a major say in world affairs.

Upon taking power, Nasser moved quickly to assume leadership of the Arab world. His boldness inspired others, such as, for example, a group of Iraqi soldiers who overthrew the Iraqi king in 1958 and made Iraq a republic. Nasser's stature in the Arab world was due in part to Egypt's importance in that world. Egypt was both an educational and publishing center for countries throughout the Middle East. The fact that Egypt had—and still has—by far the largest population of any Arab state was also a factor in Nasser's bid for leadership.

Although Nasser was extremely popular, not all Arabs were willing to accept him as a champion of Pan-Arabism. He encountered much resistance from other leaders in the region. Saudi Arabia openly supported the Muslim Brotherhood, and leaders in Syria, Lebanon, and Yemen saw Pan-Arabism as an example of Egyptian imperialism.

Nasser on the World Stage. From the start, Nasser redirected Egyptian foreign policy. He did this in a number of ways. First, he moved the country away from Britain by seeking economic aid from the world's superpowers, the United States and the Soviet Union. But he did not align himself with either one. By refusing to affiliate Egypt with either the United States or the Soviet Union, Nasser followed a policy of **nonalignment.**

In 1955, Britain, with U.S. backing, put together the Baghdad Pact, which was an attempt to create a defensive region against Soviet expansion in the Middle East. It linked Iran, Iraq, Pakistan, and Turkey in the pact, and in so doing it split the Arab world. Iraq, as the only Arab country to sign it, was denounced by Nasser. He called for the overthrow of the Iraqi government. Indeed there was a revolution in Iraq in 1958, and the new government withdrew from the Baghdad Pact soon after.

The Suez War of 1956.   The new symbol of Nasser's Egypt was to be the High Dam at Aswan on the Nile, which was to provide Egypt with much-needed electric power and control the annual flooding of the Nile. Initially, the United States and Britain were to supply the money for the dam. But when Nasser negotiated with the Soviet Union, the Western powers withdrew their support of the dam. In 1956, Nasser announced that he was taking over the Suez Canal from its French and British owners. This act that triggered the Suez War of 1956.

From the start of the Suez crisis, Britain, France, and Israel drew up military plans. Israel invaded Egypt and quickly defeated the Egyptian army. Britain and France followed with demands for the withdrawal of all forces from the area around the canal. Nasser refused, and French and British troops invaded Port Said, the city at the northern end of the canal. Many people, including both Soviet and U.S. leaders, thought the issue could have been settled without resort to force. They pressured the invading powers to end the confrontation, and the British, French, and Israelis were forced to withdraw.

Nasser emerged from the Suez War in triumph. The Suez Canal was firmly in Egypt's hands, and he had won out over non-Arab nations. For Britain, the canal proved to be less vital than had been thought. The disruption of traffic between the Mediterranean and Red seas caused little undue hardship.

The United Arab Republic: 1958–1961.   In the years after the Suez War, Nasser pursued a foreign policy designed to enlarge Egypt's influence. In the name of Pan-Arabism, Egypt combined with Syria in 1958 to form the United Arab Republic (UAR). However, the alliance never worked. Nasser treated Syria as a junior partner, almost as a province of Egypt. When he ordered Syrian political leaders to live in Cairo so as to keep them under his control, the Syrian army stepped in. The UAR broke apart in 1961.

Throughout the 1950s and 1960s, Nasser moved toward a one-party state, with increasing government control over the economy. He called his policy Arab socialism. The 1962 Charter of National Action formalized what was already a reality in Egypt. It set up the Arab Social Union, a mass political party through which the government could communicate with the people. It also called for the government to play a central role in industrializing the nation.

Under Nasser, Egypt made impressive gains domestically. Nationalization of the Suez Canal brought the country almost $200 million a year in tolls. Nasser used this money to build up Egypt's industry.

Crowds greeting Egypt's President Nasser after he announced Egypt's takeover of the Suez Canal in 1956.

In 1950 industry accounted for 10 percent of Egypt's gross national product. Twenty years later the figure had doubled. This gain, however, was undercut by failures in agriculture. Nasser did break up large land-holdings and distributed them to the poor. But rapid population growth, especially in Cairo, placed a huge burden on the country's still-struggling economy.

The Six-Day War. The Arab states had never acknowledged Israel's right to exist. Arab guerrilla bands from time to time raided Israeli's borders and conducted terror campaigns against Israeli civilians. The 1960s saw increased tensions on Israel's border with Syria. Palestinians made attacks on Israel from bases in Lebanon and Jordan and from the Golan Heights in Syria. On November 13, 1966, the Israelis struck at Jordan, leaving 18 dead and 54 wounded. Arab opinion demanded action.

Nasser responded by demanding the withdrawal of the United Nations forces that had kept the peace on the Sinai border since the Suez War. He also closed the entrance to the Gulf of Aqaba, which vessels carrying goods from the Red Sea to Israel had to pass through (see map on page 184). Israel had clearly stated that closing the gulf would lead to war. On May 10, 1967, when Jordan's King Hussein signed a mutual defense pact with Nasser, the Israelis believed they were surrounded. Egypt began moving a force of hundreds of Soviet-supplied tanks accross the Sinai desert toward Israel's borders.

On June 5, Israel launched a surprise military strike on Egypt and Jordan. Israeli bombers caught the Egyptian air force on the ground. In a few hours, the Arab world's most powerful military force was almost totally wiped out. In the Sinai Peninsula the Israelis smashed the Egyptian army, which fled in defeat. On June 9 the Israeli army reached the Suez Canal. Within a few days it had control of the entire Sinai Peninsula, including the Gaza Strip. On June 11, when the UN Security Council forced a cease-fire, the Israelis were threatening Cairo and Damascus. Pressure by the United States and the Soviet Union put an end to the war.

Israel had offered King Hussein a kind of informal separate peace. But Hussein knew that he could not agree to it and survive. In the end, Jordan lost all of the West Bank and the Old City of Jerusalem. On the Syrian front the Israelis took the Golan Heights, an area that stretched about 12 miles (19 kilometers) into Syria northeast of the Sea of Galilee. (From the Golan Heights, Syrian rockets had shelled northern Israeli settlements.) Egypt lost the Gaza Strip and the Sinai Peninsula. These losses made Middle East politics more complicated after 1967, as you will read in Chapter 8.

With Egypt beaten, Nasser resigned. Though his government and his people turned down his resignation, the loss of the war was a major defeat for him. The bold victory of Israel in the Six-Day War, as it would soon be called, shocked the Middle East.

REVIEWING THE CHAPTER

I. Building Your Vocabulary

Match the terms with the words or phrases that best define them.

mandate	nationalize	coup d'état	partition
sabra	Pan-Arabism	anti-Semitism	Zionism
nonalignment	protectorate		

1. the dream of a unified Arab state

2. an order giving one country the right to rule another

3. prejudice against Jews

4. to take over a business or industry by the government

5. the sudden seizure of power by a group of individuals in authority

6. a movement to create a Jewish homeland in Palestine

7. division

8. a policy of refusing to affiliate one's country with any of the world's great powers

9. a native-born Israeli

10. a country partly controlled by another

II. Understanding the Facts

Write the letter of the word or phrase that best completes each sentence.

1. World War I spelled the end of the
   a. Ottoman Empire.   **b.** British Empire.   **c.** French Empire.

2. Ibn Saud was Saudi Arabia's
   a. founder.   **b.** last king.   **c.** sultan.

3. The Turkish Republic did all of the following *except*
   a. abolish the sultanate.   **b.** establish universal suffrage.
   c. break ties with the Soviet Union.

4. World War I left Persia
   a. in a state of chaos.   b. a modern democratic society.
   c. a major importer of British and American goods.

5. Reza Shah's close relations with Germany in World War II led
   a. Iran to enter the war on Germany's side.
   b. to his overthrow by the British and the Russians.
   c. to war with Iraq.

6. Ahmed Ben Bella was the first prime minister of the
   newly independent nation of
   a. Algeria.   b. Tunisia.   c. Morocco.

7. The Balfour Declaration was regarded by Zionists as a
   a. British statement favoring an independent Palestine.
   b. British promise to support the establishment of a Jewish state
      in Palestine.
   c. blueprint for the Israeli constitution.

8. The Holocaust resulted in
   a. the establishment of a republic in Turkey in the Middle East.
   b. an increase in Jewish immigration to Palestine.
   c. the murder of about 600,000 Jews.

9. The Free Officers' Movement was
   a. military conspiracy to free Egypt of British influence.
   b. a popular movement to establish Egypt as a democracy.
   c. a popular movement to unite Egypt and Syria.

10. The nationalization of the Suez Canal by Egypt caused
    a. Nasser's downfall.
    b. a war with France, Britain, and Israel.
    c. an end to ties with the Soviet Union.

III. Thinking It Through

1. How did British activities during World War I help to secure its position in the Middle East after the war?

2. Describe the growing importance of oil to the Middle East and the major powers after World War I.

3. Compare and contrast modernization in Iran and Turkey.

4. How was Zionism a force for nationalism in the Middle East?

5. Why was Egypt a leader in the Arab world after World War II?

ANALYZING A SECONDARY SOURCE

As you have read, Egypt has played an important role in modern Arab affairs. Under Nasser, the country became a key player on the world stage. Egypt itself underwent major changes. Read the description of Nasser below by one of his biographers. Then answer the questions that follow.

Abdel Nasser was a remarkable man. His contribution to Egypt has guaranteed him a place in history. He gave a sense of dignity and national pride to his people. . . . He planted the seeds of a modern industrial society.

The High Dam [at Aswan] and land reclamation have increased [farm lands] by more than a million acres. As a result of land reforms introduced in 1952 and 1961, about 75 percent of the [farm] land of Egypt is now owned by those who previously were forced to work for alien masters. . . .

[Nasser overcame] the attempt by Britain and France to destroy him and his revolution in 1956. He became the hero of every Arab nationalist from the Atlantic to the Indian Ocean. But if Nasser was [praised] by the masses outside as well as within Egypt, he failed to understand his fellow Arabs. Identifying himself with their longing for some form of unity, he was misled into thinking that those who waved his banner wanted to live under it. He failed to see that, with their different backgrounds, even those Arabs who shared his [views] were bound to resent being dictated to by Cairo. He found that he had grossly overrated his capacity to place Egypt's leadership upon the rest of the Arab world. . . .

Looking back over Nasser's [time], it is difficult not to conclude that he might have done still more for Egypt's welfare and prosperity if he had not tried to do so much to [gain] her supremacy in the Arab world.

For all his faults and failures, Nasser helped to give Egypt and the Arabs a sense of dignity which for him was the hall-mark of independent nationhood. As his old [rival], Ben-Gurion, was moved to say . . . . after . . . . the Six-Day War, "I have great respect for Nasser. He is a patriot who wants to do something for Egypt."

Adapted from *Nasser* by Anthony Nutting, E.P. Dutton & Co., New York, 1972.

1. Is this a fair assessment of Nasser's career? Explain.

2. Give examples of Nasser's actions to show the success and failure of his policies.

DEVELOPING CRITICAL THINKING SKILLS

Relating Cause and Effect

In each pair of sentences, identify the cause and the effect. Then explain the relationship between them.

1. **a.** Britain and France received mandates from the League of Nations.
   b. The Ottoman Empire collapsed after World War I.
2. **a.** The Turks sought Russian aid.
   b. Greek and Allied troops invaded Turkey.
3. **a.** The French built railways, hospitals, and schools in Algeria.
   b. The Algerians were aware of their lack of political power.
4. **a.** Differences between Christians and Sunnite Muslims in Lebanon had serious consequences in the 1930s.
   b. Militias formed along communal lines.
5. **a.** Britain and the United States attempted to create a defensive corridor against Soviet expansion in the Middle East.
   b. The Baghdad Pact was signed in 1955.

ENRICHMENT AND EXPLORATION

1. Investigate the career of T.E. Lawrence, the British soldier and writer who supported Arab independence. Write a report describing Lawrence's perception of Arab philosophy, motives, and attitudes. How did he influence British policies?

2. Write a report on the 1915 massacre of the Armenians by the Turks. When did the persecution begin? Why? How many were killed? What evidence is there to support the Armenians' account of the episode? Investigate the Turkish view as well.

3. Create a map of the Middle East and North Africa. Place on the map dates each country won its freedom. In which part of the Middle East did independence come early? Where did it come late? How do you account for this?

8 More Turbulent Years (1967–1989)

The Six-Day War in 1967 set off a chain of events that altered life throughout the Middle East. Some changes were immediate. Over 1.3 million Palestinians in the West Bank, East Jerusalem, and Gaza were now living under Israeli rule. Egypt, Syria, and Jordan lost not only land but also prestige. Other states now became more important in the Arab world, especially the oil-rich countries of the Persian Gulf.

Other changes were less direct. The war led to a renewal of intense religious feelings both in the Arab world and in Israel. The war also fostered political changes. There were uprisings, revolutions, and wars throughout the 1970s and 1980s. This chapter looks at some of the changes that took place in the Middle East after 1967. As you read about them, keep in mind that no two groups or even nations responded to the events of 1967 in exactly the same way, but everyone in the region was affected.

RELIGIOUS REVIVAL

As you have read, religion has always been an important force in the Middle East. In recent years, especially since the Six-Day War of 1967, many groups in the region have called for a return to traditional Islamic values and beliefs. Europeans and Americans often call these groups **fundamentalists**. It is not a term that people in the Middle East themselves use. They see themselves as restoring religion to its proper place in the world. They want governments based on religious, rather than

MORE TURBULENT YEARS

1967-1989

1967	Arab-Israeli War
1968	*Soviet Union invades Czechoslovakia.*
1969	Muammar al-Qaddaffi takes power in Libya.
1969	*First humans land on moon.*
1970	Black September in Jordan; Sadat succeeds Nasser.
1973	*Most U.S. troops are withdrawn from Vietnam.*
1973–1974	Arab-Israeli War; Arab oil embargo
1974	Civil war begins in Lebanon.
1977	Sadat visits Jerusalem.
1978	Camp David Peace Accords
1979	Egyptian-Israeli Treaty signed in Washington; Soviet invasion of Afghanistan; Muslim extremists hold the Grand Mosque in Mecca; Iranian revolution.
1980	*Deng Xiaoping comes to power in China.*
1980–1988	Iran-Iraq War
1981	Iran frees American hostages; Sadat is assassinated.
1982	Israelis withdraw from Sinai.
1983	Israel invades Lebanon.
1985	U.S. pulls out of Lebanon; Israel withdraws from Lebanon.
1985	*Gorbachev calls for major changes in Soviet Union.*
1987	Intifada begins in Gaza, the West Bank, and East Jerusalem.
1987	*U.S. imposes sanctions against South Africa.*
1989	Ayatollah Khomeini dies; Soviets leave Afghanistan.

secular, or worldly, law, and are willing to organize and, sometimes, fight to establish such governments.

Islamic Revival.   The origins of the Islamic revival may partly be a response to the West. This response rests on the idea that the Western belief in the separation of church and state has robbed the Middle East of its moral values. As you read in Chapters 6 and 7, European technological and imperial power caused tensions within the Islamic world. These tensions sometimes expressed themselves as a crisis of faith. One example of the crisis was Sufism, which sought a mystical contact with God. Another was Wahhabism, the puritanical religious movement that led to the founding of the modern nation of Saudi Arabia. Still another was the Muslim Brotherhood, which spread from Egypt throughout the region. You have read about these movements in Chapter 7.

The Islamic religion never called for Muslims to oppose everything that was not Islamic. As you read in Chapter 5, the early Muslims of Arabia absorbed into Islam many of the cultural traditions of the peoples they conquered. Some of these foreign ideas and words can be found in the Koran itself. In Islam's great days during the Middle Ages, the law guaranteed the rights of non-Muslims such as the Christians and Jews. The key factor was control. So long as Muslims ruled, they were free to choose which foreign traits were acceptable and which were not. The West's imperialism—both in a military and an economic sense—changed all of this. For the Islamic world, the imperialist age that began in the early 1800s was an unending nightmare. A return to the strict teachings of the Koran was one response to this nightmare.

The Effects of the 1967 War.   The Six-Day War also had an impact on the Islamic revival. Israel now controlled all of Jerusalem, which is one of Islam's three holy cities. The possibility that Israel could, if it wished, deny Muslims access to the Dome of the Rock, from which Muhammad is believed to have ascended to heaven, disturbed many Muslims. The very roots of their religion, they feared, were vulnerable to attack. As a result, the Arabs tried to sway public opinion among non-Arab Muslims throughout the world. The Arab states appealed to the Muslim nations of Africa, South Asia, and Southeast Asia for support. In 1970, for example, during state visits to Indonesia and Malaysia, King Faisal of Saudi Arabia stated that Palestine was a problem for all Muslims.

The 1967 war was also a blow to Pan-Arabism. The movement reached a peak between the Arab-Israeli wars of 1956 and 1967. After

Like Muslim fundamentalists in other countries,
Algerians demand a government that is run according to
Islamic principles. They scored heavily in a 1991 general
election.

the war, Pan-Arabism no longer had the appeal it once had. Instead, people looked for answers elsewhere. Many found those answers in militant Islamic groups like the Muslim Brotherhood. Most governments in the region opposed these groups. The leaders of countries like Egypt, Syria, and Iraq were nationalists who wanted to modernize their countries and make them strong and powerful. Although some were religious Muslims, they did not want to create a **theocracy,** a government run by religious authorities.

Gamal Abdel Nasser was the first to move against such groups. Though he banned the Muslim Brotherhood, he could not destroy it. In 1981, a splinter group assassinated Anwar Sadat, Nasser's successor, who had signed a peace treaty with Israel. The following year, the Syrian army put down an uprising led by the Islamic Front, a coalition of Muslim groups that included the Brotherhood. Over 5,000 people died in the fighting. Throughout the 1980s, attempts to institute Islamic law in Sudan also led to riots and uprisings. By 1989, the militants werein control in Sudan. In 1991, Muslim groups won free elections in Algeria. They would have taken control of the country, but the Algerian army stepped in and blocked them, at least temporarily. Increasingly, fundamentalism was a force to be reckoned with throughout the region.

NO WAR, NO PEACE

In the years after the Six-Day War, while the Middle East was not at war, there was no peace in the region either. The war had proved that Israel was the dominant military power in the region. But it did not resolve the conflicts that had led to the fighting. Instead, it complicated issues.

A New Mood in Israel. When the Six-Day War war ended in 1967, the Israelis were jubilant. They had won a great victory. Before 1967, only strict Zionists had mourned the fact that the land of Israel did not include many areas of religious importance to the Jewish people. After the war, however, the nation suddenly was in possession of all of historical Israel, and Israelis of many degrees of Zionist faith were determined to keep it.

From the beginning of Israel's existence as a state, David Ben-Gurion, its first prime minister, had argued that while Zionists wanted a democratic state, a Jewish state, as well as one that included all of the historical land of Israel, it was not possible to have all three. So he claimed it was better to settle for two goals—a Jewish state that was democratic—rather than risk everything in an effort to secure all three objectives.

Ben-Gurion's political opponents never accepted his argument. But his Labor party dominated the government in the years after independence. Contrary voices had little influence until after the Six-Day War, when they steadily grew in importance. In 1973, under the leadership of Menachem Begin (BAY-gin), a new party, called Likud (li-KOOD), which means "unity" in Hebrew, was formed. It consisted of a coalition of groups that were determined to retain the territory Israel had regained during the 1967 war.

The Likud party attracted members in part because Israel then faced a set of choices like those Ben-Gurion had set forth in 1948. Israel had to decide what kind of nation it wanted to be. Again, there were only two possibilities. If Israel kept all of the land it had won, it would remain a Jewish state only by becoming less democratic, since it would have to deny citizenship to its Arab population. If Israel chose to remain democratic and keep the territories, it would lose its identity as a Jewish state because so many of its people would be Arabs. A third possibility was to remain Jewish and democratic by giving up large areas of the West Bank and Gaza. That was the option Ben-Gurion, then retired, recommended. But few Israelis agreed. As long as the Palestinians refused to negotiate, most Israelis argued for holding onto the captured territories.

Some Israelis, however, wanted action. Among them were many religious Jews. In Israel, too, as in Muslim lands, the 1967 war had prompted a religious revival. A number of strictly religious groups saw the war as an act of providence. They were determined to keep all of Jerusalem. Indeed, Israelis were united on that issue, and the government annexed East Jerusalem. However, these religious militants also believed that Israel had to keep Judea and Samaria—the Biblical names for the West Bank. In early 1968, a group of religious Jews established a settlement in Hebron near the tomb of the Patriarchs (where Abraham is said to be buried). It was a site that both Arabs and Jews consider holy. In the years that followed, others joined these pioneers. More and more Jewish settlements dotted the West Bank. These religious Jews believed they were fulfilling a holy commandment.

By 1974, this religious movement had a name—Gush Emunim (goosh em-oo-NEEM), or the Bloc of the Faithful. Although few Israelis belonged to the group, many people in the nation, including some leaders of the Labor party, had mixed emotions about the settlers. The Gush Emunim reminded them of the pioneer spirit that had created the state of Israel. They also shared the settlers' feelings about the land even though some disapproved of their methods. Increasingly, Gush Emunim became a political force in Israel. Its supporters tended to back the Likud party. By 1977, the Likud party, with the help of the Gush Emunim and other religious groups, had a majority in the Knesset. The Labor party was out of power for the first time in the nation's history. Israel was changing.

The Rise of the Palestinians. Changes were also taking place among Palestinians. After the 1967 war, many Palestinians felt they could not depend on the Arab world to win back their country. So they took more

202

action on their own. A new generation of Palestinians, born in exile after 1948, came of age in the 1970s. Many of these young people had spent their lives in refugee camps in Jordan, Lebanon, and Syria. They formed militant groups that were willing to fight for independence. Now most of these united loosely into one organization—the Palestinian Liberation Organization (PLO). The Arab League had formed the group in 1964 and controlled its movements until the 1967 war. After the war, the Palestinians took control of the organization. Led by Yasir Arafat (A-ruh-fat), the PLO stepped up its raids in Israel and the territories occupied by Israel after the 1967 war. The PLO fighters realized that they could not defeat Israel in open battle. However, they believed they might force it to withdraw from the territories through constant guerrilla action, hit-and-run raids, and terrorism attacks on Israeli settled communities and busy city neighborhoods. In response, Israel hit PLO camps wherever they were located.

For the Palestinians, the PLO, based in Jordan, was a government in exile. As such, it acted independently of Arab nations. By August 1970, the PLO had turned Jordan into an armed camp. Then, the PLO,

Yasir Arafat, chairman of the Palestine Liberation Organization, speaking at the United Nations, 1974.

Israeli soldiers clearing a captured Egyptian missile base near Suez, October 1973. The Soviet Union had supplied Egypt with weapons, although President Sadat had announced the withdrawal of Soviet advisers in 1972.

to condemn Western governments' support of Israel, started hijackingEuropean and U.S. commercial airplanes and flying them to Jordan. Rejecting this challenge to his authority, King Hussein took action against the Palestinians. In mid-September, he ordered the Jordanian Army to attack the Palestinian guerrilla camps in Jordan. Palestinians called this attack Black September. Despite Syrian aid, PLO resistance was totally wiped out. Thus Hussein freed his country of a rival for power. With Egyptian and Syrian help, the PLO moved its headquarters to southern Lebanon, leaving thousands of Palestinians still in Jordan.

Attempts at Peace. As the death toll mounted on both the Palestinian and Israeli sides, the United States tried to intervene. In 1970, it persuaded Egypt, Jordan, and Israel to accept a 90-day cease-fire and to take part in negotiations that would lead to a peace treaty. Protests immediately arose throughout the region. Syria and Iraq promptly rejected the idea of peace talks. The Palestinians dramatized their opposition by carrying out a series of airplane hijackings. Israel itself withdrew from the agreement after six members of Prime Minister Golda Meir's cabinet resigned in protest. Yet another opportunity for a settlement was lost. The possibility of another war in the Middle East was becoming more likely.

The Yom Kippur War. President Nasser of Egypt died in 1970 and was succeeded by his vice-president, Anwar Sadat. Sadat did not believe that a no-war and no-peace situation was in Egypt's best interests. In 1972, Sadat set about on a new foreign policy. His plan was to convince Israel that Arabs could fight well and could regain land lost in previous wars. On October 6, 1973, the Egyptian and Syrian armies started simultaneous surprise attacks on Israel. The choice of the day was important. For Jews, October 6 of that year was Yom Kippur, their most solemn religious day. For Muslims, it was the tenth of Ramadan, the anniversary of the Prophet Muhammad's conquest of Mecca.

The surprise attack brought Egypt an immediate advantage in the Sinai Peninsula. Yet Egypt's advantage was quickly reversed after a few days of fighting. Once again, the Israelis showed their military strength. Just as the Egyptian army was about to be surrounded, the United States and the Soviet Union arranged a cease-fire to keep the Egyptians from being humiliated.

During the war, the Arab oil nations declared an oil embargo to prevent the sale of their oil to countries supporting Israel. An **embargo** is a ban on shipping. It increased U.S. efforts to end the war. In a complex series of moves, Henry Kissinger, the U.S. secretary of state, engaged in what came to be called "shuttle diplomacy." Flying back and forth for talks with Egypt and Israel, Kissinger finally helped secure a cease-fire.

The war on the Egyptian front ended on October 24, but fighting on the Syrian front continued until May 1974. The Syrians suffered great losses in the war and were not as successful as the Egyptians in the cease-fire negotiations. They regained some land lost in the 1967 war, but they did not regain the Golan Heights. A complicated buffer zone, to be policed by the UN, was set up on the Syrian-Israeli border.

The Syrian and Iraqi Responses.   The head of Syria's government who had joined in the 1973 attack on Israel was Hafez al-Assad (ahl-ah-SAHD). He had come to power in 1970 in a bloodless coup. Assad and his supporters were military officers who belonged to the Baath (BAHTH) party, the stated aim of which was to bring socialism to every part of the Arab world. The Baathists also supported Pan-Arabism, yet they believed that Syria's national interests were more important than Arab unity. In the years after 1973, Assad set out to further Syria's interests. His foreign policy reflected that aim. For military strength, Assad relied on help from the Soviet Union.

Like his predecessors, Assad supported the PLO, but only when it was in Syria's interests to do so. When it looked as if the PLO might upset the balance of power in Lebanon and reduce Syrian influence there, Assad sent troops to Lebanon to put down the opposition. Syria's chief

Governments of the Middle East and North Africa

COUNTRY	TYPE OF GOVERNMENT	HEAD OF STATE	HEAD OF GOVERNMENT	PARTY SYSTEM	VOTING AGE
Afghanistan	Republic	President	Prime Minister	Single Party	18
Algeria	Republic	President	Prime Minister	Multiparty	18
Bahrain	Monarchy (Emirate)		Emir Prime Minister	No parties	None
Cyprus	Republic	President	President	Multiparty	21
Egypt	Republic	President	Prime Minister	Multiparty	18
Iran	Islamic Republic	President and Rahbar (religious guide or leader)	President	Two party (plus minor parties)	15
Iraq	Republic	President	President	Multiparty; one party dominant	Adult
Israel	Republic (Parliamentary Democracy)	President	Prime Minister	Multiparty	18
Jordan	Constitutional Monarchy	Monarch	Monarch (assisted by Prime Minister)	No parties	20
Kuwait	Constitutional Monarchy	Emir	Emir (assisted by Prime Minister)	No parties	21[1]
Lebanon	Parliamentary Republic	President	Prime Minister	Multiparty	21[2]
Libya	Islamic Arabic Socialist "Mass-State"	Secretary of the General People's Committee	Secretary of the General People's Committee	No parties	Adult
Morocco	Constitutional Monarchy	Monarch	Monarch (assisted by Prime Minister)	Multiparty	20
Oman	Monarchy (Sultanate)	Sultan	Sultan	No parties	None
Qatar	Monarchy (with Council of Ministers)	Emir	Emir	No parties	None
Saudi Arabia	Monarchy (with Cabinet and Consultative Council)	King	King	No parties	None
Sudan	Military Dictatorship	President	President	No parties; military	Adult
Syria	Republic	President	President	Multiparty; one party dominant	18
Tunisia	Republic	President	Prime Minister	Multiparty; one party dominant	Adult
Turkey	Republic	President	Prime Minister	Multiparty	21
United Arab Emirates	Monarchy (Federation of Cmirates)	President	Prime Minister	No parties	None
Yemen	Socialist Republic	President	Prime Minister	Multiparty	18

1 males only; voting is restricted to men who resided in Kuwait before 1920 and their male descendents.
2 all men over 21; women over 21 are eligible if they have had an elementary education.

Sources: Encyclopaedia Britannica, 1991 Yearbook; Countries of the World and Their Leaders Yearbook, 1992.

Fig.6 CH 8

rivals were Egypt and Iraq. When either seemed to gain strength or influence, Syria was quick to act. Assad wanted Syria to be the major power in the region.

By the end of the 1970s, Iraq had a very similar goal to that of Syria. After years of unrest, in July 1968 a group of Iraqi officers took control of the country. Like Syria's leaders, these Iraqis also belonged to the Baath party. Yet they, too, were more moved by Iraqi nationalism than by Pan-Arabism. Like the Syrians, the Iraqis also received military aid from the Soviet Union. The two countries differed in that Iraq's leaders were not able to take an active part in foreign affairs until 1980. They were too busy fighting a civil war at home. An ethnic group known as the Kurds had been fighting for its independence for many years. Until the Kurds were subdued, Iraq would play a relatively small role in the region. Only a few Iraqi troops fought in the 1967 and 1973 wars against Israel because they were needed at home.

Iraq differed from Syria in yet another way as well. Iraq had oil, while Syria did not. As oil prices rose in the 1970s, so did the wealth and power of the Iraqi government. By 1979, the head of that government was Saddam Hussein (sah-DAHM hoo-SAYN). Increasingly, he assumed more and more power, ruthlessly putting down all opposition to his rule. Once clearly in control of Iraqi's government and economy, he turned his attention to his neighbors.

The Egyptian Response. Egypt's President Sadat was also concerned with building a strong and powerful country, but he set out to do so in a very different way from Syria and Iraq. By the late 1970s Sadat had come to realize that peace with Israel would benefit Egypt, especially since it might mean the return of most of the Egyptian land Israel had occupied since 1967.

On November 19, 1977, Sadat made a dramatic journey to Jerusalem, where he addressed the Israeli Knesset. The visit was an important step across the psychological barriers to peace. Israelis were delighted when they heard President Sadat say ". . . we really and truly welcome you to live among us in peace and security."

Less important at the time was Sadat's insistence on certain "bargaining points," such as the withdrawal of Israeli settlements on the West Bank of the Jordan River. Israeli Prime Minister Menachem Begin was a leader of the Likud party. Still, he applauded Sadat's courage in coming to Jerusalem. The PLO saw the whole trip as a shameful betrayal. Egypt was accused of seeking a separate peace and of selling out the Palestinians.

March 26, 1979. President Anwar Sadat, President Jimmy Carter, and Prime Minister Menachem Begin standing at attention during the playing of the national anthems of the three countries. What were some of the results of the Israeli–Egyptian 1979 peace treaty signed later that day?

Peace Between Egypt and Israel. When he returned to Cairo, Sadat addressed his parliament. "I feel that the barrier of suspicion, the lack of trust and confidence, has been shattered." In September 1978 Sadat and Begin met at Camp David, Maryland, with President Jimmy Carter. Out of these talks came the Camp David Peace Accords. These **accords,** or agreements, led directly to the signing of the Israeli-Egyptian peace treaty, in Washington, on March 26, 1979.

The treaty set up full relations between Egypt and Israel. The agreement called for the exchange of ambassadors. It opened up economic and cultural ties. It ended the state of war that had existed between the two countries since 1948. The treaty set a border between the two nations. Israel would return the Sinai Peninsula, which Egypt had lost in the 1967 war. The treaty also set up a framework for discussing Palestinian autonomy.

The United States encouraged peaceful relations between the two nations. Both Israel and Egypt received several billion dollars' worth of U.S. financial aid and military equipment. Egypt made its economy more attractive to foreign investors and secured an inflow of capital from Western countries. In addition, the World Bank, a development agency connected with the United Nations, gave Egypt a sizable loan.

Still, for Sadat the price for peace with Israel was high. He failed to convince the rest of the Arab world to accept the Camp David Peace Accords. As a result, Egypt lost financial aid from the oil-rich Arab states. It was also forced to leave the Arab League. Despite these problems, Sadat tried to follow a path of development within Egypt. He started a controlled multiparty system. But as economic conditions became more difficult, Sadat became less popular in Egypt. Yet Sadat enjoyed great prestige in the West. He was seen as the molder of a moderate Arab policy.

Egypt After Sadat. The growing power of militant Islamic groups challenged Sadat's regime, however. In September 1981, Sadat ordered about 1,500 Muslim extremists arrested. To put a stop to antigovernment sermons, he ordered that all mosques be placed under direct government control. A few weeks later Sadat appeared at a military parade. There, extremists gunned him down.

Hosni Mubarak (HAHS-nee muh-BAHR-uhk), Sadat's vice-president, became Egypt's new leader. As air force commander and hero of the 1973 war, Mubarak had played a key role in Sadat's regime. Mubarak kept Egypt committed to the Camp David peace process. As a result, he gained the return of the Sinai, which began on schedule in 1982. During the years since 1973, Israel had built new communities and military bases there. The Israelis had spent billions of dollars developing the Sinai Peninsula's resources, including oil. Yet the Israeli government felt it was worth giving the Sinai back to Egypt as part of the peace process.

Mubarak also put an end to the fundamentalist riots that immediately followed Sadat's death. He released political prisoners, but was cautious toward the fundamentalists. He purged the military of extremism. And he brought back Sadat's pre-September 1981 strategy. By distinguishing between peaceful and violent Islamic groups, Mubarak tried to achieve peace with the radical fundamentalists. He also sought to end Egypt's isolation from the Arab world.

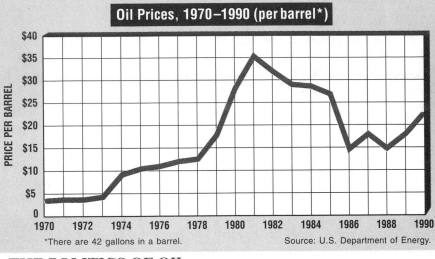

Oil Prices, 1970–1990 (per barrel*)

PRICE PER BARREL

$40
$35
$30
$25
$20
$15
$10
$5
0

1970 1972 1974 1976 1978 1980 1982 1984 1986 1988 1990

*There are 42 gallons in a barrel.   Source: U.S. Department of Energy.

THE POLITICS OF OIL

In 1973, during the October war, the Arab oil-producing countries discovered the political power of oil. As a result, Arab countries gained great influence in world affairs.

OPEC.   OPEC is a cartel that gained world attention during the 1973 war. The oil embargo resulted in a huge leap in oil prices in Europe, the United States, and Japan. Though the embargo was lifted in 1974, oil prices did not come down. OPEC had discovered its ability to have a strong influence on the world market for crude oil. Oil that had been selling for around $2 a barrel suddenly skyrocketed in price. In 1985 a barrel of oil cost almost $25.

Vast riches poured into the oil-rich states of Iran, Iraq, Libya, Algeria, and the Persian Gulf states. (The Persian Gulf states include Saudi Arabia, Kuwait, Bahrain, Qatar, Oman, and the United Arab Emirates.) In 1970, for example, Saudi Arabia received $1.2 billion from its sale of oil. The country earned $29 billion in 1974 and $101 billion in 1981. Thousands of skilled foreign workers came to work on the new construction projects and in the new industries developed in the oil-rich states. Many of these workers were Palestinians.

The great outflow of capital from the oil-importing nations brought great power to the oil-producing Arab countries. Even as the threat of an oil shortage lessened, the Arab members of OPEC used their funds to build political influence. All kinds of groups had a personal stake in OPEC because OPEC created business for everyone. Bankers, lawyers, shippers, manufacturers, scientists, and governmental agencies all sought the favor of OPEC. Its cooperation or lack of cooperation could

210

mean success or failure for an international corporation, even for a government. The power of the Arab oil producers became a key factor in international relations. Yet most Arab states had no oil. Those that have the most oil, such as Saudi Arabia, Kuwait, and Libya, have very small populations. The great oil boom of the 1970s enabled oil-rich countries like Saudi Arabia and Libya to promote Islam, although very differently.

Libya Under Qaddaffi. As you read in Chapter 6, in the years before World War I, Libya was taken by Italy from the Ottoman Empire. Libyan independence was granted in 1951, but the country kept up cultural ties with Italy. Italian laws from the colonial period continued, and non-Muslims living in Libya went about their business. In foreign affairs, Libya allowed Great Britain and the United States to keep their military bases. The Arab conflict with Israel was ignored.

In September 1969, Muammar al-Qaddaffi (moo-ah-MAHR ahl-kuh-DAH-fee) took power in Libya in a bloodless coup. Quite suddenly he ended the corrupt monarchy and started sweeping changes. He nationalized most foreign assets, including oil companies. He also expelled foreign troops and closed foreign cultural centers. Yet the nation continued to depend largely on foreign companies to help explore for oil, run the oil fields, and market oil.

At home, Qaddaffi directed money from the sale of oil to a variety of public services. The government also tried to provide a more equal distribution of income. It could do so because of its control of much of the nation's economy. Qaddaffi used oil money to build roads, airports,

Portraits of Muammar al-Qaddaffi hang on the wall of this clothing factory in Tripoli, Libya.

water ports, schools, and hospitals. The government provided low-interest loans to businesses and low-cost housing for all who needed it. Health care and education started to improve dramatically, and the standard of living reached its highest level.

Qaddaffi has often proclaimed his commitment to Islam. All laws in Libya must conform with Sharia, Islamic law. (See page 93.) But, by the mid-1970s it appeared that Qaddaffi's Islamic vision was uniquely his own. He published his ideas in a series of pamphlets called "The Green Book." (Green is a color associated with Islam because it was Muhammad's favorite color.) While he claimed to favor a democracy based on Islam, he allowed almost no democracy in his own country. Opposition to his rule was dealt with harshly, and Libyan opponents living in exile were sometimes attacked in their foreign homes.

On the international scene, Qaddaffi followed a wild, often reckless, course. As a result, Libya and the United States clashed frequently in the 1980s. In 1981, two Libyan warplanes attacked U.S. naval forces in the Gulf of Sidra off the coast of Libya. Qaddaffi claimed that the ships were violating Libyan national waters. The United States argued that the Gulf of Sidra lies well within international waters. A similar attack in 1986 ended with the loss of two Libyan ships. The U.S. government then imposed **economic sanctions** on Libya. That is, it called for a ban on trade with Libya. It also froze Libyan assets in the United States and asked all U.S. companies and workers to leave Libya.

Much of the hostility between the two nations centers around the role Qaddaffi has played in Middle Eastern affairs. Since the mid-1970s, he has given large sums of money to radical groups in Jordan, Pakistan, Egypt, Sudan, Tunisia, and Turkey in an effort to overthrow the governments of these nations. He has also been an outspoken supporter of the Palestinians. He has urged them to reject all compromises. Over the years, he has been accused of providing training camps and funds for terrorist groups.

In 1985, Qaddaffi was held responsible for terrorist attacks at airports in Rome and Vienna that killed many people, including a number of Americans. In 1986, a group he sponsored bombed a nightclub in West Berlin, killing two U.S. soldiers. In response, the United States attacked two Libyan cities with the presumed intention of killing Qaddaffi. However, Qaddaffi survived the attack and continued his support of terrorists. In 1990, Libyan agents were linked to the 1988 bombing of a commercial airliner over Lockerbie, Scotland, and Qaddaffi was condemned by the United Nations for refusing to turn the agents over to the West for criminal prosecution.

Such Western condemnation only served to strengthen Qaddaffi's support at home. Yet he became increasingly unpopular with many groups within his own country and the region. Both radicals and conservatives considered him too unpredictable to be a reliable ally.

Saudi Policy After the Oil Boom.   Like Libya, Saudi Arabia has used its oil wealth—it is the leading Arab oil exporter—to build industry and improve living conditions within the nation. It has also invested large sums of money in businesses in Europe and North America. Saudis have also used their wealth to influence foreign affairs. One of their main goals is to protect their own security. For this purpose, Saudi Arabia has spent huge sums to buy military equipment from the United States and other Western nations. Another goal has been to promote stability in the region.

During 1970s and 1980s, Saudi Arabia faced two major tests of its authority. In 1979, a group of Muslim extremists held the Grand Mosque in Mecca for two weeks. Recognizing how delicately the situation had to be handled, the government did not remove the occupiers until it had the approval of the nation's main religious leaders. In 1987, the Iranians inspired riots that disrupted the annual pilgrimage to Mecca. Over 400 people died in the fighting. The fighting was followed by explosions at Saudi oil installations. The Saudis believed the explosions were the work of Shiite workers with ties to Iran.

The Saudis responded to these threats by expanding the influence of religious authorities in affairs of state. In 1986, King Fahd emphasized the special Islamic character of his rule by adopting the title "Custodian of the Holy Places." He also granted more social and religious equality to the Shiite minority living in Saudi Arabia but limited the number of Iranians who could come to Mecca each year. At the same time, the Saudis devoted more and more of their resources to defense.

In the 1980s, Saudi Arabia used foreign aid to make new allies and reduce Soviet influence over poorer states in the Middle East. The nation has consistently opposed radical groups in the region. In the 1970s it sent troops to help put down rebellions in what was then North Yemen and in Oman. In 1979, it opposed the Camp David Accords and broke off relations with Egypt, as other Arab nations did. Yet, by late 1987, Saudi Arabia had restored relations with Egypt. It was moved to do so for two reasons. One was a deepening concern over the events in Iran that you will read about in the next section. The other was the growing Palestinian uprising in the Israeli-occupied territories. Saudi Arabia believed that Egypt could help keep peace in the region.

THE IRANIAN REVOLUTION

One of the major events of the late 1970s was a revolution in Iran. A Western ally since the early 1950s, Iran became the main center of Islamic fundamentalism. How did this happen? What impact did it have on the Middle East and the world?

Iran in the 1970s.   As you read in Chapter 7, during the Pahlavi dynasty, Iran underwent great changes. It became a modern country, but the modernization was uneven. As one of the world's largest oil producers in the 1970s, Iran benefited greatly from the oil boom. The shah of Iran was the main promoter of the first large oil price increases in the 1970s. From 1970 to 1977 Iran's gross national product jumped to an average rate of 7.8 percent. Money from oil financed a remarkable growth of investment. But not all Iranians benefited from the oil boom. The gap between rich and poor in Iran became large; and rumblings of discontent began to be heard. As the population grew, the movement of people from small villages to large towns added to social unrest. In both agriculture and industry there was a sense that too much had been tried too quickly. In foreign affairs, the shah kept up close relations with the United States. Yet he was unconcerned by the growth of a religious movement within his country. Moreover, he did not see the need for democratic reform. Instead, he continued to rule as a tyrant. He used his hated secret police and an elaborate network of informers to stamp out dissent and maintain order.

Social unrest grew in 1978. Many people were killed in demonstrations against the government. Unrest soon swept the country. In September martial law was imposed in the big cities. Shiites known as *Mujahhedin,* or "Dedicated Fighter" groups, opposed the influx of foreigners in Iran. The Western values of foreigners were held in contempt by the Mujahhedin. These extremists felt that their own Shiite values were under attack.

The Fall of the Shah.   Leading the religious opposition to the shah was Ruhollah Khomeini (koh-MAY-nee), an Islamic jurist. His honorary title was ayatollah, meaning "reflection of God." Khomeini had been in exile first in Iraq and then in France. Khomeini used his time of exile to call for the shah's abdication. With great skill, Khomeini used discontent against the Shah's policies to come to power. Relying on the country's 180,000 **mullahs,** or religious leaders, Khomeini directed a campaign against the shah from his place of exile. Khomeini's speeches were taped and smuggled into Iran. There, his supporters played them in mosques and bazaars.

In January 1979, the shah left Iran to seek medical treatment abroad. (He died in Egypt in 1980.) But the caretaker government created for the shah's absence proved unable to rule. Demonstrators took to the streets of the capital and called for Khomeini's return. Celebrations greeted the ayatollah's return from exile in February 1979.

Ayatollah Ruhollah Khomeini was Iran's spiritual and revolutionary leader. Shown here with his son, he led the fight to overthrow the shah and transform Iran into an Islamic republic. He opposed the modernization of Iran and encouraged the taking of Americans hostage in 1979.

Iranians protesting against the United States outside the U.S. embassy in Tehran during the hostage crisis, 1979.

The Islamic Republic of Iran.   In April 1979, Khomeini won a landslide victory in a referendum, making Iran an Islamic Republic. Immediately, a program was designed to increase the Islamic element in Iranian life. For example, Iran's Western-style divorce laws were repealed. Women were required to wear veils in public places. Non-Muslims were forced from government office. The school system was made to conform with Islamic law. What Khomeini and others called for was a theo-cracy, a government ruled by religious authorities.

Efforts were made to stamp out Western influence in Iran. The United States was a particular target of the new regime because of the nation's close ties to the shah. The leaders of the Islamic Republic attacked Western popular culture and tried to ban its music. Many Western-educated Iranians—especially the professionals—fled the country. Under the leadership of the Islamic Republic, opponents of the government were arrested and put to death. The regime was dominated by a sense of crisis. In November 1979, after the shah had been let into the United States for medical treatment, student supporters of the revolution took control of the U.S. embassy in Tehran. They demanded that the shah be returned to Iran for trial. They seized 66 U.S. citizens and kept 52 of them hostage until January 1981. This caused a crisis with the United States that had a major effect on the U.S. elections of 1980. After the election, the United States worked out a secret deal to sell arms to Iran in return for the freeing of the hostages.

CASE STUDY:

The Fall of the Shah of Iran

Fereydour Hoveyda was the Iranian ambassador to the United Nations under the shah. After the revolution, he wrote an account of the shah's reign. In the following passage, he describes protests against the shah in late 1978. These events took place during the Shiite holy days of Muharram, which mark the assassination and martyrdom of the Imam Hussein (see Chapter 4).

On Sunday, December 11, hundreds of thousands of people held a procession in the center of Tehran. . . . In an unprecedented development the banners fluttering above the heads of the crowd indicated not only mourning for the martyr, but also a political purpose. Huge portraits were carried high. Slogans against the Shah rippled in the wind—"Death to the Shah!" "Death to the American Cur!" "Victory is near," "Khomeini is our leader," and so on. People from all walks of life could be found in the throng. There were workers, intellectuals, merchants from the bazaar, women with or without the concealing chador, clerics in black, green, or white turbans, children, adolescents, the wealthy in European dress, the poor in rags.

Next day the people of Iran flooded on the main streets of their principal towns in millions. Except in Esfahan, where violent clashes occurred, they all showed the same calm, the same discipline, and above all the same determination. But the Shah and his advisers seem not to have realized the deep significance of these events.

The masses were demanding the departure of the Shah; Khomeini's intransigence [stubbornness] hardened; and the opposition was consolidating its strength. Yet the Shah, closeted in the palace, discussed the command of the army and studied plans which had long since been overtaken by the movements of events. It was Byzantium all over again.

Adapted from Fereydour Hoveyda, *The Fall of the Shah*. Wyndham Books, 1980.

1. What groups were opposed to the shah?
2. What was the shah's reaction to the crisis in his country?

The Soviet Invasion of Afghanistan. The loss of Iran's support seemed especially vital to the United States after the Soviet Union invaded Afghanistan in 1979. The event took on special importance because of its effect on the relationship between the United States and the Soviet Union.

The Soviets claimed to be acting defensively when they sent more than 100,000 troops to Afghanistan. They said they were securing their own borders by supporting a communist government caught up in a civil war. The United States saw the move as an aggressive act. The situation led to a major disagreement between the two nations in the early 1980s. By 1988, however, the two sides in the civil war had reached a stalemate. That year the Soviets began to withdraw their troops. By February 1989, the last Soviet soldier had left Afghanistan. Fighting between different Afghan groups, however, continued. To the surprise of many, the Afghan communists managed to keep control of the country long after the Soviets were gone.

The Iran-Iraq War. In September 1980, Iran's civil disorder made the country seem vulnerable. Iraq decided to take advantage of that vulnerability by invading Khuzistan, Iran's southwestern oil-producing province. Reflecting an age-old rivalry between the two powers, Iraq believed it could make quick territorial gains at its neighbor's expense. It also wanted to stop the Iranians from supplying the Kurds in Iraq with military weapons.

Iran's army proved more capable than Saddam Hussein, Iraq's leader, expected. Iran's Khomeini government, appealing to religious fervor, recruited many volunteers, including young teenagers, to fight on the Iraqi front. Boys were told that a beautiful afterlife was theirs if they died for their country. In 1982, the Iranians took the offensive and threatened Iraqi territory. Though their troops did not get very far, they rejected a UN resolution in 1983 calling for a cease-fire. In 1984, the United States condemned Iraq's use of chemical warfare. Iraq denied having used such weapons.

In 1984 Iraq agreed to a UN cease-fire resolution and to peace proposals by Islamic groups. Iran turned down these efforts. Instead, it called for the ouster of Iraq's government as a precondition for peace. For a time, it looked as if Iraq might be defeated economically rather than militarily since the fighting cut off Iraqi oil shipments through the Persian Gulf.

Saddam Hussein survived by calling for aid from other Arab states, many of whom feared the spread of Iran's Islamic revolution. By the end of 1987, Hussein had received about $60 billion from Saudi Arabia and other countries along the Persian Gulf. He used the money to buy weapons from the Soviet Union and Western Europe. The United States and the Soviet Union tried to stay neutral, fearing the consequences of victory by either side. But by early 1988, the United States was finding it harder to stay out of the war. Its warships were used to escort Kuwaiti oil tankers carrying Iraqi cargoes through the Persian Gulf.

Now almost completely isolated, Iran was desperate. Only Iraq's enemies, Israel and Syria, offered it support. With no hope of winning the war, the ayatollah's government turned to the United Nations for a settlement. In August 1988, a cease-fire was arranged, and the war, which cost hundreds of thousands of lives on both sides, finally ended. Saddam Hussein hailed the war as an Iraqi victory. In fact, it was not. Although he had managed to recover some territory in early 1988, his nation's economy was in ruins. Many wondered what he might do to restore Iraq's fortunes.

CRISIS IN LEBANON

The years between 1975 and 1991 in Lebanon were marked by a civil war that was one of the most destructive in recent history. Tens of thousands of Lebanese were killed in the fighting, and economic losses were enormous. When the war appeared to have ended in 1991, the peace was so fragile that it seemed as though the war might erupt again at any moment. The origins of the civil war went back many years and were extremely complex.

Lebanon to 1975. Following the end of the French mandate in 1941 and the establishment of an independent parliamentary democracy in 1943 (see Chapter 7), Lebanon seemed to have achieved prosperity. Located on a beautiful corner of the Mediterranean, its capital, Beirut, became a popular spot for vacationing Middle Easterners. It was also a major banking center for the region. Despite a civil war in 1958, when U.S. Marines first intervened in Lebanon, it seemed to be on a stable course. Furthermore, the country managed to remain neutral during the Arab-Israeli wars of 1956 and 1967.

The calm in Lebanon was only on the surface, however. From independence on, major changes were taking place. The most important was urbanization. After Lebanon became independent, about 40 percent of the people moved to Beirut. Before long four out of five Lebanese were living in cities. Beirut reflected the lack of unity of the country as a whole. Each district of the city took on its own religious identity, reflecting the Muslim and Christian mix of the people. The well-off, middle class in Beirut and other cities were mostly Christians and Sunnite Muslims. The poorer people, mostly in the south and in rundown sections of the cities, were Shiite Muslims. They were the most politically powerless group in the country.

The immediate trigger of the civil war was the new role of the Palestinians in Lebanon. After the 1970 Black September period in Jordan, the Palestinians saw Lebanon as their last refuge. By 1973 about one person in ten in Lebanon was Palestinian. Landless and poor, Palestinian workers identified with Lebanon's rural poor, who were mostly Muslim. With Egypt on the road to peace with Israel, the Palestinians believed their cause would soon be forgotten by the Arab world and that they would be suppressed.

The Civil War, 1974–1976. Although the National Pact of 1943 lasted for more than 30 years, the militias founded in the 1930s never broke up. As you recall, militias in Lebanon were really private armies. The arrival of Palestinians increased the number of Muslims in Lebanon. Even without the Palestinians, Muslims had become the majority in Christian-dominated Lebanon. Non-Muslims felt their political position was threatened.

When the Palestinians began to use Lebanon as a base of operations against Israel, Lebanese politics entered a crisis. Sunnites supported these operations. Christians were generally opposed to them. Frustrated by the political stalemate, the Muslims felt that legal means could not bring results, so they decided to abandon the National Pact. The Muslims believed the National Pact had given the Christians a permanent position of superiority in the country's political affairs.

Increasing activity by the militias led to the unofficial partition of Lebanon into Christian and Muslim regions. Thus, the factions returned to their pre-1943 positions. The Christians—especially one faction in the south—moved toward greater cooperation with Israel. The Muslims worked for a greater voice in Lebanese affairs.

In 1975 and 1976, the country was torn apart by intense fighting. The government almost ceased to exist. The army, made up of all religious groups, proved unable to restore order. During the summer of 1976, the Israelis invaded and occupied much of southern Lebanon. Israeli leaders said this was to prevent continued Arab attacks across the

Beirut, Lebanon, 1978. It is estimated that 600,000 to 900,000 people fled the country during the civil war from 1974 to 1976.

border against Israeli towns and villages. From the east, about 20,000 Syrian soldiers and 450 tanks crossed the Syrian-Lebanese border.

The result of these invasions was the partition of the country along the Green Line. This line passed through the center of Beirut, dividing the city from east to west along the main road to Damascus. By the end of November 1976 most of the fighting had come to an end.

Renewed Tensions. In mid-March 1978, Israel invaded southern Lebanon again. The stated purpose was to destroy Palestinian military bases. Israel also wanted to pressure the Lebanese government to limit PLO raids into Israel. Eventually, a small UN force replaced the Israeli force. But Israel continued to supply arms and money to the Christians in the south.

The continued fighting among the various factions damaged the prestige of Lebanon's leaders. Only the Phalangist (fuh-LAN-jist) party, backed by a right-wing Christian coalition, appeared to have any real strength. This alarmed Syria. To counter the success of the Phalangists, the Syrians supported an opposing coalition of Palestinians and Muslim leftists. No solution appeared to lessen the bitterness caused by hatred, mistrust, and the continued loss of life.

The Israeli Invasion of 1982.   On June 6, 1982, Israel launched a massive invasion of Lebanon. The purpose was now to wipe out the PLO in Lebanon and set up a friendly government on Israel's northern border. The Israelis announced a limited invasion of southern Lebanon. But then the Israeli army continued marching north to Beirut. In the long run, it proved a costly mistake for all involved.

At first, Israel's plan seemed successful. Syrian forces were defeated. The PLO retreated to West Beirut. The Arab states did little but protest. From late June to August the Israelis hesitated to attack the PLO in the crowded streets of West Beirut. Instead, they blockaded the area and bombed it from afar in an effort to force the PLO and Syrian troops to leave the city. The siege of Beirut became a world media event. The suffering it caused put Israel in a bad light. Many supporters of Israel became critical of Israeli Prime Minister Begin's policy.

Children biking in a Palestinian refugee camp in Beirut, 1985. Many buildings had been destroyed by fighting between Christian militia and Palestinian fighters.

Through diplomatic efforts by the United States, a solution was reached. A peacekeeping force of U.S., French, and Italian troops went to Lebanon to oversee a cease-fire. Members of the PLO were forced to leave Beirut and sent to other Muslim countries. Thus, Israel appeared to have succeeded in its policy of breaking the power of the PLO. But Israel's attempt to create a stable government in Lebanon proved far more difficult.

After West Beirut was occupied by the Israelis, the Lebanese Phalangists killed about a thousand Muslim Palestinians in two refugee camps. The act was meant as revenge for the assassinatiion of the Christian Lebanese president. Israel's investigation found no direct Israeli involvement, but it did criticize high Israeli officials. The high loss of life caused by the Phalangists' attack on the camps cost Israel some of its support.

The Continuing Cycle of Violence. Although the Israeli invasion of Lebanon was a military success, it proved very costly. Israel's continued presence in Lebanon radicalized Shiite supporters of the Iranian revolution. In 1983, a radical suicide mission destroyed the U.S. embassy in Beirut. This was followed, in October, by more terrorist attacks.

One attack killed 58 French soldiers. Another attack destroyed the barracks of the U.S. Marine peacekeeping force, killing 237 Americans. Following these terrorist incidents, U.S. troops were pulled out of Lebanon. Israeli forces began their pullout in 1985.

After the U.S. and Israeli withdrawals, the major power in Lebanon was Syria. By 1992, a Syrian-backed government controlled Lebanon, and Syrian troops helped it maintain order. Syrian president Assad wanted to make Lebanon part of "Greater Syria," as it was before the French mandate.

The degree to which Syria controls the country could be seen in the 1991 release of Western hostages held by various extremist groups in Lebanon. UN representatives worked closely with the Syrian government to accomplish the release of the hostages. They also worked with Iran, which continues to influence many Shiite groups in Lebanon. The Lebanese government played only a small role in the negotiations.

The Growing Influence of the Palestinians. The Palestinians were deeply involved in the civil war in Lebanon. By 1989, they had reestablished their bases in southern Lebanon so that they could continue their attacks on Israel. At the same time, the PLO pursued its goals through diplomatic action. The PLO was not, however, a united group. It was an uneasy coalition of factions, some of which were very radical. The divisions within the PLO made it difficult for the group to follow a single course of action. Terrorist attacks by extremists often undid the efforts of Palestinian diplomats. Still, Yasir Arafat managed to win support from many countries in Asia and Europe. He moved in this direction in 1988 when he announced that the PLO recognized Israel's right to exist and renounced the use of terrorism.

Many wondered what the Palestinians' next step would be. Few expected it to come from the people of the West Bank and Gaza. Yet it was Palestinians in these Israeli-held territories who launched a strategy that held the world's attention for months. On December 9, 1987, Palestinians throughout Gaza took to the streets to protest the death of four Palestinians. The four had been killed the day before when their truck was rammed by an Israeli-driven car. Within a day, the rioting had spread to the West Bank and East Jerusalem. Soon the protest grew into a continuing series of stone-throwing attacks by Palestinian men and boys on Israeli soldiers that became known as the **intifada** (in-tuh-FAH-duh), or uprising.

In the uprising known as the intifada, Palestinians in Israeli–held territories attacked Israeli troops with rocks and slashed the tires of Israelis. The intifada resulted in the deaths of hundreds of Palestinians and many Israelis.

No single event caused the intifada. It was the result of 20 years of tight military rule by Israel in the occupied territories. Although Israel never annexed Gaza or the West Bank as it had Jerusalem, it seemed clear to many Palestinians that Israel had no intention of giving up either territory. Year by year, there were more and more Israeli settlements in the occupied zones. The Palestinians were increasingly frustrated and angry with Israel's attitude toward the territories and with their own dismal economic conditions. The intifada in its early days reflected that anger and frustration.

Palestinian leaders quickly realized that the intifada could be their strongest weapon against Israel. It kept the Palestinian problem on the front pages of every major newspaper in the world. It also increased sympathy for their cause. Most importantly, they hoped that the prospect of fighting the intifada for years to come would change the way Israelis viewed the territories. A cycle of Palestinian protests followed by harsh responses by Israeli soldiers continued through the early 1990s. It led to the deaths of hundreds of Israelis and Palestinians.

The uprising placed considerable pressure on Israel. It also placed pressure on others in the region. Soon after the intifada began, King Hussein of Jordan responded to the uprising by giving up all claims to the West Bank, leaving it free for the Palestinians to claim. Hussein's move surprised the Israelis. They had considered him their best hope of achieving some kind of settlement of the territories without dealing directly with the PLO. Israel had refused all along to negotiate with the PLO, which only reluctantly had accepted Israel's right to exist as a state and still followed a policy of terrorism. The government believed further that negotiations would in effect recognize the legitimacy of the Palestianians' claim to the occupied territories.

The PLO also felt pressure. The group had not planned the intifada, nor could its leaders control the movement. If the PLO were to continue to represent the interests of all Palestinians, it had to make progress toward a Palestinian homeland.

REVIEWING THE CHAPTER

I. **Building Your Vocabulary**

Write the word or words that complete each of the sentences below.

intifada	cartel	theocracy
guerrilla	attrition	embargo

1. A government ruled by religious authorities is considered a(n) _____.

2. A combination of commercial groups working together to limit competition is a(n) _____.

3. A war in which one side tries to wear down the other is called a war of _____.

4. A fight that uses hit–and–run tactics rather than open battles is called _____ warfare.

5. A ban on shipments to a country is called a(n) _____.

II. **Understanding the Facts**

Write the letter of the word or phrase that best completes or answers each of the following.

1. The 1967 Arab-Israeli war dealt a blow to
   a. the United States.   b. Muslim religious groups.
   c. Pan-Arabism.

2. After the 1967 war, the PLO decided to
   a. settle in Lebanon.   b. step up guerrilla raids in Israel.
   c. recognize Israel.

3. Israelis regarded the land they won in the Six-Day War as
   a. a bargaining point in working out a peace agreement.
   b. land that was rightfully theirs.
   c. land of interest to no one in the region.

4. Egypt's performance in the 1973 Yom Kippur War allowed Sadat to
   a. resign.   b. seek a settlement with Israel.
   c. seek aid from the Soviet Union.

5. As a result of the Camp David Accords,
   a. Egypt and Israel signed a formal treaty.
   b. the PLO was invited to participate in negotiations with Israel and Egypt.
   c. President Anwar Sadat gained popularity in the Arab world.

6. In 1970, Jordan's King Hussein regarded the PLO as a group
   a. he respected and admired.
   b. that was trying to take control of his country.
   c. he wanted to keep in Jordan for as long as possible.

7. Israel invaded Lebanon in 1982 because it hoped to
   a. annex the nation.   b. stop the civil war there.
   c. end raids by Palestinians in southern Lebanon.

8. After the fall of the shah in Iran,
   a. an Islamic republic was proclaimed.
   b. Khomeini went into exile in France.
   c. a caretaker government succeeded in transforming the country into a democracy.

9. Iran received help in its war with Iraq from all of the following countries *except*
   a. Syria.   b. Saudi Arabia.   c. Israel.

10. Iraq received help in its war with Iran from all of the following countries *except*
    a. Kuwait.   b. Saudi Arabia.   c. Israel.

III. Thinking It Through

1. How was the Islamic religious revival a response to European imperalism?

2. What effect did the Israeli capture of Jerusalem have on
   a. the Muslim world?   b. Jews?

3. a. What are OPEC's goals?   b. To what extent has OPEC succeeded in meeting those goals?

4. Contrast Libya's foreign policy with that of Saudi Arabia.

5. What strategy did Khomeini use to topple the shah of Iran?

DEVELOPING CRITICAL THINKING SKILLS

Identifying Cause and Effect

Identify at least one cause and one effect of each of the following events.

1. the Islamic revival
2. the Gush Emunim movement
3. the increasing independence of the PLO
4. Black September
5. the 1973 Yom Kippur War
6. the Camp David Accords
7. the intifada
8. the Israeli invasion of Lebanon
9. the Islamic Republic of Iran
10. the Iran-Iraqi War

INTERPRETING A CHART

The chart on page 206 outlines the governments of the Middle East as of 1992. Study the chart and answer the following questions.

1. What kind of government did Jordan have?
2. Who was the head of Morocco's government?
3. In which country was an election most likely to involve several political parties: Libya, Kuwait, or Turkey?
4. What is the title of the head of the government in Israel?
5. What is unique about Iran's government?

ENRICHMENT AND EXPLORATION

1. Use an encyclopedia to research the recent history of one country in the Middle East that was not discussed in detail in this chapter. How have the key events described in this chapter affected that nation?
2. Plan a television interview with a major figure in the Middle East. Plan questions that focus on current affairs as they relate to the person interviewed and his or her country. Have someone role–play that figure and present the interview to the class.
3. Debate the Israeli-Palestinian conflict with a classmate.

9 The Middle East and the World (1989–Present)

The 1990s began with dramatic changes in the world. First, the great empire that the Soviet Union had built in Eastern Europe crumbled. Then the Soviet Union itself disappeared. In its place were more than a dozen competing republics. With the Soviet Union's collapse, the rivalry between the United States and the Soviet Union came to an end. The Cold War that had defined world affairs since World War II was over.

The Middle East, like other regions of the world, had to adjust to this new reality. Nations there took a hard look at their alliances and re-evaluated their foreign policies. Some saw opportunities in the new world order. One of the first to do so was Iraq. It shattered many long-held beliefs in the Middle East, as you will read.

WAR IN THE PERSIAN GULF

On August 2, 1990, Iraq invaded Kuwait (koo-WAYT), its small neighbor that lies between it and the Persian Gulf. Within six hours, Iraq had seized the nation's capital. The Kuwaiti ruler and his family fled to Saudi Arabia as Iraq's president, Saddam Hussein, proclaimed that Kuwait was now the "nineteenth province" of Iraq.

On the Way to War. In 1990, Iraq was the main military power in the Persian Gulf, as a result of its long war with Iran. During the war, Iraq had built one of the largest armies in the world and one of the best equipped. After the war ended in 1988, the Iraqis continued to add to their stock of weapons. They did so even though the nation owed $80 billion to other Gulf states and to the United States, Japan, and various European nations.

THE MIDDLE EAST AND THE WORLD

1989-Present

1989	Ayatollah Khomeini dies.
1989	*Chinese student demonstrations in Tiananmen Square are crushed.*
1989–1990	*Communist governments fall throughout Eastern Europe. Cold War ends.*
1989–1990	Massive immigration of Soviet Jews to Israel begins.
1990	*Nelson Mandela is released from South African prison.*
1990	Iraq invades Kuwait.
1990	*Germany is reunited.*
1991	Persian Gulf War; release of Western hostages in Lebanon
1991	*Soviet Union collapses.*
1991	*South Africa abandons apartheid policy.*
1991–1992	Israelis and Arabs take part in Middle East peace talks. Arab states woo Central Asian republics.
1992	Saudi Arabia liberalizes its government.

Saddam Hussein had hoped that oil sales would enable him not only to pay for his military expansion but also to help discharge Iraq's debts. However, when oil prices fell in the late 1980s, he was quick to place the blame on neighboring countries. In May 1990, Hussein accused Kuwait of deliberately keeping oil prices low by overproducing in violation of agreements reached by the OPEC nations. In July, he charged that Kuwait was stealing Iraqi oil by drilling at a slant across the border between the two nations. He demanded $2 billion in payment. He also announced that Iraq would not repay the loans it had received from Kuwait during the Iran-Iraq War.

Kuwait was ready to negotiate these differences with Iraq, when Hussein increased his demands. Now he claimed that Kuwait had no right to the Gulf islands of Bubiyan (boo-bee-YAHN) and Warba (WAHR-buh). Both, he said, were part of Iraq. The dispute over ownership of the islands had been a long-standing one between the two countries.

The Kuwaitis left a meeting with the Iraqis on August 1 believing that negotiations had just begun. But the next day Saddam sent his armies into Kuwait. The Iraqi army quickly overwhelmed the Kuwaitis and began a campaign of destruction and looting that alarmed and dismayed the outside world. A number of Kuwaitis, most of them in the resistance, were rounded up. Some of them were tortured and slain; others were shipped to prisons in Iraq. The Kuwaiti government later alleged that the Iraqis had killed about 1,000 people. Iraqi occupation forces also severely damaged Kuwait's water, electrical, and telephone services. They stole billions of dollars' worth of gold from Kuwaiti banks and removed billions of dollars in goods from Kuwaiti stores and shipped them to Iraq.

The Iraqi attack was part of Saddam's goal to dominate the Persian Gulf and even the Arab world. Saddam did not believe that the other Gulf states would challenge an invasion of Kuwait. He knew that they, too, were angry with Kuwait's refusal to honor OPEC agreements. He felt that other Arab nations were even less likely to come to Kuwait's aid. After all, many resented the way the Kuwaitis displayed their wealth. He was equally confident that the United States and other Western nations would not take action, either, especially now that the Soviets posed no threat in the region. So Hussein felt he had nothing to lose and everything to gain when he ordered the invasion of Kuwait.

The Arab Response.   Saddam clearly miscalculated. Without exception, the Arab nations were outraged. The invasion of Kuwait marked the first time in modern history that one Arab state had invaded another. On August 10, 1990, Egypt held a special meeting of the Arab League to deal with the crisis. The leaders who gathered in Cairo were united in their condemnation of Iraq. They disagreed only on how to respond to the invasion. Jordan, Yemen, Libya, Algeria, and the PLO insisted that the problem must be settled within the Middle East by the people of the Middle East. Saudi Arabia and Egypt disagreed. They believed that outside help was critical.

Indeed, Saudi leaders had already asked the United States to send troops to defend Saudi Arabia, free Kuwait, and ultimately destroy Saddam Hussein's army. The Saudis had the backing of the other Gulf states. It was an extraordinary request. Countries that had long opposed the United States as what they had called "an imperialistic supporter of Zionism" were now asking the Americans for protection against another Arab nation. Jordan, Yemen, and the PLO could not accept the Saudis' solution. Therefore, they refused to support the **coalition,** or alliance, that was forming in response to the invasion.

Response from Abroad. World reaction to the invasion was swift. Led by the United States, one nation after another condemned Iraq. The UN Security Council passed a resolution demanding an immediate Iraqi withdrawal. It had the support not only of the United States but also of the Soviet Union. Although no UN member nation wanted another war in the Middle East, none was willing to allow Iraq to control the Persian Gulf. They feared Iraq would hold the largest oil reserves in the world up for ransom. The Middle East has over 65 percent of the world's known oil reserves. Nearly half of those reserves are in Saudi Arabia and Kuwait, both of which border on Iraq.

On August 6, the UN General Assembly imposed **economic sanctions** on Iraq. UN members agreed not trade or conduct other business with Iraq. Two days later, the first U.S. troops arrived in Saudi Arabia. Their mission was to defend Saudi Arabia against further Iraqi aggression. They were quickly joined by soldiers from Britain, France, Italy, Egypt, Syria, and the other Gulf states. These forces operated under the code-name Desert Shield.

Peace Efforts. As troops from 28 countries gathered in Saudi Arabia, a number of nations tried to act as peacemakers. The Soviet Union was among them. But as its power declined, so did its influence over the region. Leaders in the Middle East, such as King Hussein of Jordan, also tried repeatedly to find a way to avoid war. They, too, failed.

Iraq did respond to the peacemakers. Saddam Hussein offered to withdraw from Kuwait if the Israelis agreed to pull out of the West Bank and Gaza. It was an attempt to lure Arab states away from the coalition by turning the conflict into a war against Israel. The coalition, however, held firm. Feelings against Hussein ran high after he ordered U.S. and British nationals in Kuwait to be taken as hostages to Iraq. There, he declared, they would be held as "human shields" in locations that were likely targets of attacks.

Meanwhile, the Desert Shield buildup continued, as did pressure on Iraq. On November 29, the UN called on Iraq to release the hostages and withdraw from Kuwait by January 15, 1991. If it did not do so, force

An Israeli father and his son after an Iraqi Scud missile smashed into their Tel Aviv home in the Persian Gulf War. Israel agreed not to retaliate against Iraq for missile attacks in order to sustain the coalition against Saddam.

Like the father and son in the picture on the previous page, this mother and her child were bombed out of their home in the Gulf War. Baghdad was heavily damaged by allied air attacks in the war.

would be used. On December 6, Hussein let the hostages go. Chances for peace seemed brighter, but Iraq was firm in its refusal to give up Kuwait. A January 1991 meeting between James Baker, the U.S. secretary of state, and Tariq Aziz, Iraq's foreign minister, ended in a stalemate. War now seemed inevitable.

Operation Desert Storm. By January 1991 over 460,000 coalition forces had been assembled in Saudi Arabia and about 330,000 Iraqi troops were on alert in or near Kuwait. The Iraqis were deployed in a "sword and shield" defense. That meant that coalition forces would have to fight through the border fortifications—the shield—only to face the elite Iraqi Republican Guard tank units—the sword. But the coalition planned to use air power to weaken Iraq and cut off its forces in and around Kuwait before launching a ground assault. The offensive called Operation Desert Storm began on January 16, 1991.

For 40 days, bombs lit up the skies over Iraq and Kuwait. Iraqi military targets along the front suffered heavy damage. Baghdad and other Iraqi cities were also hit. The Iraqis responded by firing Soviet-made Scud missiles at cities in Israel and Saudi Arabia. The Iraqis hoped the attacks on Israel would pull that country into the fighting. If Israel entered the war, Hussein was sure, the Arabs would leave the coalition. Israel, however, refused to retaliate, and the coalition stood firm.

As the coalition prepared for a ground war, members gave Iraq one more chance to pull out of Kuwait. There was no reply. On February 24, the coalition launched the ground war. The sweeping ground attack quickly flushed Iraqi forces out of Kuwait. Just 100 hours later, the war was over.

A BITTER PEACE

Although Hussein agreed to a cease-fire, his forces set about 600 of Kuwait's oil wells on fire before they left the country. More than 100 oil wells were partially damaged and gushed out of control. The cease-fire terms required Hussein to pay for the repairs of these wells.

At home, Hussein faced a civil war led by Shiite Muslims in the south and Kurds in the north. The coalition hoped that the unrest in Iraq would lead to Hussein's overthrow. It did not. Hussein put down the revolts at home and strengthened his grip on the nation. Despite further air attacks by the Allied coalition when Hussein failed to meet cease-fire terms, he remained in power. Many people in the west regarded the failure to remove Hussein as a major failure.

The Kurds of northern Iraq were among those who suffered the most as a result of the Gulf War. Saddam Hussein had long attacked these people, who wanted an independent country of their own.

When Iraq invaded Kuwait, a Saudi official remarked bitterly, "Pan-Arabism is dead, and so are its supporters." A Palestinian who served in the Jordanian government told reporters, "Whatever Saddam did, right or wrong, has brought to the surface many of the hidden feelings and hidden conflicts within Arab societies." Those feelings did not disappear when the war ended. Instead, they seemed to grow stronger.

Differing Views.   To Westerners, the war was fought over two issues. The first was a moral issue. A large country with a huge army had invaded a small defenseless nation in peacetime. It was this action that had led President Bush to call Hussein "a Hitler." The second issue was economic. The West was not willing to let Hussein control the world's supply of oil. To the people of the Gulf states, the issues were equally clear-cut. The Iraqis had to be stopped before they took over all six Gulf nations. To other Arabs, the issue was far more complicated.

Millions of Arabs throughout the Middle East admired Saddam Hussein not as a person but as a symbol. A Jordanian journalist wrote,

> Even though most Arabs don't support the invasion of Kuwait, Saddam Hussein's fearlessness in standing up to our enemies, Israel and America, appeals to a new spirit of the Arab world—a spirit that says, "We'd rather die on our feet than live groveling [cringing] on the ground."

Hussein was cheered even in nations that supported the coalition, including his recent enemy, Iran. At the same time, few people in the region had much sympathy for Kuwait. Although the Kuwaitis had given or loaned large sums of money to countries throughout the region, people regarded them with hostility and envy.

The Persian Gulf States.   Kuwait is one of the six oil-rich nations of the Persian Gulf. They are the richest nations in the region even though they are the poorest in every resource but one—oil. It is a resource they are determined to protect. In 1981, during the Iran-Iraq War, Saudi Arabia, Kuwait, the United Arab Emirates, Bahrain, Qatar, and Oman banded together to form the Gulf Cooperative Council (GCC). Tiny in population and led by conservative royal families, the six have much in common. For one thing, they are all vulnerable to attack. In the 1980s, they feared a possible attack not only from Iran but from internal radical Arab groups as well. Iraq's invasion of Kuwait in 1990 heightened their anxieties. None was strong enough to protect itself from Iraq—not even Saudi Arabia, the most powerful of the six.

Saudi Arabia's Stake in Peace.   Saudi Arabia has two important sources of income. One comes from the annual *hajj*, or pilgrimage, to Mecca. Each year, two million pilgrims converge on the holy cities of Mecca and Medina for between two and six weeks.

The other source of income for Saudi Arabia is its oil. It is critical to the nation's political and economic stability. When oil prices are high, the country prospers, and there is little disagreement in the nation. When oil prices are low, however, the kingdom is far less stable. For example, in the 1980s, falling oil prices and declining production cut Saudi earnings from $102 billion in 1980 to $28.5 billion in 1986. As revenues fell, the Saudis tried to cut spending. In a country where almost all economic development is created by the government, this decline had serious consequences.

Saudi Arabia is trying to balance modern and Islamic ways. It combines the world's most modern technological advances with a very strict interpretation of Islamic law. For example, the Saudis spend huge sums building up-to-date medical and engineering schools. The nation's solar-energy technology (coordinated with the U.S. Department of Energy) ranks with the best in the world. At the same time, the Saudis also strive to preserve their Islamic heritage. Religious leaders have considerable power in the kingdom.

Saudi Arabia changed enormously as the kingdom has developed its oil fields. Education is one example of those changes. In 1950, there were virtually no college graduates in the kingdom and few high school graduates, all of whom were men. Women could not attend school.

Within ten years, thousands of students were being educated in schools that included a number of newly built universities. Thousands of others were studying in the United States and Europe. Among the students were hundreds of girls and young women. Still, even though Saudi Arabia, like other Gulf nations, has a serious shortage of workers, women do not have many opportunities to use their training. They can work only in segregated schools, offices, and businesses. They are not permitted to deal directly with men who are not family members.

In 1992, King Fahd took a significant step in the direction of liberalizing the government. Yielding to the Saudi middle class and members of the royal family who had been educated in the West, he announced a new written constitution. Also influencing the king was a new spirit in Saudi Arabia that followed the Iraqi invasion of Kuwait and the presence of foreign troops in the country.

The new plan of government decentralized power, which had been in the hands of the ruling family, and provided for a bill of rights for the

Saudis in traditional clothing at an audio and video electronics store in Riyadh.

first time. A new system by which future kings were to be chosen made it possible for younger members of the royal family to succeed to the throne. The reform set up a Consultative Council of 60 Saudi citizens to advise the cabinet and suggest new laws. Although the king was careful to state that the changes were based on the Koran and the Sharia, the new bill of rights banned a number of human rights violations that had been carried out by religious extremists. These had included raiding and searching people's homes and arresting people who held parties or danced to loud music. The new laws restricted the right of the government to arrest, punish, and spy on its citizens. Steps to protect individual liberties were also expected to benefit women, who had been harshly criticized by Islamic fundamentalists for such practices as eating in public restaurants and patronizing shopping centers.

Kuwait and the Other Smaller Gulf States.   The other Gulf states are much smaller than Saudi Arabia, but they face similar problems. The United Arab Emirates is a loose federation of seven sheikhdoms. Abu Dhabi (AH-boo DAH-bee), the country's capital, accounts for 90 percent of its land, 75 percent of its oil, and half of its population. Just 30 years ago, the city was a mud-brick fishing village. Soon after oil was discovered, it was transformed into a bustling, modern city. Today, Abu Dhabi has wide avenues, palaces, and high-rise apartment buildings. The city also has cheap huts for its largely immigrant labor force.

238

CASE STUDY:
The Problems of Oil Wealth

The decline in oil revenues in the mid-1980s created a number of social and economic problems for countries that had come to rely on the oil boom of the 1970s.

Most people in Saudi Arabia live . . . in drab, prefabricated apartment buildings on treeless streets. They are not rich by Western standards. Half the Saudi population eats little meat and lives in unsanitary housing. More than three quarters are illiterate. [By the mid-1980s, illiteracy had been reduced to about 50 percent.] Disease is rampant, infant mortality is high, and life expectancy is low. Saudi oil revenues are about $15,000 to $20,000 per capita, but personal income is only a fraction of this. Most of the revenues go for foreign labor, foreign goods, and foreign investments. . . .

To [ease] the high cost of living, the government provides a wide range of subsidies. The state pays premium [high] wages and collects minimal [very small] rents on its properties. It sells goods, especially food, at below cost, and charges only a fraction of the market price for energy. Bus and plane fares are subsidized. The state covers medical expenses and student fees. It assists almost every commercial or agricultural venture with inexpensive land and interest-free loans. The Saudi government helps young couples to marry, by paying $7,000 toward a woman's bride-price. Citizens have come to depend on subsidies to smooth the way for virtually every endeavor. They may turn against the government if the supports are withdrawn.

Foreign workers are perhaps the greatest potential source of danger for the sheikhdoms. They constitute . . . 60 percent in Saudi Arabia . . . . With rare exceptions, however, foreign workers cannot become citizens (in Saudi Arabia that requires a special royal decree) and do not enjoy the easy life of the native-born. They earn lower wages, lack full legal rights, and are excluded from the political process.

Source: Daniel Pipes, "The Middle East: The Curse of Oil Wealth," *The Atlantic*, July 1982, pp. 19-25.

1. How did Saudi Arabia use some of its oil wealth for its citizens?
2. Why are foreign workers a potential danger to the oil sheikhdoms?

Bahrain (bah-RAYN) is an **archipelago,** or chain of islands, about 13 miles (21 kilometers) off the coast of Saudi Arabia. The country consists of the large island of Bahrain and some 33 tiny coral islands. Before oil was discovered in 1932, its main industry was pearl diving. About two thirds of Bahrain has no fresh water and most of the country's soil is not suited to farming. As a result, the country relies heavily on imports. The same is true of Qatar (KAH-tuhr) and Oman (oh-MAHN).

Kuwait is also a small nation—about the size of New Jersey. Like the others, it would be a very poor nation without oil. Oil revenues have helped turned Kuwait into a modern **welfare state.** That is, it offers its citizens a wide range of free social services. All citizens are entitled to free education and health care. Even telephone service is free. Taxes barely exist except for those on imports.

Yet beneath the wealth, there were problems even before the Gulf War. Despite all of the money Kuwait spent on economic development in the 1970s and 1980s, its economic structure did not really change. It remained totally dependent on oil and oil-related businesses. The huge inflow of money from oil sales allowed the ruling family to import more and more goods and services. It also allowed the Kuwaitis to invest heavily in companies in Europe and North America. Those investments have been valued at over $100 billion. The ruling family hopes that the investments will help support Kuwait long after the oil runs out.

Kuwait, like other countries in the Persian Gulf, has become dependent on imports. It buys not only food and other necessities from abroad but also technology and labor. At the time of the invasion, nearly 60 percent of the population and more than 75 percent of the labor force was foreign, mostly Palestinian, Egyptian, Yemeni, and Pakistani. These foreign workers did everything from sweeping the streets to running key government agencies. Yet they could not own property or become citizens even if they had lived in the country for years. The Kuwaitis did not trust their foreign workers and feared they would be disloyal in time of war. The foreigners, in turn, felt unappreciated and exploited. The Gulf War brought those feelings to the surface.

Kuwait After the War.   When the war was over, Kuwait set out to punish its foreign workers even though most had remained loyal to Kuwait and some had even fought in the resistance. The government directed most of its anger toward two groups of its population. One group was the nation's 350,000 Palestinians. The other group was made up of the approximately 100,000 foreigners who came from what it called "the bad countries"—nations that had supported Saddam Hussein or remained

240

neutral. Kuwait treated the Palestinians particularly harshly. Kuwait's ambassador to the United States told reporters, "If people pose a security threat, as a sovereign country, we have the right to exclude anyone we don't want."

About 230,000 Palestinians had left Kuwait at the time of the invasion. They were not permitted to return. Almost all of those who had stayed in the country during the war lost their jobs. Some were imprisoned. Others were killed for "collaborating with the enemy." A Kuwaiti official tried to explain the hostility this way:

> We were the most vocal supporters of the PLO, and we gave plenty, more than $60 million in the past six years alone. And that doesn't count the five percent of Palestinians' salaries we deducted for direct transmittal to Yasir Arafat [the PLO leader]. Who would not feel betrayed?

The Palestinians also felt betrayed. They argued that they had served the Kuwaiti government loyally. Yet their reward was banishment. Where did the thousands of Palestinians go? A few found refuge in Sudan. Some returned to the West Bank and Gaza. Most went to Jordan. Their presence there increased tensions in an already tense area.

The Kuwaitis replaced the Palestinians with workers from Bangladesh, India, and Sri Lanka. By late 1991, these new foreign guest workers were arriving at a rate of one thousand a week. Most could not speak Arabic, however. In jobs that required the ability to speak the language, the Kuwaitis turned to Arabs from countries that had supported Operation Desert Storm. Egyptians took over some of the jobs once held by Palestinians. Syrians took over others. But even they were not fully trusted. The Kuwaitis offered them only short-term contracts and allowed only a few to bring their families.

The Saudi Response. The Saudis also vowed to "never forgive and never forget the betrayal" of the Arab nations that sided with Iraq. Like Kuwait, Saudi Arabia stopped payments to the PLO. It also cut off aid to Jordan and cancelled all trade agreements with that country.

Saudi Arabia also moved against Yemen, which was the only Gulf state that had not supported the coalition against Iraq. During the war, the Saudis expelled 800,000 guest workers from Yemen. They had done nothing wrong. They had not demonstrated against Saudi policies or committed acts of sabotage. They were forced to leave the country solely because they came from a country that did not support the war.

Saudi Arabia replaced its Yemeni and Palestinian workers with recruits from South and Southeast Asia. It no longer trusted its Arab neighbors—not even those who had supported the war. A Saudi official complained, "Whenever the Egyptians and Syrians look into our eyes, they see dollar signs."

Defending the Gulf.   That lack of trust was evident in the spring of 1991. In March, just after the war ended, the GCC met with Egypt and Syria in Damascus. They agreed to cooperate on economic matters and to build an all-Arab peacekeeping force in the Persian Gulf for security. But by April, Saudi Arabia and Kuwait were backing away from the idea. By May, they were encouraging Egypt and Syria to withdraw their soldiers from the Gulf. In doing so, plans for a Gulf security arrangement with Arab military participation came to an end.

The Gulf states chose to secure their borders in a different way— one that would have been unthinkable before the invasion of Kuwait. They openly turned to the United States for help. In September 1991, the United States and Kuwait signed an agreement that called for a U.S. military presence in the nation for a period of ten years. Saudi Arabia took a similar step. The kingdom entered into an arrangement that allowed the Saudi army to double in size. The new troops were to be armed and trained by the United States, which, however, would not establish bases in Saudi Arabia. The Saudi government feared criticism at home if U.S. soldiers were too visible.

The Arms Race.   Saudi Arabia was not the only nation in the Middle East that expanded its army after the Gulf War. Every country in the region was doing the same. There seemed to be no end to the arms race in the Middle East. The region is one of the world's main markets for military equipment. Nations there account for about 35 percent of the world's arms trade. In the 1980s alone, the region spent over $500 billion on defense. As a result, the Middle East is probably the most heavily armed region in the world. Most Middle East nations spend anywhere from 10 to 30 percent of their total income on defense. Some countries in the region spend far more. (See the chart on page 243.) Continuing conflicts there have been a gold mine for arms dealers on every continent. With so much spent on arms, the money available for economic development is limited. At the same time, the risk of yet another war in the region is heightened.

The Arabs and the Israelis fought their first war in 1948 with weapons left over from World War II. That war and every war since then

Armed Forces of Countries in the Middle East and North Africa

COUNTRY	SIZE OF ARMED FORCES (in thousands)	PERCENTAGE OF POPULATION IN ARMED FORCES	MILITARY BUDGET (in millions of dollars)	MILITARY EXPENDITURE AS PERCENT OF GNP
Algeria	126	0.52	1,784	3.4
Egypt	452	0.85	6,086	7.8
Iran	654	1.26	20,800	6.6
Iraq	1,000	5.69	28,030	22.5
Israel	191	4.44	6,001	13.8
Jordan	82	NA	631	14.8
Lebanon	22	NA	NA	8.2
Morocco	193	0.78	1,138	6.0
Saudi Arabia	68	0.54	13,560	16.5
Turkey	647	1.56	2,664	3.9

NA = Not available

Sources: U.S. Statistical Abstract, 1991; Encyclopaedia Britannica, 1991 Yearkook; The Universal Almanac, 1991 (for Jordan only).

have set off a scramble for newer and more powerful weapons. For example, the Gulf War speeded up Iran's buildup of arms. It purchased aircraft and major weapons from the former Soviet Union, China, and North Korea. After the Soviet Union collapsed in 1991, Iran turned to the financially hard–pressed nations of Eastern Europe, which put their military equipment up for sale.

During the Gulf War, many people wondered who had armed Saddam Hussein. The disquieting answer was that almost everyone involved in Operation Desert Storm had helped build the Iraqi army. The Soviet Union, France, Britain, Germany, and the United States each had sold millions of dollars' worth of military equipment to Iraq. Saudi Arabia, Kuwait, and other nations along the Persian Gulf had lent Hussein the money to pay for that equipment and even purchased some of it for him. Some of the countries did so because they feared an Iranian victory in the Iran-Iraq war more than they feared Saddam. Others

In the uncertain peace that followed the Persian Gulf War, Israel continued to maintain an active aircraft industry to keep its equipment in readiness.

saw a chance to profit from conflicts in the region. Indeed, many of the nations that sold arms to Iraq also supplied Iran with weapons. Some also sold arms to every other country in the region as well.

After the Gulf War, the UN tried to destroy Iraq's military capacity, particularly its nuclear capabilities. It sent inspection teams to Iraq, and, despite the roadblocks put in their way by the Iraqi military, they managed to identify the country's nuclear stockpiles. The plan was then to force Iraq to destroy its nuclear weapons.

A number of nations were also concerned about the arms potential of other nations in the region. They hoped to end the arms race by limiting all weapon sales in the region. Experts have argued that these efforts will not stop the arms race. They point out that countries that want weapons are bound to get those weapons in one way or another. Israel and Egypt, for example, build much of their own military equipment. Furthermore, Israel also has nuclear capability. Although Iran denies it, some fear that Iran does as well. The experts maintain that the arms race will end only when there is genuine peace in the region.

A Push for Peace. When the Gulf War ended, the United States was the dominant power in the Middle East. It decided to use its power and influence to ease tensions in the region. The United States reasoned that the spirit of mutual interest that had held the Arab coalition together against Saddam could result in a renewed interest in the peace process.

Therefore, the United States, together with the Soviet Union, issued an invitation to a Middle East peace conference. The peace talks began in Madrid, Spain, in October 1991 and then shifted back and forth between Washington, D.C., and Moscow. For the first time, Israelis faced Syrians, Jordanians, Lebanese, Saudis, and even Palestinians across a conference table instead of on a battlefield. Although little real progress was made in the early stages of the talks, the meetings were an important first step on the road to peace.

Peace talks between Israel and its Arab opponents that began in 1991 made slow progress. What does this cartoon tell you about why this may have been the case?

A WINDOW OF OPPORTUNITY

The end of the Cold War left a gap in the Middle East. Then came the Gulf War. It, too, brought fundamental changes in the way countries in the region regarded one another and the way they viewed Western nations. As nations adjusted to the new conditions, a so-called "window of opportunity" to bring about changes in the region opened. The United States used that window to arrange the peace talks. Countries in the region also took advantage of it.

Israel and the United States.   In the years before the late 1980s, immigration of Jews to Israel had slowed down to the point where it seemed as though Israel was in danger of losing its Jewish majority. Then, in 1989, the Soviet Union, which had stubbornly refused to allow Jews to leave the country, changed its policy. Anyone who wished to emigrate was now allowed to do so. Within two years, more than 300,000 Soviet Jews had settled in Israel and another 600,000 were expected over the next three years.

For Russian immigrants who could not find work Israel set up food distribution centers. Many of those who had been engineers, doctors, and teachers in Russia had to accept such low–paying jobs as street sweepers and kitchen workers.

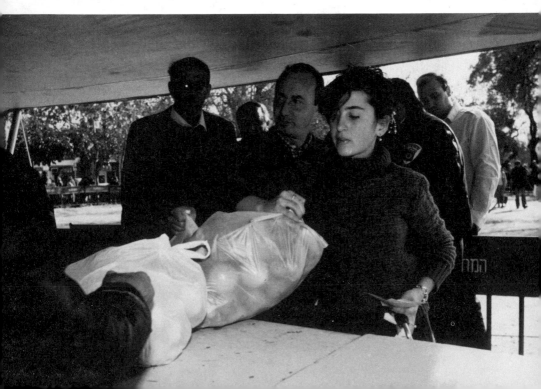

The arrival of so many people in such a short time presented Israel with a number of problems. The nation had to build houses, find jobs, and provide public services for the newcomers at a time when it was facing severe economic problems. Unemployment was already high when the immigration began. The arrival of so many newcomers also increased tensions in the West Bank and Gaza. It fueled Palestinians' fears that Israel would build new settlements for them there. Actually, most of the new arrivals were settled within Israel itself. The increase in the number of settlements in the territories came, as before, from Israelis who moved there to secure Israel's hold on the territories.

With the arrival of the newcomers, Israel saw an opportunity to develop high-tech industries that would make the most of the immigrants' special skills. Over 40 percent of the Russians were college graduates. About 25 percent were engineers, and many others also had scientific training. To build these new industries, however, Israel needed billions of dollars. Banks were unwilling to lend the government that much money without a guarantee that it would be paid back. Israel did not have the resources to guarantee the loan so it asked the U.S. government to do so.

Israel saw the loan guarantees as a humanitarian gesture. After all, the Russian Jews were victims of discrimination. Israel also believed that the United States owed it a debt for its part in the Gulf War. Without Israel's restraint after having been hit by Iraqi missiles, the coalition might not have held together. Loan guarantees allow Israel to borrow money from banks with the United States guaranteeing repayment.

The U.S. government argued that no loan guarantee is ever risk free. Besides, it maintained, the United States did not owe Israel a debt. If anything, the opposite was true. The United States had done Israel a favor by taking care of the Iraqi threat.

Behind these arguments, however, lay a more basic matter. The U.S.'s major objective was to secure a lasting peace in the Middle East. That meant settling the Palestinian issue. The heart of the U.S. plan was to persuade Israel to exchange territory for peace. The United States wanted Israel to give up all or part of the West Bank and Gaza in return for a guarantee of peace by the Arabs. Even while the loan talks were going on, new settlements were being built. The United States, therefore, tied its granting of loan guarantees to an Israeli promise to freeze settlements in the occupied territories. Continuing Israeli settlements there, the United States argued, would complicate the peace process and increase tensions in the region. In the early 1990s, this issue strained relations between the two allies.

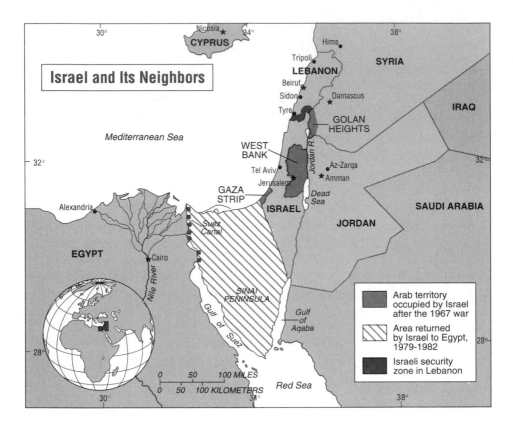

Israel and Its Neighbors

Mediterranean Sea

CYPRUS
Nicosia

Tripoli
Hims
SYRIA
LEBANON
Beirut
Sidon
Damascus
Tyre
GOLAN HEIGHTS
IRAQ

WEST BANK
Tel Aviv
Jordan R.
Az-Zarqa
Amman
Jerusalem
GAZA STRIP
Dead Sea
ISRAEL
SAUDI ARABIA
JORDAN

Alexandria
Suez Canal

EGYPT
Cairo
Nile River

SINAI PENINSULA
Gulf of Suez
Gulf of Aqaba

Red Sea

	Arab territory occupied by Israel after the 1967 war
	Area returned by Israel to Egypt, 1979-1982
	Israeli security zone in Lebanon

0   50   100 MILES
0   50   100 KILOMETERS

Ending Israel's Isolation.   Israel saw yet another opportunity in the early 1990s to achieve an important goal. It had a chance to end the isolation that had resulted from the Six-Day War in 1967. A number of nations, led by the Soviet Union, had cut off diplomatic relations with Israel to protest its occupation of the West Bank and Gaza. Now Israel worked to end that isolation. The first sign of change came when Russia resumed diplomatic relations with Israel in 1991. The Russians did so because they wanted to play a role in the Middle East peace talks. They could not do so unless they had diplomatic relations with all of the nations involved in those talks. The Russians were also trying to build better relations with the West, and recognition of Israel was part of that effort.

In 1975, the Soviet Union had helped the Arab states pass a UN resolution stating that Zionism was a form of **racism**. Racism is the practice of discrimination against a group of people because of their race. As a result of that resolution, many countries—particularly countries in Asia and Africa—had closed their embassies in Israel. In December

248

1991, Russia worked with the United States to overturn that resolution. Among those who supported the move were the newly freed nations of Eastern Europe and ten Islamic countries. The vote ended Israel's isolation. Many nations were now willing to re-establish ties with Israel.

These renewed diplomatic ties not only strengthened Israel's position in the world. They also encouraged trade and investment at a time when the nation needed both. As one Israeli diplomat explained, "When we were boycotted by the world, it was difficult to attract investment here. This should change now." Within two months of the UN vote, China and India had opened embassies in Israel, and a number of African nations planned to do the same. As the Israeli diplomat predicted, with diplomatic relations came trade talks.

Changes in Syria.   Syria, too, responded to the changing realities of the world. In the past, it was militantly anti-American. Indeed, as late as 1992, Syria was on the United States list of nations that support terrorist activity. The United States does not provide economic aid or favorable terms of trade to any nation on the list. As the Cold War ended, the Syrians looked for ways to build a better relationship with the United States. With the breakup of the Soviet Union, they could no longer count on the Russians for help.

The Gulf War provided Syrian President Hafez al-Assad with an opportunity to show Syria's good will, and he took full advantage of it. Syria supported the coalition in the Persian Gulf with troops. When the war ended, Syria continued to show its interest in winning U.S. approval. In 1991, it agreed to take part in the peace talks with Israel. It also worked with Iran to secure the release of the remaining Western hostages in Lebanon in December 1991.

The benefits of cooperation were immediate. Saudi Arabia gave Syria $2 billion in aid for its help in the war. Assad used the money to purchase weapons from Czechoslovakia as well as Scud missiles from North Korea. At the same time, he increased Syria's control over Lebanon. After disarming the militias there, Syria persuaded the nation to sign a "treaty of brotherhood and cooperation." The treaty severely limited Lebanese independence and brought Assad closer to his dream of re-establishing "Greater Syria." (See Chapter 8.) No one objected— not even the United States.

Iran's Shift.   Until 1989, Iran was even more isolated than Israel. Relations with the West and most countries in the Middle East were openly hostile. However, even before Ayatollah Khomeini's death in 1989, the

Iranians were seeking ways to build bridges to the West and to their Arab neighbors. Iran's economy was in bad shape, and it needed all the help it could get. The Gulf War provided such an opportunity.

Although Iran did not send troops to fight in the war, it did support the trade embargo against Iraq. In return, the United States relaxed its own embargo against Iran by allowing U.S. purchases of Iranian oil. When the U.S. hostages were freed in Lebanon, the last of the economic sanctions against Iran were lifted. Iran also restored relations with France and Britain and tried to end its feuds with most of the Gulf states.

Opportunity in Central Asia. In building new bridges, Iran focused most of its attention on the six Islamic republics that emerged in the southern part of what was once the Soviet Union. Kazakhstan (kuh-zahk-STAHN), Uzbekistan (ooz-bek-i-STAHN), Tajikistan (tah-jeek-ee-STAHN), Kyrgyzstan (keer-giz-STAHN), Azerbaijan (ahz-uhr-beye-JAHN), and Turkmenistan (turk-men-i-STAHN) all joined the Commonwealth of Independent States that replaced the Soviet Union. Yet the six have more in common with countries in the Middle East than with the mostly Slavic republics in the new Commonwealth. Indeed the people of Tajikistan speak a language that is of Persian origin. Like Iran, Azerbaijan is home to many Shiites. Islamic leaders in Tajikistan and Uzebekistan have already developed links to mullahs in Iran. They would like to turn their countries into Islamic states much like the one in Iran.

Turkey has also shown a strong interest in the republics. It, too, has opened diplomatic relations with all six and is building strong economic ties. The Turks feel that they have an historical kinship to Central Asia. At present, they also have more influence over the republics than Iran does. An Azerbaijan leader explained why: "Our priorities in foreign policy are those countries which have achieved political and economic development, and we like the Turkish example of turning all heads to the West."

Saudi Arabia, too, has taken steps to establish ties with the Central Asian republics. In 1992, King Fahd offered to pay the expenses of Muslim pilgrims from Uzbekistan to Mecca and to finance the restoration of mosques and religious sites in that republic. In addition, the Saudis have available money for education and the development of energy resources. Saudi Arabia, as well as Turkey, are both motivated by a desire to blunt Iran's influence with the republics, most of whose people are Sunnite Muslims.

WINDS OF CHANGE

As the West pushed for peace in the Middle East, some countries in the region began to focus less on the issues that divide them and more on common concerns. The nations of the Middle East are, in fact, linked in many ways. Some of those ties are the traditional ties of language and religion. Others are geographic. When the Iraqis set fire to Kuwaiti oil fields during the Gulf War, the environmental damage affected every country along the Gulf. Still other links are economic and social.

Economic Links.   As countries in the region have modernized, a problem in one country may be quickly felt throughout the region. Events in Jordan at the time of the Gulf War suggest some of those links. In 1991, Jordan had an unemployment rate of about 35 percent. Conditions there were aggravated by the arrival of 300,000 Palestinians expelled from the Gulf. A number of people recalled that when oil prices fell in the mid-1980s, many Palestinians also lost their jobs in the Gulf states. That loss almost destroyed Jordan's economy. It also hurt the economies of Israel's occupied territories. The money the Palestinians sent home had played an important role in keeping those economies stable.

Jordan was also hurt by the UN's trade embargo on Iraq. Iraq is one of Jordan's main trading partners. Jordan also traded with the Gulf states. When that trade was cut off in 1991 as punishment for Jordan's stand during the Gulf War, the nation faced an economic crisis. It also faced a political crisis as the Muslim Brotherhood and other militant Islamic groups capitalized on the crisis to gain power. It was those same groups that made it impossible for King Hussein to support the Gulf states during Operation Desert Storm. There was a danger that they would have started a civil war in Jordan if the government had tried to support Kuwait. By the early 1990s, there was a growing recognition that few problems in the region were purely local.

Sharing Resources.   Almost every resource in the Middle East is shared. Kuwaiti and Iraqi oil comes from the same underground oil fields. Israel and Jordan pump water from the same aquifers, or underground sources of water. In fact, every country in the region shares water supplies with several other nations.

Water is the most valuable resource in the Middle East. As one government official explained, "Water is our life." Life is more costly in the Middle East than in any other region in the world. Water costs twice as much in the Middle East as it does in North America and five times as

Feeding the Middle East's rapidly growing population is a problem for all countries in the region. Oman, one of the few countries with a reliable source of water, has established experimental farms like the one shown to increase its food supply.

much as in Southeast Asia. As a result, even traditional enemies have found ways to cooperate on a daily basis. Jordan and Israel are officially still at war. Yet the two have drawn their water from the same rivers, aquifers, and lakes for over 40 years.

Many people believe that the region's limited water resources would be better managed if countries there cooperated more fully. Indeed, almost every country in the region has a scheme to expand its water resources if only there were peace in the Middle East. Turkey would like to build what it calls a "peace pipeline" that would pump water from rivers in northern Turkey to drier lands farther south. At the same time, Turkey has been involved in disputes with Syria and Iraq over control of the Euphrates River. Turkey would like to build a dam on the river, but the other two countries fear that this would give Turkey too much power over their share of the water of the Euphrates.

Israel would like to pool resources with its neighbors and build a desalination plant that would turn the salty waters of the Mediterranean Sea into fresh water. King Hussein of Jordan would like to build a dam on the upper Yarmuk River to provide badly needed water for the

Jordan Valley and the city of Amman. Jordan cannot build the dam without Israeli approval, however. The World Bank will not lend money for an international water project without the agreement of all of the countries affected by it. Israel is not willing to approve the project without being assured that it will get a fair share of the water.

Unless projects such as these become reality, many people fear that the next war in the region will be over water rather than oil. A scientist at Jordan University says, "Relative to the number of people in Jordan, Israel, and the occupied territories, there is not enough water." Israelis agree. Both nations draw water from the Jordan River, which flows into the Dead Sea. The two nations use so much of the water of the Jordan that the level of the Dead Sea is said to be dropping. They also share an aquifer that lies beneath the West Bank. That is part of the reason the Israelis are reluctant to give up the territory. They claim that if they lost the territory, they would be giving up about 25 percent of their water supply. Their fears are heightened by a drought in the region. In 1991, the Sea of Galilee, which supplies almost one-third of Israel's water needs, was at its lowest level in over 60 years.

The Gulf states also face a water crisis. During Operation Desert Storm, water tankers were given as high a priority as tanks and weapons. Most of the nations along the Gulf rely almost totally on their desalination plants for fresh water. Saudi Arabia alone produces 30 percent of all the desalinated water in the world. Kuwait and other Gulf states are equally dependent on their desalination plants. During the war, the Iraqis wiped out much of Kuwait's capacity to make fresh water. The first ships to dock in Kuwait after the war carried water—not medical supplies, food, or other equipment.

Communication Links.   Ports are an important part of every nation in the region. So are airports. Nations are also linked by a network of highways, pipelines, and railroads. Some of those links were visible during the Gulf War. The embargo on the sale of Iraqi oil would have been impossible without Turkey's help, for Iraq's pipeline to Europe runs through Turkey. Other links are less noticeable.

People throughout the region listen to the same music and see the same movies. They also watch the same TV shows. Since 1985, the 22 nations that belong to the Arab League have been linked by two satellites. These satellites are controlled from a ground station in Saudi Arabia with a back-up station in Tunisia. The system, known as **Arabsat,** allows for the transmission of international telephone calls, radio and TV programs, electronic mail, fax services, and teleconferences.

By 1987, Arabsat was relaying local television programs to countries throughout the Arab world. The Arabsat network also broadcasts live events, ranging from prayers at the grand mosques of Mecca and Medina to soccer matches between countries in the region. In addition, the network gives local broadcasters access to global television news services like the U.S.-based Cable News Network (CNN). Many believe that in years to come Arabsat will be used to expand educational opportunities. Even the most remote village will have access to literacy programs, health-care information, and even college-level courses.

In most countries of the region, the government controls the press, radio, and television. Yet governments everywhere are finding it harder and harder to stop the spread of information and ideas. Militant Islamic groups as well as moderate Arab reformers have learned to use the new technology to bypass government censors. One way is through audio and video cassettes. Tapes are copied and then smuggled from one country to another. In richer countries like Saudi Arabia, people use computer networks and fax machines to exchange ideas. Information travels more quickly today than ever before.

It is easy to see how unrest in one country can quickly spread to others. Yet the links that unite the Middle East offer opportunities for peace as well. Many people believe that with those links the Middle East has an opportunity to improve the lives of its people and end the conflicts that have divided the region for so long.

Chapter 9:

CHECKUP

REVIEWING THE CHAPTER

I. **Building Your Vocabulary**

Match the definitions with the correct terms.

economic sanctions   archipelago   welfare state
aquifer   racism   coalition

1. an underground source of water

2. a chain of islands

3. a country that offers citizens a wide range of social services

4. refusal to trade or do business with a country

5. discrimination against people because of their race

II. **Understanding the Facts**

Write the letter of the word or phrase that best completes each of the following sentences or answers each of the following questions.

1. Saddam Hussein invaded Kuwait for each of the following reasons *except* that:
   a. he hoped to dominate the Persian Gulf.
   b. he wanted to punish Kuwait for its support of Iran in the Iran–Iraq War.
   c. he wanted to be the leader of the Arab world.

2. During Operation Desert Storm, Syria
   a. supported Kuwait.   b. supported Iraq.   c. stayed neutral.

3. During Operation Desert Storm, Israel
   a. supported Kuwait.   b. supported Iraq.   c. stayed neutral.

4. Jordan, Yemen, and the PLO did not think that Saudi Arabia should
   a. ask the United States for help.   b. support Kuwait.
   c. attack Iraq.

5. Which was an outcome of the Gulf War?
   a. an end to the arms race in the Middle East
   b. the overthrow of Saddam Hussein
   c. the liberation of Kuwait

6. Which of the following was not a member of the Gulf Cooperative Council?
   a. Saudi Arabia
   b. Yemen
   c. the United Arab Emirates

7. Which word or phrase best describes the relationship between
   the Gulf states and their foreign workers?
   a. mutual respect
   b. resentment
   c. cooperation

8. What effect did the Gulf War have on the arms race in the
   Middle East?
   a. no effect
   b. decreased the arms race
   c. set off a scramble for newer and more powerful weapons

9. Which of the following events helped Israel end its isolation in
   the early 1990s?
   a. the end of the Cold War
   b. the Iraq invasion of Kuwait
   c. the immigration of Russian Jews

10. Syria tried to improve its relationship with the United States by
    a. recognizing Israel.
    b. helping secure the release of the hostages.
    c. taking control of Lebanon.

11. In the early 1990s, Iran wanted to
    a. ally with Iraq.
    b. restore relations with the West.
    c. invade Kuwait.

12. Economic sanctions against Iraq hurt the economy of
    a. Israel.
    b. Egypt.
    c. Jordan.

13. The most valuable resource in the Middle East is
    a. water.
    b. oil.
    c. iron ore.

14. Arabsat provides for the transmission of all of the following
    except
    a. television programs.
    b. electronic mail.
    c. video cassettes.

15. The Middle East peace talks of 1991–1992 were sponsored by
    a. the United States and the former Soviet Union.
    b. Lebanon.
    c. the United Nations.

III. **Thinking It Through**

1. What problems do the Gulf nations share? How do those problems affect other countries in the region?

2. Name two effects that the end of the Cold War had on the Middle East.

3. Name two effects that Operation Desert Storm had on the Middle East.

4. a. How does water unite people in the region?
   b. How does it increase tensions in the region?

5. How has Arabsat helped to unite the people of the Middle East?

DEVELOPING CRITICAL THINKING SKILLS

I. **Supporting Generalizations**

List facts in this chapter that support the following generalizations.

1. New alliances are forming in the Arab world.

2. The year 1991 was critical in the Middle East.

3. The year 1991 was one in which the Middle East conducted "business as usual."

II. Interpreting a Chart

Use the chart on page 243 to answer the following questions:

1. Which country has the largest army?

2. Which spends a larger percent of its gross national product (GNP) on the military: Morocco or Israel?

3. Which country has the larger army: Egypt or Iran?

4. Which country has a greater share of its population in the military: Algeria or Iraq?

5. What does the chart suggest about the effect of the arms race on the Middle East?

ENRICHMENT AND EXPLORATION

1. Find out more about foreign guest workers in the Middle East. What countries do they come from? Why do they travel from nation to nation in search of work? What skills do they have?

2. Find out more about the Kurdish population in Iraq. How do the Kurds differ from other groups in the region?

3. Prepare a report on the six Islamic republics that were once a part of the Soviet Union. How are they linked to nations in the Middle East?

4. Interview someone who took part in Operation Desert Storm. Ask about how he or she was transported to the war region, what living conditions were like, whether or not he or she saw action and of what kind, how he or she felt about the experience. Share the interview with the class.

5. Research Secretary of State James Baker's efforts to set up the Middle East peace talks in 1991. What problems did he encounter? Was he able to overcome them?

Glossary

Altaic language: a family of languages that includes Turkic, Tungisic, and Mongolian subfamilies

aquifer (AK-wuh-fuhr): underground source of water

archipelago (ahr-kuh-PEL-uh-goh): a chain of islands

astrolabe: an instrument used to calculate a ship's latitude by measuring the position of the stars

anti-Semitism: prejudice against Jews

arable land: land suitable for farming

Ashkenazim (ash-kuh-NAHZ-im): Jews of central and eastern Europe and their descendants

astrolabe: an instrument used to calulate a ship's latitude by measuring the position of the stars

authenticate: to eastablish the truth or reliability of

ayatollah (eye-uh-TOH-luh): religious leader of the Shiite community

Bedouin: a Middle Eastern nomad

bitumen (bi-TOO-muhn): asphalt used as a cement or mortar

bride wealth: payment to the bride by or on behalf of the groom

caliph: a title for the religious and civil head of a Muslim state and successor to Muhammad as civil and spiritual head of Islam

calligraphy: beautiful or elegant handwriting

capital: money or other wealth used for the production of more wealth

capitulations: immunity from local laws and taxes conceded by Muslim rulers to subjects of Western countries

caravanserai (kar-uh-VAN-suh-reye): in the Middle East, an inn where caravans stopped for the night

cartel: a group of businesses or governments formed to regulate prices or output of a product

cash crops: food or other crops raised to be sold

censor: to examine writings and pictures to make sure they do not contain objectionable material and, if necessary, to have them changed or to ban them entirely.

city-state: a state consisting of a city and its surrounding lands

civilization: a complex culture, often including written records and specialized skills

coalition: a temporary alliance between states or parties for the purpose of joint action

coup d'état (koo day-TAH): a sudden overthrow of a government

covenant: an agreement by two or more parties

culture: a people's learned ways of living

cuneiform (kyoo-NEE-uh-form): writing in the form of wedgelike symbols

deforestation: the clearing of forests

département (day-pahr-tuh-MAHN): an adminstrative district of France

desalination: the removal of salt from sea water to make it drinkable; sometimes called "desalinization"

desertification: the process of becoming arid or desert land

dialect: the form of a language spoken in a particular region or locality

dhimmis (THIM-eez): Non-Muslims in Muslim regions who were allowed to practice their faiths and organize their own communities

Diaspora: the dispersion of Jews outside Palestine after the Babylonian exile in 586 B.C.

domestication: making plants or animals fit for living in close association with and for the advantage and use of human beings

dynasty: a succession of rulers who are members of the same family

Druze (drooz): a Muslim religious group centered in Syria, Lebanon, and Israel

economic sanctions: refusal to trade or do business with a country to force that country to change certain policies

embargo: restriction placed on trade with a country

emir (uh-MEER): a ruler or prince in some Muslim countries

erode: to wear away or destroy by degrees

extended family: a family group that includes in one household near relatives in addition to the father and mother and their children

Fertile Crescent: the semicircle of fertile land from the southeast coast of the Mediterranean to the Tigris and Euphrates rivers

genocide (JEN-uh-seyed): the systematic killing of a whole national, ethnic, or religious group

ghazis (GAH-zeez): Ottoman frontier fighters, especially Muslim soldiers fighting non-Muslims

hadith (hah-DEET): traditions guiding the Islamic community

hajj (haj): Muslim rite of pilgramage to Mecca

Hatt-i Humayan: the Ottoman imperial edict of 1856 that was the major Turkish reform edict of the 19th century

headmen: village leaders chosen by the local heads of households or appointed by the central government

hieroglyphics (heye-uhr-oh-GLIF-iks): a system of writing with picture symbols used by the ancient Egyptians

hijra (HIJ-ruh): the flight of Muhammad from Mecca in A.D. 622. Also spelled *hejira* and *hegira*

Holocaust: the sytematic killing of six million Jews by the Nazis before and during World War II

hydroelectric: pertaining to the production of electricity by water power

hydroponics: growing plants using water containing nutrients

illiteracy: the state of being unable to read or write

imam (i-MAHM): a local leader of Muslim congregational worship

Indo-European languages: a family of languages spoken by people who originally lived in a region extending from India to western Europe that now includes most of the languages spoken in Europe and many of those spoken in southwestern Asia and India

infant mortality rate: the number of babies who die before reaching the age of one year, per 1,000 live births

institution: an organization of people with a common purpose; an established custom or system

intifada (in-tuh-FAH-duh): the attack of Palestinians in the West Bank, Gaza, and East Jerusalem on Israelis that began in 1987 seeking to end the Israeli occupation of these places

Islam: the Muslim religion that regards Allah as the supreme deity and Muhammad as his prophet

Ismailis: members of a Shiite sect who believed that the Koran was a general guide to living rather than merely a statement of beliefs

janisseries (JAN-uh-ser-eez): elite corps of the Ottoman army loyal to the sultan alone

jihad (ji-HAHD): a holy struggle waged on behalf of Islam

jizya (JIZ-yuh): a poll tax placed on non-Muslims by Muslim rulers

Judaism: the Jewish religion

Kaaba (KAH-buh): a cube-shaped building in Mecca that includes a black stone sacred to Muslims

khan: a medieval ruler of China or of Turkish or Mongol peoples

kibbutz (ki-BOOTS): a collective Israeli community in which both land and labor are shared

Knesset (KNES-et): the Israeli legislature

Koran (koh-RAHN): the book of writings sacred to Muslims and accepted by them as revelations made to Muhammad by God through the angel Gabriel, and one of the main sources of Islamic law, literature and culture. Also spelled *Quran*

kufiya (kuh-FEE-yuh): a Middle Eastern head covering made of folded cloth held in place by a headband

Law of Return: a law enacted by Israel in 1948 that gives every Jew the right to immigrate to Israel

life expectancy: the number of years that an average newborn baby can be expected to live

Maghrib (MUH-gruhb): Northwest Africa, chiefly Morocco, Algeria, and Tunisia. Also spelled *Maghreb*

Mamelukes: former Turkish slave soldiers who ruled Egypt

mandate: a commission by the League of Nations to a country to administer a region or a country

medrassa (muh-DRAS-uh): an Islamic college

mercenary: a professional soldier who serves for pay in a foreign army

Mesopotamia: the Greek-derived name for "the land between the rivers," meaning the land between the Tigris and Euphrates rivers, now part of present-day Iraq

Messiah: an anointed person who would be the savior of a people

mihrab (MEE-rahb): a niche or place in the wall of a mosque that faces toward Mecca

millet: a non-Muslim religious community within the Ottoman Empire

minaret (min-uh-RET): a slender tower attached to a mosque from which the call to prayer is made

minbar (MIN-bahr): the pulpit in a mosque

monotheism: the belief in and worship of one God, a doctrine that is common to Judaism, Christianity, and Islam

monsoons: winds that change direction with the seasons, especially winds blowing to and from the Indian Ocean

moshav (moh-SHAHV): a cooperative community in Israel in which each family owns its own land

mosque: a Muslim place of communal worship

muezzin (moo-EZ-uhn) a Muslim crier who calls the people to prayer

Muslim (MUZ-luhm): a follower of Islam

nationalism: loyalty and devotion to a nation, especially as expressed by praising one's nation above all others and by promoting its culture and interests

nationalize: to transfer privately owned resources or industries to government ownership or control

Neolithic Age: the latest period of the Stone Age during which the earliest farming and the domestication of animals took place, believed to have begun in the Middle East about 12,000 years ago

nomads: people who have no fixed home but move from place to place in a regular pattern to fill their flocks' need for grazing land

nonalignment: the policy by a country of avoiding being closely allied with any of the more powerful countries of the world

nuclear family: a family consisting of father, mother, and children

oasis: a fertile or green area in a dry region

obsidian: volcanic glass, usually black

Palestine Liberation Organization (PLO): the political organization that represents the Palestinian people in their goal to establish Palestine as a national state

Pan-Arabism: the movement to establish a single, unified Arab state that cuts across national boundaries

pasha (puh-SHAH or PASH-uh): a title that was used by civil and military officials of high rank in Ottoman lands

pastoralism: a way of living based on livestock raising as the main economic activity

patriarchal: pertaining to rule by men, with the father as the head of the family

Pax Romana: the "Roman peace" that lasted from 31 B.C. to A.D. 180 during which the Romans fought few outside enemies

petroleum: an oily liquid refined for use as gasoline

pharaoh: ruler of ancient Egypt

phosphate: a mined substance used as a fertilizer

plateau: an elevated piece of land

pogrom: an organized massacre of Jewish people

polygamy: the practice of a person having more than one spouse at a time

population density: the number of inhabitants in a given area

prophet: one who is regarded as a spokesperson for God as though under divine guidance

protectorate: a state or territory controlled by a stronger country

purdah (PUR-duh): the seclusion of women from public observation

Ramadan (RAM-uh-dahn): the ninth month of the Muslim year, a period of daily fasting from sunrise to sunset

reforestation: the renewal of a forest by planting seeds or young trees

refugee: a person who flees from his or her country to escape danger

ruralization: the introduction of the customs, attitudes, and ways of living in a city by rural people

sabra: a native-born Israeli

Semitic: pertaining to the Afro-Asiatic family of languages that includes Arabic and Hebrew

Sephardim (suh-FAHR-dim): Jews who originated in Spain and Portugal but were driven out and their descendants

service industries: industries that provide aid or services rather than goods or products

shah: a ruler of Iran

Shari'a (shu-REE-uh): Islamic law based primarily on the Koran

sheikh (shayk or sheek): an Arab chief

Shia (SHEE-uh): one of the two great sects of Islam. Shiites believe in Ali and the Imams as the only rightful successors of Muhammad and in the messianic return of the last recognized Imam.

Shiite (SHEE-eyet): a Muslim of the Shia branch of Islam

subsistence crops: food raised by the farm family for their own use without any surplus for sale

Sufism (SOO-fiz-uhm): a Muslim sect or movement that places great emphasis on individual worship, piety, and mysticism

Sunni (SOON-ee): one of the two great sects of Islam, it follows the orthodox tradition and recognizes the first four caliphs as the rightful successors of Muhammad.

Sunnite (SOON-eyet): a Muslim of the Sunni branch of Islam

sultan: a ruler of a Muslim state

suq (sook): a marketplace in the Middle East. Also spelled *souk* and *sook*

sura (SOOR-uh) a chapter of the Koran

synagogue: Jewish house of prayer, assembly, and study

Talmud: the authoritative collection of legal interpretations of Jewish law and customs and commentaries on these interpretations

Tanzimat: the intensive Westernizing reform movement that began in 1839 and was enforced by the Ottoman government

tax-farming: the practice of delegating the collection of taxes by a ruler to lower officials, with these officials retaining a portion of the money they collect

terrorism: the deliberate and systematic murder, maiming, and menacing of innocent people to inspire fear for political purposes

theocracy: a government ruled by religious authorities

Torah (TOH-ruh): the first five books (Genesis, Exodus, Leviticus, Numbers, and Deuteronomy) of the Old Testament

traditional: conforming to an inherited, established, or customary way of doing things

ulema (ooh-luh-MAH): Muslim scholars in religion and law

unleavened: pertaining to bread made without yeast

urbanization: the shift of the population of a country that consists largely of rural dwellers to one of city dwellers

Wahabis (wah-HAH-beez): members of a puritanical Muslim group founded in Arabia in the 1700s and revived in the 20th century

water table: the upper limit of the ground saturated with water

welfare state: a govenment that offers its citizens a wide range of free social services

ziggurat (ZIG-oo-rat): an ancient Mesopotamian temple tower consisting of a terraced pyramid with outside staircase and a shrine on top

Zionism: the movement that was established to promote the establishment of a Jewish state in Palestine and that now supports the continued existence of Israel as such a state

Bibliography

Chapters 1-2

Bacharach, Jere L. *A Middle East Studies Handbook*. 2nd ed. Seattle: University of Washington Press, 1986.

Bates, Daniel and Amal Rassam. *Peoples and Cultures of the Middle East*. Englewood Cliffs, NJ: Prentice-Hall, 1983.

Beaumont, Peter et al. *The Middle East: A Geographical Study*. London: Wiley, 1976.

Beck, Lois and Nikki Keddie, eds., *Women in the Muslim World*. Cambridge, MA: Harvard University Press, 1978.

Binder, Leonard, ed. *The Study of the Middle East*. New York: Wiley, 1977.

Bulliet, Richard W. *The Camel and the Wheel*. Cambridge, MA: Harvard University Press, 1975.

Fernea, Elizabeth W., and Basima Q. Bezirgan, eds. *Middle Eastern Muslim Women Speak*. Austin: University of Texas Press, 1977.

Fisher, W.B. *The Middle East: A Physical, Social and Regional Geography*. London: Methuen, 1978.

Goitein, S.D. *Jews and Arabs: Their Contacts Through the Ages*. New York: Schocken, 1974.

Hazelton, Lesley. *Israeli Women*. New York: Simon and Schuster, 1978.

Longrigg, Stephen H. and James Jankowski. *The Middle East: A Social Geography*. Chicago: Aldine, 1970.

Chapters 3-6

Davis, Fanny. *The Ottoman Lady: A Social History from 1718 to 1918*. New York: Greenwood, 1986.

Denny, Frederick Mathewson. *An Introduction to Islam*. New York: Macmillan, 1985.

Grabar, Oleg. *The Formation of Islamic Art*. Rev. ed. New Haven, CT: Yale University Press, 1987.

Hallo, William W. and William K. Simpson. *The Ancient Near East: A History*. New York: Harcourt Brace Jovanovich, 1971.

Johnson, Paul. *A History of the Jews*. New York: Harper & Row, 1987.

Mango, Cyril. *Byzantium: The Empire of New Rome*. New York: Scribner, 1981.

Newby, Gordon D. *A History of the Jews of Arabia*. Columbia, SC: University of South Carolina Press, 1988.

Norwich, John J. *Byzantium: The Early Centuries*. New York: Knopf, 1989.

Roberts, D.S. *Islam: A Concise Introduction*. San Francisco: Harper & Row, 1982.

Watt, W. Montgomery. *Muhammad: Prophet and Statesman*. London: Oxford University Press, 1961

Whitting, Philip, ed. *Byzantium: An Introduction*. New York: New York University Press, 1971.

Chapters 7-9

Ammar, Hamed. *Growing up in an Egyptian Village*. New York: Octagon, 1967.

Abou-Seif, Leila. *Middle East Journal: A Woman's Journey into the Heart of the Arab World*. New York: Scribner, 1990.

Chaliand, G. et al., eds. *People Without a Country: The Kurds and Kurdistan*. London: Zed Press, 1980.

Collins, Larry and Dominique Lapierre. *O Jerusalem!* New York: Pocket Books, 1980.

Crystal, Jill. *Kuwait*. Boulder, CO: Westview Press, 1991.

Davison, Roderic H. *Turkey*. Englewood Cliffs, NJ: Prentice-Hall, 1968.

Devlin, John F. *Syria: Modern State in an Ancient Land*. Boulder, CO: Westview Press, 1983.

Eban, Abba. *Autobiography*. New York: Random House, 1977.

Farouk-Sluglett, Marion and Peter, *Iraq Since 1958: From Revolution to Dictatorship*. New York: St. Martin's Press, 1991

Fisher, Sydney Nettleton and William Ochsenwald. *The Middle East: A History*. 4th ed. New York: McGraw-Hill, 1990.

Friedman, Thomas L. *From Beirut to Jerusalem*. New York: Farrar, Straus and Giroux, 1989.

Friedman, Norman. *Desert Victory: The War for Kuwait*. Annapolis, MD: Naval Institute Press, 1991.

Frye, Richard N. *Persia*. New York: Schocken, 1968.

Gilmour, David. *Lebanon: The Fractured Country*. New York: St. Martin's Press, 1984.

Glass, Charles. *Tribes with Flags: A Dangerous Passage Through the Chaos of the Middle East*. New York: Atlantic Monthly Press, 1990.

Goldschmidt, Arthur, Jr. *A Concise History of the Middle East*, 4th ed., Boulder, CO: Westview Press, 1991.

Haim, Sylvia G., ed. *Arab Nationalism: An Anthology*. Berkeley: University of California Press, 1974.

Halabi, Rafik. *The West Bank Story: An Israeli Arab's View of Both Sides of a Tangled Conflict*. New York: Harcourt Brace Jovanovich, 1981.

Hitti, Philip K. *History of the Arabs*. New York: Macmillan, 1961.

Horne, Alistair. *A Savage War of Peace: Algeria, 1954-1962*. New York: Viking, 1978.

Hourani, Albert. *A History of the Arab Peoples*. Cambridge, MA: Harvard University Press, 1991.

Keddie, Nikki R. *Roots of Revolution: An Interpretive History of Modern Iran.* New Haven, CT: Yale University Press, 1981.

Lamb, David. *The Arabs: Journeys Beyond the Mirage.* New York: Random House, 1987.

Laqueur, Walter and Barry Rubin, eds. *The Israel-Arab Reader : A Documentary History of the Middle East Conflict.* 4th rev. ed. New York: Penguin Books, 1987.

Lewis, Bernard. *The Arabs in History.* New York: Harper & Row, 1977.

Meir, Golda. *My Life.* New York: Dell, 1976

Monroe, Elizabeth. *Britain's Moment in the Middle East, 1914-1971.* 2nd ed. Baltimore, MD.: Johns Hopkins Press, 1981.

Mortimer, Edward. *Faith and Power: The Politics of Islam.* New York: Random House, 1982.

Peretz, Don. *Intifada: The Palestinian Uprising.* Boulder, CO: Westview Press, 1990.

Quandt, William B. *Camp David: Peacemaking and Politics.* Washington, DC: The Brookings Institution, 1986.

Raban, Jonathan. *Arabia: A Journey Through the Labyrinth.* New York: Simon & Schuster, 1980.

Sachar, Howard M. *A History of Israel: From the Rise of Zionism to Our Time.* New York: Knopf, 1979.

————— *A History of Israel, Volume II: From the Aftermath of the Yom Kippur War.* New York: Oxford University Press, 1987

Sadat, Anwar. *In Search of Identity: An Autobiography.* New York: Harper & Row, 1978.

Saikal, Amin. *The Rise and Fall of the Shah.* Princeton, NJ: Princeton University Press, 1980.

Sampson, Anthony. *The Seven Sisters: The Great Oil Companies and the World They Shaped.* New York: Bantam, 1976.

Sciolino, Elaine. *The Outlaw State: Saddam's Quest for Power and the Gulf Crisis.* New York: Wiley, 1991.

Shipler, David. *Arab and Jew: Wounded Spirits in a Promised Land.* New York: Times Books, 1989.

Stillman, Norman A. *The Jews of Arab Lands: A History and Source Book.* Philadelphia: Jewish Publication Society of America, 1979.

Voll, John Obert. *Islam: Continuity and Change in the Modern World.* Boulder, CO: Westview Press, 1982.

Wilber, Donald. *Iran: Past and Present,* 9th ed. Princeton, NJ: Princeton University Press, 1981.

Wright, Robin. *In the Name of God: The Khomeini Decade.* New York: Simon and Schuster, 1989

————— *Sacred Rage: The Wrath of Militant Islam,* Rev. ed. New York: Simon and Schuster, 1986

Yergin, Daniel. *The Prize.* New York: Simon and Schuster, 1991.

Index

Abbas the Great, 138
Abbasids, 102, 109-110, 112, 114, 117, 122, 126, 128
Abdallah, 84
Abd-al-Malik, 99
Abd-al-Rahman I, 112
Abd-al-Rahman III, 112-113
Abdul Aziz, 150, 151
Abdul-Hamid II, 151, 154
Abraham, 86
Abu Bakr, 97
Abu Dhabi, United Arab Emirates, 238
Aden, Gulf of, 8
Aegean Sea, 18, 66
Afghanistan, 10, 163, 218
agriculture, 11-18, 23-24, 110, 128
    domestication of plants, 57-58
    Israel, 185
    Nile Valley, 64
Akkadians, 62
Alawites, 3
Albania, 154
Alexander the Great, 70
Alexandria, Egypt, 31, 70, 100
Algeria, 113, 137, 153, 173, 200, 232
Algerian National Liberation Front, 173
Alhambra, 125
Ali, 97-98, 99
Ali ibn al-Abbas, 102, 109
Allah, 90
alphabet, 67, 168
Altaic languages, 5
American University of Beirut, 40, 147
Amman, Jordan, 12, 32, 253
Anatolia, 9, 12, 60, 66-67, 126, 135-137
Ancient Eastern Church, 76-77
anesthesia, 123
Anglo-Persian Treaty (1919), 169
Ankara, Turkey, 32, 168
an-Najaf, 99
anti-Semitism, 177, 178
apostles, 75-76
Aqaba, Gulf of, 191
aquifer, 252, 253
Arab High Committee, 179
Arabia, 83, 87, 147
Arabian-American Oil Co. (Aramco), 166
Arabian Peninsula, 5, 7, 8, 10, 83, 102, 165
Arab-Israeli wars, 182-183, 186, 187, 219, 242
Arab Israelis, 50
Arabian Sea, 8
Arabic language, 4-5, 40, 99, 111, 113, 115, 117, 118, 119, 122, 124, 147, 166, 173, 183

Arabi Pasha, 152
Arab League, 182, 209, 232
arable land, 13
Arabs, 86, 99, 100-102, 117, 184
Arabsat, 254
Arab Socialist Union, 190
Arafat, Yasir, 203, 224, 241
Arameans, 66
archaeology, 57, 247
archipelago, 240
architecture, 124-125, 138
Aristotle, 73, 115
Armenian Orthodox Church, 77
Armenians, 5, 117, 167
arms, 242-244, 249
arts, 124, 138
Ashkenazim, 241
al-Assad, Hafez, 205, 223, 249
Assyrians, 62, 67
astrolabe, 120
astronomy, 119-121
Aswan High Dam, 23, 190
Atatürk. See Kemal, Mustafa.
Atlas Mountains, 8
Austria, 156, 163-164
authentication, 93
Averroës (Abu al-Walid Muhammad ibn Rushd), 124
Avicenna (Abu Ali al-Husayn ibn Sina), 122-123, 124
ayatollah, 98-99, 214-217
Azerbaijan, 250
al-Azhar, Cairo, 40-41, 118
Aziz, Tariq, 234

Baath party, 205, 207
Babylon, 62
Babylonians, 47, 62, 67
Badr, battle of, 87
Baghdad, Iraq, 12, 31-32, 102, 109, 111, 112, 119, 122, 126, 128, 138, 234
Baghdad Pact (1955), 189
Bahrain, 6, 99, 236, 240
Baker, James, 234
Baki, 138
Balfour Declaration, 164-165, 177-178
Balkan wars, 154
Bangladesh, 241
bankruptcy, 144, 151
al-Banna, Hasan, 188
Baradaeus, Jacob, 77
bargaining, 36
Basra, 9

Battani, 120
Bay of Bengal, 110
bedouins, 47, 89, 110
Beersheba, Israel, 12
Begin, Menachem, 16, 201, 207, 222
Beirut, Lebanon, 12, 31, 148, 219,
    221, 222, 223
Belgrade, 137
Ben Bella, Ahmed, 173
Ben-Gurion, David, 185, 201
Bendjedid, Chadli, 173
Berbers, 115, 117
Bethlehem, 75
bey, 138
Bible, 13, 67, 68, 73, 74, 84, 202
bimarastan, 122
birth rate, 46, 240
al-Biruni, 120, 124
bitumen, 58
Black Sea, 9, 10, 18, 142, 145, 164
Black September, 203, 220
Bosporous, 9, 34, 72
Boumedienne, Houari, 173
Bourguiba, Habib, 174
Bubiyan, 231
Buddha, 73
burial, Islamic, 95
Bush, President George W., 236
Byzantine Empire, 72, 77, 83, 100, 115,
    127, 136

Cable News Network (CNN), 254
Cairo, Egypt, 12, 31, 32, 33, 35, 115, 116,
    124, 126, 137, 147, 190, 191, 232
calendar, 76, 86, 168
caliphs, 97, 99, 102, 109-110, 113, 119, 126,
    128
caliphate, in Spain, 112-113
calligraphy, 38, 94
camels, 13-14
Camp David Peace Accords, 208, 213
Canaan, 67
Canaanites, 66
canals, 12, 13, 61, 111, 152
capital, 18, 184
capitulations, 144, 145
caravans, 87, 110
caravanserai, 110
Carter, President Jimmy, 208
Carthage, 70
Casals, Pablo, 244
cash crops, 15-18, 23
Caspian Sea, 10, 138, 171
Catherine the Great, 145
censorship, 254
Ceylon, 110
Chalcedon, Council of, 76
Chaldeans, 62
Charter of National Action (1962), 190

chemistry, 120-122
China, 101, 243, 249
Christianity, 75-77, 114-115, 127, 141, 152,
    241
Christians, 32, 48, 85, 99, 112, 114, 135,
    137, 139, 141, 148, 150, 199, 220-221
cities, 31-42, 49
city dynasties, 126
city-state, 60
civilization, 8, 55, 58-61, 67, 117
climate, 12, 55
coal, 20
Commonwealth of Independent States,
    250. See also Soviet Union.
compass, 110
Confucius, 73
Constantine, Roman emperor, 72, 75
Constantinople, 72, 102, 115, 136, 138,
    141, 168
conversion, 114, 115
Coptic Orthodox Church, 76
Corinth, 70
cotton, 15, 18, 65, 111, 118, 145, 152
Council of Chalcedon, 76
coup d'état, 171, 175
covenant, 74
Crimean War, 149-150
crucifixion, 75
Crusades, 127-128
cultural exchange, 58-59
culture, 3, 55, 58-59, 70
cuneiform, 61
Cyprus, 168

Damascus, Syria, 12, 31-32, 99, 108, 109,
    111, 119, 124, 129, 148, 174, 191, 221,
    242
Dar al-Harb, 102
Dar al-Islam, 102
Dardanelles, 9, 164, 167
Darius, Persian king, 70
David, Hebrew king, 67
Dead Sea, 18, 57, 253
deforestation, 13
de Gaulle, Charles, 173
de Lesseps, Ferdinand, 152
dentists, 241
département, Algeria as, 173
desalination, 23, 252-253
deserts, 7-8, 10, 12
Desert Shield, Operation, 232
desertification, 13
dhimmis, 114
dialects, 4
Diaspora, 67, 74, 176-177
Diaz, Bartholomew, 144
Diocletian, Roman emperor, 72
Disraeli, Benjamin, 152
divorce, 140, 170, 216

Dome of the Rock, 32, 86, 199
domestication, 57-58
dress, 41, 118, 128
Druze, 3
dynasties, 32, 65, 126, 148, 169

earthquakes, 9
Eastern Orthodox Church, 115
economics, 12-25, 35
economic sanctions, 212, 232, 250
Ecuador, 20
Edessa, Greece, 76
education, 39-41, 93, 117-118, 122, 147,
    170-171, 188, 212, 237, 240, 254
Egypt, 3, 6, 8, 12, 35, 100, 114-115, 126,
    145, 152-153, 242, 244
    in 20th century, 187-192
    ancient, 32, 65-66
    and Arab League, 182
    independence, 163
    invades Israel, 182
    life expectancy in, 41
    under Mamelukes, 128-129, 148
    Napoleon in, 147
    oil exploration, 166
    Ottoman conquest, 137
    and Persian Gulf War, 232
    and Saudi Arabia, 213
    and Six-Day War, 191-192
    unifies, 64-65
    and United Arab Republic, 190-191
    and World War I, 164
    and Yom Kippur War (1973), 204-205
El Alamein, battle of, 187
Elburz Mountains, 10, 13
emir, 185
England, 145
Erech, 60
erosion, 11, 13
Ethiopian Jews, 48
Euphrates River, 8-9, 12, 25, 111, 112, 252
exploration, 144
extended family, 34, 46
extremists, 209, 212, 213, 223, 238, 254
Ezekiel, 74

Fahd, King, 213, 237, 250
Faisal, King, 164-165, 174
family life, 45-46, 49-50
Farouk, King, 187
Farsi, 40
Fatima, 126
Fatamids, 126
Fertile Crescent, 8, 12, 77
Fez, Morocco, 113
First Crusade, 128
First Zionist Congress, 177
Five Pillars of Islam, 88-90
food, 14-18, 43, 57, 59, 111, 112, 118, 128,

184, 240
France, 145, 146, 164, 214, 250
    and Crimean War, 149-150
    independence of Middle Eastern
      colonies, 173-174
    in North Africa, 152-153
    and Persian Gulf War, 232, 243
    Revolution, 145-146
    and Suez crisis, 190
    and Suleiman, 137-138
Franks, 101
Free Officers Movement, 188
fundamentalism, 197-200, 209, 214-216,
    238

Gabriel, 85, 90
Galilee, Sea of, 13, 191, 253
Gallipoli Peninsula, 164
Gama, Vasco da, 144
Gaza Strip, 183, 185, 191, 201, 224-225,
    233, 241, 247, 248
Geber. See Jabir ibn Hayyan.
Genghis Khan, 128
geography, 7-12, 119-120, 251
Germany, 156, 163-164, 171, 178-182, 187,
    243
ghazis, 135
glass, 111
Golan Heights, 191, 205
Golden Horn, 34, 136
government
    Islam, 96
    Israel, 183
    Jordan, 185-186
    Ottoman, 138-141
    Saudi Arabia, 237-238
    separated from church in Turkey,
      167-168
    in villages, 44-45
Great Britain, 145, 146, 147, 166
    and Crimean War, 149-150
    and Iran, 168-169, 250
    and Israel, 177-178
    and Jordan, 185-186
    and North Africa, 152-153
    and Palestine, 178-179
    and Persian Gulf War, 232, 243
    and Suez crisis, 190
    and World War I, 164-166
Great Depression, 178
Greater Syria, 176, 223, 249
Greece, 70, 148, 168
Greek Orthodox Church 76, 149
"The Green Book" (Qaddaffi), 212
Green Line, 221
Guide to the Perplexed (Maimonides), 115
Gulf Cooperative Council (GCC), 236,
    242
Gush Emunim, 202

hadith, 91, 93, 118
Haifa, Israel, 184
hajj, 32, 89-90, 120, 213, 237
Hammurabi, 62, 63
    Code of, 62
Hapsburgs, 137, 142, 163
Harun al-Rashid, 112
Hasdai ibn Shaprut, 115
Hashemite Kingdom of Jordan, 164, 186
Hassan II, 174
Hatt-i Humayun, 150
headmen, 44-45
health care, 32, 41-42, 46, 240
Hebrew, 5, 40, 48-49, 115, 183
Hebrews, 66, 67
Hebron, 202
Hellenistic civilization, 70
Herod, 71-72
Herodotus, 12
Herzl, Theodor, 177
hidden imam, 98-99
hieroglyphics, 65
Hijaz, 87, 164, 165, 185
Hijra, 86
Hisham, caliph, 102, 109
Hitler, Adolf, 47, 179
Hittites, 66, 67
Holocaust, 179
holy war, 102
hospitality, 48-49, 94
hospitals, 122, 212
hostages, 216, 223, 233-234, 249
House of Wisdom, 119
housing, 33-34, 35-36, 49-50
Hoveyda, Fereydour, 217
Hulagu Khan, 128
Hungary, 137, 142, 163-164
Husayn, imam, 98, 217
Hussein, Abdullah, King, 185-186, 191,
203, 225, 232, 251, 253
Hussein, Saddam, 207, 218-219, 229, 231-
236, 243
hydroelectric projects, 22-23
hydroponics, 25
Hyksos, 65

illiteracy, 19, 168, 170, 239, 254
imam, 93, 98
imperialism, 151-152
India, 101, 110, 119, 241, 249
Indian Ocean, 11
individual, and Islam, 93-95
Indo-European languages, 5-6
Indonesia, 101, 117
industrial growth, 19-20
Industrial Revolution, 145
infant mortality rate, 41-42, 43
inflation, 144
institution, Islam as, 96-99

intifada, 224-225
inventions, 120
Iran, 3, 5, 9, 11, 12, 20, 22, 32, 98, 99, 110,
163, 223, 243, 244, 249-250
    modernization, 170-172
    oil exploration, 166
    and OPEC, 210
    revolution, 214-217
Iran-Iraq War, 218-219, 231, 243
Iraq, 3, 8, 9, 12, 20, 22, 98-99, 109, 110, 114,
126, 163, 165, 189, 250, 251, 252
    and Arab League, 182
    independence, 163
    invades Israel, 182
    oil in, 166, 207
    and OPEC, 210
    and Persian Gulf War, 229-236
Iraq Petroleum Co., 166
irrigation 11-12, 13, 15, 23, 57, 60, 110, 184
Isaiah, 74
Isfahan, Persia, 138, 171
Ishmail Pasha, 152
Islam, 2-4, 32, 73, 77, 83-102, 113-114,
126, 188
    civilization, 117-125
    expansion, 100-102
    Five Pillars of, 88-90
    and individual, 93-95
    as institution, 96-99
    revival, 197-199, 209, 213
Islamic Empire, 97-98, 102, 109,
113-117, 126
Islamic Front, 200
Islamic Republic of Iran, 216
Ismail, 138
Ismailis, 98, 126
Israel, 3, 6, 8, 12, 16, 18, 32, 47-50, 67,
75, 179-185, 201-202, 244, 245, 248-249,
251-252
    agriculture, 185
    culture, 241-244
    daily life, 49-50
    economy, 184-185
    education, 40
    immigration to, 48, 178-179, 184, 246-
247
    infant mortality rate, 42
    leadership, 185
    and Lebanon, 220-225
    life expectancy in, 41
    loan guarantees, 247
    peace with Egypt, 208
    and Persian Gulf War, 233, 234-235,
247
    and Six-Day War, 191-192
    social welfare, 41-42
    state created, 182-183
    and Yom Kippur War (1973), 204-205
Israelites, 67

271

Istanbul, Turkey, 31, 34, 72, 168
Italy, 136, 153, 187, 211, 232

Jabir ibn Hayyan, 120-122
Jacobites, 77
janisseries, 139, 142, 146
Jeremiah, 74
Jericho, 57, 58
Jerusalem, Israel, 32, 67, 72, 74, 87, 137, 176, 177, 182, 183, 184, 191, 199, 202, 224-225
Jesus, 73, 75, 76, 84
Jewish National Fund, 177
The Jewish State (Herzl), 177
Jews, 32, 47-50, 72, 74, 75, 77, 85, 86, 87, 99, 114-115, 127, 139-141, 164, 176-178, 179-185, 246
jihad, 102, 135
jizya, 114
Jordan, 6, 11, 18, 251, 252, 253
    and Palestine, 185-186
    and Palestinians, 203, 220, 225, 241
    and Persian Gulf War, 232
    and Six-Day War, 191
Jordan River, 183, 185, 253
Judah ha-Levi, 115
Judaism, 3, 32, 67, 73-74, 77
Judea, 72, 202. *See also* Israel and Palestine.

Kaaba, 84, 86, 87, 90
Karbala, Iraq, 32, 98, 99
Kemal Atatürk, Mustafa, 167-168
khans, 128
al-Khawarazmi, 119
Khazakhstan, 250
Khomeini, Ayatolla Ruholla, 214-219
Khuzistan, 218
kibbutz, 50
Kish, 60
Kissinger, Henry, 205
Knesset, 183, 184, 202, 207
Koran, 4, 38-40, 73, 84, 85, 87, 90-91, 94, 95, 118, 125, 126, 199, 237-238
Kuchuk Kainarji, Treaty of, 145
kufiyah, 118
Kurdistan, 126
Kurds, 5, 40, 43, 207, 235
Kushites, 65
Kuwait, 6, 20, 22, 23, 166, 210-211, 229, 231-236, 238, 240-241, 242, 243, 251, 253
Kyrgyzstan, 250

Labor party, 201-202
land, 12-13, 44, 172
Land Reform Law, 172
language, 4-6, 40, 71, 111, 119, 124, 141, 147, 173, 183, 250
latitude, 120

law, 46, 61, 62, 71, 74, 75, 93, 95, 96, 99, 113, 114, 138, 140, 150, 168, 170-171, 197-199, 211, 212
Law of Return, 48, 184
League of Nations, 165, 174, 179
Lebanon, 3, 6, 8, 12, 99, 164-165, 205, 249
    and Arab League, 182
    civil war, 219-225
    independence, 174-176
    invades Israel, 182
    and Six-Day War, 191
Lebanon Mountains, 13
Lepanto, battle of, 138
Likud, 201-202, 207
Libya, 153, 210-213
life
    early Islamic, 118-120
    in ancient Egypt, 65-66
    in cities, 33-42, 46-47
life expectancy, 41
linen, 111, 118
literacy, 40
literature, 124, 138, 147
Little Caucasus mountains, 9
livestock, 13-14, 118
Lloyd George, David, 178
longitude, 120
Lydians, 66, 67

Macedonia, 154
Maghreb, 113
Mahan, Alfred Taylor, 1
Mahmud II, 146
Maimonides (Moses ben Maimon), 115, 116
Mamelukes, 128, 129, 137, 147, 148
al-Mamun, 119
mandate, 165, 174, 178, 185-186
Marathon, battle of, 70
Marcus Aurelius, Roman emperor, 71
Marmara, Sea of, 9
Maronite Church, 77
marriage, 45-46, 62, 95, 118, 139, 140, 141, 239
Martel, Charles, 101
Masada, 72
mathematics, 61, 65, 119
Mecca, 32, 37, 84-86, 87, 88-90, 95, 102, 119, 120, 126, 137, 213, 250
medicine, 61, 65, 116, 119, 122-123, 237
Medina, 32, 86, 87, 90, 102, 137, 237
meditation, 85
Mediterranean Sea, 8, 10, 66-67, 136
medrassa, 93
Meir, Golda, 185, 204
Menes, Egyptian king, 65
mercenaries, 126-127, 141, 146
Mesopotamia, 57, 62, 70, 110, 138
messiah, 75, 93, 98

metric system, 168
Midhat Pasha, 151
migration, 33, 43-44, 46-47, 62, 67
mihrab, 37, 125
millet, 140, 150
Mimar Sinan, 138
minaret, 37, 89, 124
minbar, 37
mineral resources, 18
Mit Abul-Kum, Egypt, 16-17
mitzvah, 202
Mocha, Yemen, 11, 111
money, 67
Mongols, 128-129
monotheism, 59, 67, 84, 117
monsoons, 11, 110
Morocco, 18, 101, 113, 174
Mossaddegh, Muhammad, 171
Moses, 50, 67, 74
mosques, 32, 36-39, 89, 124, 209, 250
Mosul, Iraq, 111
Motherland party, Turkey, 168
mountains, 9-10
Mount Lebanon, 176
Mu'awiya, 98, 99
Mubarak, Hosni, 209
muezzin, 38, 89
Muhammad, 73, 83-88, 90-93, 97, 117, 126, 199
Muhammad Ali, 148
Muhammad II, 136
Muhammad V, 174
Muhammad V, 154
Muharam, 217
Mujahhedin, 214
mullahs, 214, 250
Muscat, Oman, 31
music, 124, 253
Muslim Brotherhood, 187-189, 199-200, 251
Muslims, 2-3, 32, 36-38, 48, 83-84, 86, 87, 93-95, 220. See also Islam and Ottoman Empire.
Musta'sim, 128

Naguib, General, 187
Napoleon Bonaparte, 146, 147
Nasser, Gamal Abdel, 187-192, 200, 204
nationalism, 146, 148, 152-153, 154, 177, 200, 207
nationalization, 18, 171, 190, 211
National Pact, 176, 220
Navarino Bay, battle of, 148
navigation, 120
Nazareth, 75
Nebuchadnezzar, 67
Negev Desert 13
Nelson, Horatio, 147
Neolithic Revolution, 57-58

Nestorian Church, 76, 115
New Kingdom, Egypt, 65
New Order, 146
New Testament, 73, 75
Nile, battle of the, 147
Nile River, 8, 9, 11, 31, 59, 64-65
nitric acids, 120
nomads, 5, 47, 77, 87, 126
North Africa, 6, 101, 113, 114-115, 126, 129, 138, 152-153, 184, 187
North Atlantic Treaty Organization (NATO), 168
North Korea, 243
nuclear family, 34
nuclear weapons, 244

oases, 7, 14-15
obsidian, 58
October War. See Yom Kippur war.
oil, 20-22, 166, 231, 232, 236, 237, 238, 251
    embargo, 205, 210
    politics of, 210-213
    wealth, 21-22, 35, 40, 42, 172, 207, 210-211, 213, 232, 239, 240
Old Testament, 73, 74, 75
Oman, 3, 6, 11, 22, 213, 236
Oman, Gulf of, 8
Omar Khayyam, 124
Operation Desert Storm, 234-235, 243
Organization of Petroleum Exporting Countries (OPEC), 20-22, 210-211, 231
Oriental Orthodox Church, 76-77, 115
Osman I, 135
Ottoman Empire, 32, 135-145, 148-151, 163-165. See also Turkey.
Ottoman Turks, 102, 128, 129, 135-156

Pahlavi, Mohammad Reza Shah, 171-172
Pahlavi dynasty, Iran, 170-172, 214
Palestine, 5, 67, 74, 127-128, 129, 149, 178-183, 185-186, 208
Palestine Liberation Organization (PLO), 203-204, 205, 207, 221, 222-225, 241
Palestinians, 202-203, 220-225, 240-241, 245, 247, 251
Pan-Arabism, 189, 199, 207, 236
pashas, 139
pastoralism, 9
Pax Romana (Roman Peace), 71-72
Peace Accords, Camp David, 208
peace efforts, 204, 223, 245, 247
peasants, 44-47, 61, 65, 110, 115, 168
People of the Book, 114
People of the Pen, 139
People of the Sword, 139
Persepolis, Persia, 70
Persia, 100, 126, 129, 138. See also Iran.
Persian Empire, 74, 77, 83, 100
Persian Gulf, 8, 43, 110, 164-166, 218-219

Persian Gulf states, 6, 210, 229-246, 251
Persian Gulf War, 21, 229-236, 240, 249,
　253
Persians, 5, 70, 83
petroleum. *See* oil.
Phalangists, 221, 223
pharaoh, 65, 67
Philistines, 67
philosophy, 124, 144
Phoenicians, 66-67
phosphates, 19
pilgrims, 89-90, 213, 250. *See also* hajj.
pioneers, in Israel, 181
plateau, 8, 12
Plato, 73
poetry, 61, 124
pogroms, 177
poll tax, 114
polygamy, 167-168
Pontic Mountains, 9
population, 7, 33, 43-44, 46, 214, 238
Portugal, 144
postal system, 99
pottery, 111
press, 150, 254
priests, Sumerian, 60
prophet, 74, 84
protectorate, 153, 169-170
purdah, 94
pyramids, 65

al-Qaddafi, Muammar, 211-213
Qajar dynasty, 169-170
Qatar, 236, 240
Qum, Iran, 32

railroad, 150
rainfall, 10-11, 12, 14
Ramadan, 85, 89, 92, 120, 205
Ramses II, Egyptian pharaoh, 67
al-Razi, Muhammad ibn Zakariya, 122
Reconquista, 112
Red Sea, 8, 87, 136
reforestation, 13
refugees, 43, 186, 202, 223, 235
religion, 3-4, 32, 34, 36-39, 50, 59, 96
　Christianity, 75-77
　Egyptian, 65
　Hebrews, 67
　Islam, 36-39, 83-86, 87-93, 119-120,
　　197-199
　Judaism, 73-74, 76, 202
　Sumerian, 60
religious freedom, 112, 114
Republican Guard, 234
revolution, age of, 145-146
Reza Khan, Shah, 170-171
Rhodes, 137
Richard the Lion-Hearted, 127

river valleys, 7-9
rock and roll, 244
Roman Catholic Church, 115, 149
Roman Empire, 70-72
Rommel, Erwin (Desert Fox), 187
Rothschild, Lord, 178
Rubaiyat (Omar Khayyam), 124
Rub' al-Khali (Empty Quarter), 8
rugmaking, 18
Ruling Institution, 138-139
ruralization of cities, 46-47
Russia, 142, 145, 146, 148-150, 156, 163-
　164, 168-169. *See also* Soviet Union.
Russo-Turkish War, 154
Ruth, Book of, 68-69

sabras, 184
al-Sadat, Anwar, 16-17, 200, 204, 207, 208-
　209
Safavids, Persian, 138, 142
Sahara, 7
Saint Sophia, 136
Saladin, Seljuk ruler, 127
Salamis, battle of, 70
Salat, 88-89
Sassanid Persians, 110
Saud, Ibn, 165, 166
Saud dynasty, 147, 237
Saudi Arabia, 20-22, 23, 32, 147, 163, 165,
　199, 254
　and Arab League, 182
　education in, 40-41
　medical care, 42
　and OPEC, 210
　since oil boom, 213
　and Persian Gulf War, 232, 234, 236,
　　241-242, 243
　society, 237-238, 239
Saul, Hebrew king, 67
Sawm, 89
schools, 39-41, 93, 216, 237
scientific achievements, 119-123
Scud missiles, 233, 234-235, 249
Selim I, 137, 138
Selim III, 146
Seljuk Turks, 126-127
Semites, 5
Sephardim, 141, 241
Serbia, 136
service industries, 20
shah, 138, 171-172, 214-217
Shahada, 88
shantytowns, 33-34
Sharia, 93, 98, 212, 238
sharif, 126
Sharif Husayn, 164, 165, 185
Shatt-al-Arab River, 9
sheikhs, 110, 238
Shi'at Ali, 98

Shiite Muslims, 3, 93, 97-99, 109, 126, 138, 213, 214, 217, 220, 223, 235, 250
shipping, 110
shopping, 34-36
shuttle diplomacy, 205
Sidon, 111
Sidra, Gulf of, 212
Sinai Desert, 67, 191
Sinai Peninsula, 8, 191, 205, 208-209
Six-Day War, 191-192, 199-200
Slave Institution, 139, 142
slaves, 62, 65, 66-67, 74, 75, 110, 117, 139
social welfare, 41-42
Socony-Vacuum Company, 166
Socrates, 73
solar energy, 237
Solomon, Hebrew king, 67
Soviet Union, 48, 171, 189, 205-207, 218, 231, 232, 243, 245, 246, 248, 249, 250. *See also* Russia and Commonwealth of Independent States.
Spain, 101, 111, 112-113, 114-115, 123, 137-138, 141, 174, 245
Sri Lanka, 110, 241
Standard Oil of California, 166
Standard Oil of New Jersey, 166
steel, 111, 120
subsistence crops, 15
Sudan, 148, 200, 241
Suez Canal, 8, 35, 152, 166, 187
Suez Canal Company, 152, 166, 190-191
Suez War (1956), 190
Sufism, 126, 199
Suleiman the Magnificent, 137-138
sultans, 115, 136, 138-139, 147, 150, 151, 154, 164, 167, 187
Sumerians, 60-61
Sunni Muslims, 3, 97-99, 138, 220, 250
suq (marketplace), 34, 232
sura, 90
Sykes-Picot Agreement, 164, 165
synagogues, 74
Syria, 3, 8, 12, 18, 60, 100, 128, 129, 147, 164, 165, 205, 207, 241, 249, 252
    and Arab-Israeli wars, 206
    and Arab League, 182
    independence, 174-176
    infant mortality rate, 42
    invades Israel, 182
    and Lebanon, 221, 223
    and Six-Day War, 191
    and United Arab Republic, 190
    and Yom Kippur War (1973), 205
Syrian Desert, 77
Syrian Orthodox Church, 77
Syrian Protestant College, 147

Tabka dam, 25
Tajikstan, 250

Taj Mahal, 125
Talas, battle of, 101
Talmud, 74, 114, 115
tambourines, 124
Tamerlane, Mongol ruler, 129
Tanzimat, 150
Taurus Mountains, 9, 83, 102
taxes, 99, 110, 112, 113, 114, 115-117, 139, 142, 146, 150, 240
Technion, Haifa, 40
Tehran, University of, 170
Tel Aviv, Israel, 31, 184
television, 253
temperatures, 7, 12
Ten Commandments, 67, 74
terrorism, 182, 188, 203, 212, 223-225, 249
Texas Oil Company, 166
theocracy, 200, 216
Thermopylae, battle of, 70
Third Crusade, 128
The Thousand and One Nights, 112, 124
Tigris-Euphrates valley, 57-62, 100, 128
Tigris River, 8-9, 11, 12, 31, 58, 111, 112
Timur, 129
Torah, 74
Tours, battle of, 101
trade, 34-36, 58-59, 65-66, 84-85, 87, 89, 110-111, 112, 128, 136, 144, 232, 240, 242, 249, 250, 251
Trans-Iranian Railway, 171
Transjordan, 164, 165, 182, 185-186
transportation, 20
Treatise on Smallpox and Measles (al-Razi), 122
Tripoli, 153
Truman, Harry S., 179
Tunisia, 91, 113, 114, 153, 174, 254
Turkey, 5, 9, 12, 18, 32, 60, 154, 163, 250, 252
    modernization, 167-168
    Republic, 167-168
    secular law in, 96
    Seljuk Empire, 126-127
    women in, 94
    and World War I, 164-166
    See also Ottoman Empire.
Turkmenistan, 250
Tyre, 111

ulema, 93, 98, 139
Umar, caliph, 97, 113
Umayyads, 99, 107-109, 112-113, 114
Um Kulthum, 95
United Arab Emirates, 6, 20, 42, 210, 236
United Arab Republic (U.A.R.), 190-191
United Nations, 179, 205, 218, 221, 223, 232, 244, 248, 251
    and Six-Day War, 191
    and Persian Gulf War, 231-236

United States, 164, 168, 177-178, 182, 184, 189, 204, 205, 208-209, 211, 212, 214, 216, 223, 231, 232, 234, 235, 242, 244, 245, 247, 248-249
Ur, 60, 62
urbanization, 43-44, 219-220
Ur-Nammu, Sumerian king, 61
Uthman, 97
Uzbekistan, 250

Venezuela, 20
Vienna, 137, 142, 143, 212
villages, 44-47
volcanoes, 58

Wahhabis, 147-148
Wahhabism, 199
Warba, 231
water, 7-12, 23-25, 31, 240, 251-253
Weizmann, Chaim, 177, 185
West Bank, 183, 185, 186, 191, 201-202, 207, 224-225, 233, 241, 247, 248, 253
Western oil companies, 20, 166
Western Wall of the Second Temple, 32, 74
wheat, 58
White Paper, 179
White Revolution, Iran 172
women
    in Algeria, 173-174
    and Code of Hammurabi, 64
    education of, 41
    and family life, 45

in Iran, 170, 216
Islamic, 46, 94-95, 118
in Israel, 184
in Saudi Arabia, 237-238
status, 46
in Turkey, 167-168
World Bank, 209, 253
World War I, 156, 163-166, 169
World War II, 47, 187
World Zionist Organization, 177
writing, 61, 65, 88, 118

Xerxes, Persian king, 70

Yarmuk River, 253
Yathrib. See Medina.
Yemen, 3, 8, 11, 163, 166, 182, 213, 232, 241
Yiddish, 48
Yom Kippur War, 204-205
Young Turks, 151, 154-155
Ypsilanti, Alexander, 148
Yugoslavia, 142

Zagros Mountains, 10, 58
Zakat, 89
Zayd ibn Thabit, 90
ziggurats, 60
Zionism, 47, 176-185, 201, 247, 248-249
Zoroaster, 73
Zoroastrianism, 83
Zoroastrians, 114